"The breakthrough of this book is the treatment of 'ethereal' leadership traits with respect, not with awe. The authors demystify the idea of a guiding vision and what it means to empower people, without trivializing these vital concepts. This is at once a practical book and an inspiring one."

— *Tom Peters, author of* **Thriving on Chaos**

"Chock-full of pertinent, on-the-job examples, this volume shows the many ways leaders can encourage their employees to greater productivity."

—*BOOKLIST*

"Readable, interesting, and up-to-date. Highly recommended."

—*LIBRARY JOURNAL*

"Highly readable, compelling, and full of stories about real leaders."

— *Warren Bennis, Distinguished Professor of Business Administration, University of Southern California, author of* **Why Leaders Can't Lead**

"The principles and concepts captured in *The Leadership Challenge* have proven useful in our work with top Motorola executives—and valuable not only in the U.S., but worldwide."

—*Richard Wintermantel, director, Organization and Human Resources, Motorola, Inc.*

"Kouzes and Posner have put their words and ideas behind the central issue of competitive business success—leadership!"

—*Regis McKenna, Chairman/CEO of Regis McKenna Inc.*

"This book really helps people to turn challenges into leadership. An excellent approach for continuous improvement."

—*Michael S. Roskothen, executive vice-president, Colgate-Palmolive Europe*

"A very good read for managers and executives who are interested in finding ways to understand and practice constructive, positive leadership. There is much that is written about empowering others to perform well and to be inspired by what they do. This book provides a way of making such a concept practical and useful in organizations. . . . a very accessible book with a nice blend of academic concepts and practical illustrations that are useful."

—Peter J. Frost, executive director, Organizational Behavior Teaching Society, and coauthor of **Organizational Reality**

"Kouzes and Posner have done a fantastic job of codifying the things we all must do if we are to lead and not just manage. Both practical and uplifting."

—Ron Zemke, Performance Research Associates, Inc., coauthor of **Service America!**

"This book just might convince you that you can be a leader—that leaders are not born but made. It dispels the myth that leadership talent is confined to special people or resides in special positions and does an outstanding job of revealing leadership as the process of getting the best from yourself and from others. If I had to recommend one book that really shows how to enlist others in a leader-follower relationship, this would be it."

—Perry Pascarella, vice-president–Editorial, Penton Publishing

"Customer service is the make-or-break factor in business. No company can triumph in service unless leaders drive the process hard. Kouzes and Posner offer business visionaries the keys to service-driven organizations of the 1990s."

—Bill Davidow, author of **Marketing High-Technology** *and coauthor of* **Total Customer Service**

The Leadership Challenge

James M. Kouzes
Barry Z. Posner

Foreword by Thomas J. Peters

The Leadership Challenge

*How to Get Extraordinary
Things Done
in Organizations*

 Jossey-Bass Publishers

San Francisco • Oxford • 1990

THE LEADERSHIP CHALLENGE
How to Get Extraordinary Things Done in Organizations
   by James M. Kouzes and Barry Z. Posner

Copyright © 1987 by: Jossey-Bass Inc., Publishers
                     350 Sansome Street
                     San Francisco, California 94104
                             &
                     Jossey-Bass Limited
                     Headington Hill Hall
                     Oxford OX3 0BW

Library of Congress Cataloging-in-Publication Data

Kouzes, James M., date
   The leadership challenge.

   (The Jossey-Bass management series)
   Bibliography: p.
   Includes index.
   1. Leadership.   2. Executive ability.   3. Management.
   I. Posner, Barry Z.   II. Title.   III. Series.
HD57.7.K68 1987   658.4′092   87-45428
ISBN 1-55542-211-X (alk. paper)

Manufactured in the United States of America

The paper in this book meets the guidelines for
permanence and durability of the Committee on
Production Guidelines for Book Longevity of the
Council on Library Resources.

JACKET DESIGN BY JUDY HICKS

FIRST EDITION
      First paperback printing: February 1990
      Second paperback printing: July 1990

Code 9039

The Jossey-Bass Management Series

Consulting Editors
Organizations and Management

Warren Bennis
University of Southern California

Richard O. Mason
Southern Methodist University

Ian I. Mitroff
University of Southern California

Contents

Foreword

In an important sense, Jim Kouzes and Barry Posner do not do their work justice. Its vital themes are no longer "nice to do" or "ways to get better." They are "must do," if the American economy is to survive as we know it, let alone thrive.

Banking and semiconductor and soup making businesses are under brutal competitive attack. In the past, it may have seemed as if steel, cars, and chemicals were the only industries in trouble, but the problem has infested almost all of our manufacturing and service industries.

The problem stems from low productivity and questionable quality and service across the board. In our bigger firms, this is compounded by an inability to act fast.

The pace of change is already unprecedented, and it is still accelerating. Our response, often as not, is (1) to mindlessly shove tasks and jobs to offshore partners, (2) to grasp, by means of a merger, at any apparent "fast growth" straw, and (3) to beg Washington and Tokyo for mercy, through protectionist legislation and making the dollar as worthless as possible.

We must end excuse making and look for new organizational models fit for the new world. New survivors will welcome change rather than resist it and realize that people power, not robot power, is our only long-term choice.

It is for those who seek to be part of the revolution in organizing that Kouzes and Posner write.

Management is dead, at least as we know it, the authors believe. I disagree. Sadly, management as we know it is not dead. But it darned well ought to be!

The difference between managers and leaders, say Kouzes and Posner, is the difference between day and night. The former honor stability, control through systems and procedures, and see *passion* and *involvement* as words not fit to pass adult lips. Leaders thrive on change; exercise "control" by means of a worthy and inspiring vision of what might be, arrived at jointly with their people; and understand that empowering people by expanding their authority rather than standardizing them by shrinking their authority is the only course to sustained relevance and vitality.

Management, the authors contend, has been treated as a mechanical discipline. Alternatively, leadership has been treated as mystical and ethereal. Give a synonym test and the word most associated with leadership will unfailingly be *charisma,* whatever that is.

The breakthrough this book offers is the treatment of "ethereal" leadership traits with respect, but not awe. The authors demystify the idea of a guiding vision and what it means to empower people, without trivializing these vital concepts. This is at once a practical book and an inspiring one. You will find no arrogant how-to lists spelling out the ten-day leadership awakening diet. But you will find an incredibly rich menu of examples with which any manager—oops, would-be leader—at any level can identify.

You will read of love and passion and enthusiasm and inspiration and listening and enabling and vision creation. But you won't be asked to go to a mountaintop to contemplate your navel for six months, nor will you be asked to put your firm's people through extensive "touchy-feely" sessions, as the early seventies' organizational enrichment programs came to be disparagingly called.

Instead, you will hear from factory managers to facilities managers on subjects ranging from manufacturing to services, health care, government agencies, education—the works. They've turned around unionized plants, semiconductor operations, classrooms, military operations, and retail stores. They are tough, not soft, though they freely and unselfconsciously acknowledge the emotional content of their lives as leaders.

The parade of leaders with whom the reader visits merits special praise. I and others who have dealt with some of these themes have been justly criticized for emphasizing male leaders, and those who run huge organizations. This book has as many heroines as heroes. And it features many more middle managers than chief executives. I can think of no other book on leadership that does either of these things, let alone both.

The book is a "tough read." It is written simply, clearly, and practically, and is chock-a-block with pragmatic examples. But in the end, it asks you to challenge your most deeply cherished assumptions. Don't read it in one sitting. Read, pause, and reflect. You, the reader, are being asked to make nothing less than a revolution. In the end, though, please act. The manager-to-leader revolution is not optional if you are interested in your children's well-being.

August 1987   Thomas J. Peters
                                 Coauthor of
                                 In Search of Excellence and
                                 A Passion for Excellence

Preface

> People cannot be managed. Inventories can be
> managed, but people must be led.
> ——*H. Ross Perot, Founder,*
> *Electronic Data Systems*

The Leadership Challenge is about how leaders get extraordinary things done in organizations. It is about the practices leaders use to turn challenging opportunities into remarkable successes.

There are no shortages of challenging opportunities to radically alter the world in which we live and work. The opportunities for leadership are available to all of us everyday.

There are countless opportunities to regain market shares lost in competitive battles. Opportunities to restore and rebuild our deteriorating central cities. Opportunities to substantially improve the quality of domestically manufactured products. Opportunities to offer unmatched service to the customer. Opportunities to launch a revolutionary new product that may start an entire new industry.

More than ever there is need for people to seize these opportunities to lead us to greatness. Yet there seems to be a reluctance to answer the cry for leadership. Why?

We believe this cautiousness results not from a lack of courage or competence but from outdated notions about leadership. Just about everything we have been taught about traditional management prevents us from being effective leaders. And just about every popular notion about leadership is a myth.

Our first leadership challenge is to rid ourselves of these traditions and myths. They foster a model of leadership antithetical to the way real-life leaders operate. They also create unnecessary barriers to the essential revitalization of our organizations.

Myths, Traditions, and Realities

Traditional management teaching would have us believe that the ideal organization is orderly and stable. Yet, when successful leaders talk about their personal best achievements, they talk about challenging the process, about changing things, about shaking up the organization.

At the same time, leadership myth portrays the leader as a renegade who magnetizes a band of followers with courageous acts. In fact, leaders attract followers not because of their willful defiance but because of their deep respect for the aspirations of others.

Traditional management teaching focuses our attention on the short term, the Wall Street analysts, the quarterly statement, and the annual report. Yet, in the leadership cases we have examined, all the effective leaders had a long-term future orientation. They looked beyond the horizon of the present.

A new folklore developing about leadership suggests that leaders are prescient visionaries with Merlin-like powers. To be sure, leaders must have a vision, a sense of direction, but the vision need not show any psychic foresight. It can spring from original thinking or represent the inspiration of someone else. It can be celestial or mundane.

Traditional management teaches us that leaders ought to be cool, aloof, and analytical—separating emotion from work. Yet when leaders discuss the things they are the proudest of in their own careers, they describe feelings of inspiration, passion, elation, intensity, challenge, caring, kindness, even love.

Leadership myth says that leaders are "charismatic," that they possess some special gift. At best this distorts our appreciation of leaders. At worst it can lead to hero worship and cultism. To be sure, leaders must be energetic and enthusiatic. But, a leader's dynamism does not come from special powers. It comes from a strong belief in a purpose and a willingness to express that conviction.

Traditional management teachings tell us that the job of management is primarily one of control. The control of resources, including time, money, materials, and people. Leaders know that the more they control others, the less likely it is that people will excel. Leaders do not control. They enable others to act.

Leadership myth tells us that it is lonely at the top. Not so. The most effective leaders we know are involved and in touch with those they lead. They care deeply about others, and they often refer to those with whom they work as family.

Tradition suggests that leaders direct and control others by giving orders and by issuing policies and procedures. But we know that leaders' deeds are far more important than their words. Credibility of action is the single most significant determinant of whether a leader will be followed over time.

Myth associates leadership with superior position. It assumes that when you are on top you are automatically a leader. But leadership is not a place, it is a process. It involves skills and abilities that are useful whether one is in the executive suite or on the front line.

The reality is that leadership is oxymoronic. For the people we studied, leadership was indeed a heated affair, full of exhilaration and fun. But it was also exhausting, stressful, and rigorous. Leadership is disciplined passion.

The Leadership Challenge is a book about leading people. Not merely managing them. Leadership begins where management ends, where the systems of rewards and punishments, control and scrutiny, give way to innovation, individual character, and the courage of convictions.

The Leadership Challenge presents an alternative to the standard traditions and myths. It offers a set of leadership practices that are based on the real-world experiences of hundreds of ordinary people who have answered the cry for leadership. This book contains a set of practices that can form the foundation for the development of a new generation of leaders.

We have written this book to help you develop your abilities to get extraordinary things done in organizations. We believe you are capable of developing yourself as a leader far more than tradition has ever assumed possible.

Who Should Read This Book?

The fundamental purpose of *The Leadership Challenge* is to assist managers and nonmanagers alike in furthering their abilities to lead others to get extraordinary things done. The leaders we have worked with and learned from have these major goals in enhancing their leadership capabilities:

- Assessing their strengths and weaknesses as leaders.
- Learning how to inspire and motivate others toward a common purpose.
- Acquiring skills in building a cohesive and spirited team.
- Putting these lessons to use more regularly.

This book is designed to help anyone with the desire to lead achieve these major learning objectives.

Overview of the Contents

The first two chapters introduce you to our point of view about leadership. In Chapter One we describe the five practices of exemplary leadership revealed in our research. Through examples from leaders we studied we discuss the actions they took to get extraordinary things done. We conclude Chapter One with the Ten Commitments of Leadership—ten ways you can put the leadership practices to use in your organization.

The leader's tale, however, is only half the story. To be a leader you have to have followers. In Chapter Two we describe the results of our survey of the characteristics that followers most admire in their leaders. It turns out that followers are also in agreement about the essentials of leadership, the most important of which is credibility.

In Chapters Three through Twelve we explore each of the five practices and the ten commitments in turn. The discussions are built on the results of our research, and we expand our understanding of leadership by drawing on the research of other scholars. We also illustrate each practice with case examples that we think best exemplify it. Each chapter concludes with a set of recommendations on how you can put the practices to use in your organization.

In Chapter Three we see how, when successful leaders talk about their personal best achievements, they talk about searching for opportunities to innovate and change things. The real motivator, it turns out, is the challenge of the adventure, not the material rewards.

In Chapter Four we learn that the source of most innovation is external to the leader's organization, and therefore the leader must keep the lines of communication open. We find that innovation also brings risk, so leaders accept the mistakes that result from experimentation and make every effort to learn from them.

In Chapter Five we talk about how leaders look beyond the horizon of present time and imagine how things could ideally be several years ahead. Leaders have a sense of direction and a purpose beyond the moment.

In Chapter Six leaders tell us that vision is not enough to transform organizations. Unless it can be effectively communicated, people will not enlist in making the dream a reality. We see how leaders are positive and expressive in their presentation of their personal agenda.

The leaders we studied are involved and in touch with those they lead. They care deeply about others, and they often refer to those with whom they work as family. In Chapter Seven we explore how leaders foster collaboration and build effective teams.

In Chapter Eight we examine how leaders create a climate in which it is possible for others to do their best. We see how leaders enable others to be in control of their own lives.

In Chapter Nine leaders show us how they serve as models for what followers are expected to be and do. In Chapter Ten we discuss how leaders build commitment through a process of incremental change and small wins. In Chapters Eleven and Twelve, we discuss how leaders sustain the commitment to achieve excellence by recognizing individuals and celebrating successes. Leadership is work, but it is also fun.

Finally, we discuss how the most effective leaders are those who first learn to lead themselves. We treat leadership as a learnable set of practices. In so doing we hope to demystify it, and show how it is within all of us to lead. In the concluding Chapter Thirteen, we discuss how people learn to become leaders. We

also offer guidance on how you can continue your own growth
and development. And for those who wish to know more about
how we conducted this research, in the appendixes we include
some information on our research methodology.

Doing Our Best as Leaders

The Leadership Challenge began as a research project in
1983. We wanted to know what leaders did when they did their
"personal best" at leading, not managing, others. These were
experiences when, in their own perception, these managers set
their own individual leadership standard of excellence.

The personal best survey consisted of 38 open-ended questions. Questions such as: Who initiated the project? How were
you prepared for this experience? What special techniques and
strategies did you use to get other people involved in the project?
How would you describe the character or feel of the experience?
What did you learn about leadership from this experience? The
survey generally required one to two hours of reflection and
expression. More than 550 of these surveys were collected. A
short, two-page form was completed by another group of 780
managers. In addition, we conducted 42 in-depth interviews. All
of the people in the study were middle- and senior-level managers
in private- and public-sector organizations. (A complete list of
survey questions can be found in Appendix A.)

Every manager in the study had at least one leadership
story to tell. Many had several. The stories they told seldom
sounded like textbook management. They were not logical cases
of planning, organizing, staffing, directing, and controlling.
Instead, they were tales of dynamic change and bold actions.

In one case, for example, manufacturing productivity was
improved over 400 percent in one year; in another, quality
improvements moved products in three months from last to first
on a customer's vendor list; in yet another, the company grew
fivefold in sales and 750 percent in profits over six years. There
were cases of start-ups, developments of revolutionary new products, phenomenal positive shifts in employee morale.

In the not-for-profit and public sectors, we learned of a
model educational assistance program, the establishment of a

unique drug counseling center, the planning of an association conference, and an award-winning U.S. Army unit.

From an analysis of the personal best cases, we developed a model of leadership. We then wrote the *Leadership Practices Inventory* to enable us to measure the leadership behaviors we uncovered. Finally, we put all this to the test by asking over 3,000 managers and their subordinates to assess the extent to which the managers we studied used the practices. (See Appendix B for more information about the *Leadership Practices Inventory*.)

The results have been striking both in their refutation of the leader stereotype and in their consistency. Leaders do exhibit certain distinct practices when they are doing their best. And this behavior varies little from industry to industry, profession to profession. Good leadership, it seems, is not only an understandable but also a universal process.

Leadership, we concluded, is not the private reserve of a few charismatic men and women. It is a process ordinary managers use when they are bringing forth the best from themselves and others.

The Future of Leadership

The domain of leaders is the future. The leader's unique legacy is the creation of valued institutions that survive over time. We hope this book contributes in some measure to the revitalization of organizations everywhere and to the creation of new enterprises. The most significant contributions leaders make is not to today's bottom-line but to the long-term development of people and institutions who prosper and grow.

But more than that, we want to convince you, the reader, that leadership is important not only in your dealings with others but equally in your own career. It is the leader who reaches the summit in any field.

Because leadership development is ultimately self-development, in the end, the leadership challenge is a personal challenge.

Santa Clara, California   James M. Kouzes
August 1987   Barry Z. Posner

Acknowledgments

Don Bennett, a Seattle businessman and one of the leaders we had the privilege to interview for this book, is the first amputee ever to climb Mount Rainier. That's 14,410 feet on one leg and two crutches. We asked Don to tell us the most important lesson he learned from his celebrated achievement, and without hesitation he said: "You can't do it alone."

We wish we had been the first to say that. While writing a book is certainly a very different feat from climbing a mountain, the lesson is the same. This book is the result of the loving, caring, generous assistance, advice, support, and encouragement of scores of people. If it were not for all of them there would be no book.

It is hard to pinpoint the beginnings of the project that led to this book. If memory serves us correctly, two people deserve recognition for giving us the kick start we needed. Our earliest recollection is of a parking-lot conversation with Donna Kouzes about the characteristics of individuals who perform at high levels. We thought it would be interesting to apply this idea to leaders, and in her usual enthusiastic and energetic style, Donna began to collect the stories and cases that became the sources of ideas and inspiration for this book.

Tom Peters gave us that important initial nudge up the mountain. Shortly after the publication of *In Search of Excellence,* Tom conducted a workshop with us at Santa Clara University. Tom led the first day of the seminar, and we led the second day. In an effort to help participants apply the excellence lessons to their own organizations, we utilized a technique we called "Personal Best Leadership Cases." That was the genesis of the research methodology we subsequently used with more than 500 leaders. Tom's generosity of mind, heart, and spirit continues to overwhelm us. We deeply appreciate his kind and useful comments in the Foreword to this book.

Jerry Fletcher, a teacher, counselor, and friend, guided us in the development of our personal best questionnaire. Jerry has successfully helped hundreds of people determine their patterns of high performance, and his approach was the model for ours.

We were moved to laughter and tears, awe and inspiration, as we listened in on the uplifting experiences of hundreds of men and women who accepted the leadership challenge. They are the ones who taught us what it really means to get extraordinary things done in organizations. You will meet many of these inspiring folks as you read this book. The book is about them and their colleagues: the people who really made things happen. We are forever grateful to them for sharing their lives with us, and we hope we have represented them well.

We owe an immense intellectual debt to some very special colleagues and friends. Sitting across the dinner table from Warren Bennis one night, we sketched the early findings from our research. Warren encouraged us to write a book about it. We thank him for the vote of confidence and for his brilliant insights into leadership. Roger Harrison is the first scholar we know of who had the courage to openly talk about the place of love in leadership. He gave us the courage to do the same. Rosabeth Moss Kanter was another mentor and teacher. We learned much from her, especially about the importance of empowerment. Rosabeth's research on innovation also offered many insights into the relationship between leadership and change. Warren Schmidt was an early collaborator on the power of values in personal and organizational life. Values are of immense importance in leadership and Warren was among the very first to see that. Given the disturbing ethical dilemmas of the mid 1980s in both government and business, we are glad to have had Warren as a coach. Charles O'Reilly and David Caldwell have strongly influenced our thinking. Their research on credibility, commitment, and corporate culture contributed significantly to our thinking on the foundation of leadership.

One of the ways we tested our ideas about leadership was to conduct workshops and seminars. Many people graciously agreed to be part of our experiments. They filled out questionnaires, asked others to do the same, participated in experiential exercises, and joined in on endless discussions. We want them to know that they are the real heroes of this book.

In those early workshops, several people added great value to our initial designs. Ann Bowers and Ranny Riley joined us as staff for the very first public session on "Getting Extraordinary Things Done in Organizations." Ann's and Ranny's extensive experience, creative insight, and dedicated efforts contributed to the development of many of the early activities.

Randi DuBois, Reno Taini, and Ricky Tam are the team from Pro-Action who invented the Ropes Course and gave us firsthand experience with physical challenge. They also showed us how important trust is in the willingness to risk.

We also thank David Sibbet for his advice and counsel on training design. His graphic representations of our work are exceptional. Reiko Takao produces the graphics for our slides and transparencies, and Elwood Mills does the photographic work. Paige Johnson designed and produced elegant and striking brochures, posters, and monographs, which brought our words to life through artful images. Without their assistance, we would never be able to show the complete story of what leaders do.

We owe a special debt of gratitude to Tom Melohn. Not only was Tom one of the leaders we had the good fortune to study, but he has generously given his time and passion to the many people who participated in several of our public seminars. Major General John Stanford is another leader who has been a role model to those who have taken part in our programs.

In any experimental work, people must take risks on behalf of the experiment. We were so fortunate that there are some brave risk takers in many of our client corporations. One who took a chance on us was Sue Cook. When she was manager of employee development for Apple Computer (she is now with the Tom Peters Group), Sue challenged us to make our concepts more relevant to the dynamic environments of growing companies. Sue also urged us to develop the "Leadership Practices Inventory" so managers could measure themselves on the behaviors we identified from the personal best cases. Thank goodness we followed her suggestion. We also wish to thank Trish Cutler Silber, Dorothy Largay, Candy DeSantis, and Pat Sharp of Apple for their early support and encouragement.

Another organization that took a risk on us was Tektronix. Earl Wantland, Stan Kouba, Eddie Ward, Pat Willard, Karen Kolodziejski, and the rest of the module five design team enabled us to advance our ideas yet another step. We also congratulate them for winning the Human Resource Development Award from the American Society for Training and Development for their Manager of Managers Program. We are honored to share in that adventure.

Nan Strauss was an early believer in what we were doing, and she made an innovative adaptation of some of our work to leadership development within Hewlett-Packard. Nan also introduced us to Olle Bovin of Hewlett-Packard S.A. in Geneva. Olle is an enthusiastic and profoundly positive individual who gave us the opportunity to try out our ideas in Europe.

Göran Wiklund and Jan Backelin are two Swedish friends and colleagues who brought us into contact with the warm and accepting people of Sweden and made us feel welcome in that country.

André Morkel, at the University of Western Australia, invited us to participate in the Advanced Management Program there and we began exploring cross-cultural hypotheses about leadership. Lynton Hayes and Brian Carroll at the Australian Institute of Management were gracious and enthusiastic in promoting our conversations, interactions, and data collections to Australian executives. We are also appreciative of Russ Barnett's efforts, which enabled us to work with the top executive team at Bristile.

We give special thanks to David Kaiser of Control Data; Ann Ryan, Lynn Ulrich, Jim Colwick, and Paul Witt of Tandem; Sue Arnold and Jim O'Malley of the Internal Revenue Service, Western Region; Boyd Clarke and Ron Crossland of AT&T; Ken Best and Steve Bradbury of McDonnell Douglas; and Neil Love of General Electric. They invited us into their organizations, giving us the chance to test our concepts with their managers. More recently, David Chrislip, Michael Doyle, and Joan McIntosh of Interaction Associates have become collaborators in providing leadership experiences for those interested in self-development.

Moving from the realm of testing ideas to committing them to paper was a difficult transition for us. Author and reporter Michael S. Malone helped us write down our thoughts and served as the editor of the first rough draft. Our developmental editor, Liz Currie, enabled us to transform the first rough draft into a finished manuscript. Liz's thorough and specific feedback not only helped to improve this book, but her coaching taught us a great deal about the art of writing. Thanks, too, to Jayne Pearl of the Tom Peters Group, for her editorial assistance. The true art of editing and publishing was masterfully practiced by the family of professionals at Jossey-Bass, Inc., Publishers. Their confidence in us and patience with us was overwhelming. Without their support there would be no book, only loosely connected ideas.

Our manuscript went through several drafts, and with us every step of the way was Liz Caravelli to greet us with a smile, produce the copy with amazing speed, and wish us success. Liz's help was a blessing, and we will always remember her tireless efforts on our behalf.

If there were an honor roll for hard work and dedication, it would go to the staff of the Executive Development Center at Santa Clara University. Joy Congdon gracefully managed the production of our executive programs as we focused our energies on the research and writing. Without Joy the Center would not exist. Judy Kasper typed early drafts of the mansucript and always showed her concern for us. Kelly Leahey, Kim McFarlane, and Elvia Torres kept the word processor and duplicating machines humming. Marion Krause put her trusty Santa Clara M.B.A. lessons to use at the Center, making our lives easier and the Center more efficient. They have all been able to keep laughter in their hearts, through dozens of revisions and reams of duplicating paper.

This book is dedicated to our families. We had to literally close the door on them on countless evenings and weekends. Of all the aspects of writing we hated the most, that was it. Our parents, Tom and Thelma Kouzes, and Delores Gearhart and Henry Posner, were early role models of leadership and continue to encourage our hearts. Donna Kouzes was an initial collaborator and a frequent contributor of cases and suggestions. Jackie Schmidt-Posner provided perspective and balance as well as editorial advice and insight. Amanda Posner was a delightful dis-

xxviii   Acknowledgments

traction. Donna, Jackie, and Amanda were constant sources of
love and warmth, inspiration and insight. Our public appreciation of their sacrifices, their steadfastness, and their support is
long overdue. They are living examples of what it means to care
about and care for others.

Yes, as Don Bennett said, "You can't do it alone." This
book is coauthored, and we could not have done it without each
other.

And we could not have done it without all of the folks
mentioned above, and more. They made this book possible.

We love you all.

J.M.K.
B.Z.P.

The Authors

James M. Kouzes, formerly director of the Executive Development Center (EDC), Leavey School of Business and Administration, Santa Clara University, has recently been named president of the Tom Peters Group/Learning Systems, Inc. He is founder of the Joint Center for Human Services Development at San Jose State University, which he managed from 1972 until 1980. An experienced educator and consultant, Kouzes has trained more than 15,000 managers and professionals since 1969.

Kouzes's interest in leadership began while he was growing up in Washington, D.C. In 1961 he was one of a dozen Eagle Scouts from across the United States to be selected to serve in John F. Kennedy's Honor Guard at the Presidential Inauguration. He served as a United States Peace Corps volunteer from 1967 to 1969.

Kouzes is the author of numerous articles and chapters in edited volumes on management education, leadership, and organization development. He received the Hubert H. Humphrey Memorial Award for the best article of 1983 from the *Journal of Health and Human Resources Administration.* He received his B.A. degree (1967) from Michigan State University in political science and a certificate (1974) from San Jose State University's School of Business for completion of the Internship in Organizational Development. He is a member of Certified Consultants International, serves on the American Management Association's Human Resource Council, and is a past member of the board of the Organization Development Network.

Barry Z. Posner is professor of management and director of Graduate Education and Customer Service, Leavey School of Business and Administration, Santa Clara University. He is responsible for managing the school's M.B.A. program, which involves more than 1,200 students from nearly 500 different companies, and focuses on the working professional by relating rigorous scholarship to managerial decisions. Posner is an internationally recognized scholar and educator and has received his university's Distinguished Faculty Award.

Posner's interest in leadership began during the turbulent unrest on college campuses during the late 1960s, while participating in and reflecting on the balance between energetic collective action and chaotic and frustrated anarchy. At one time, he aspired to be a Supreme Court Justice, but realized that he would have to study law, and redirected his energies into understanding people and organizational systems.

Posner is the author and coauthor of more than sixty scholarly articles, several monographs for the American Management Association, and a book, *Effective Project Planning and Management: Getting the Job Done.* He received his B.A. degree (1970), with honors, from the University of California, Santa Barbara, in political science, his M.A. degree (1972), from the Ohio State University in public administration, and his Ph.D. degree (1976) from the University of Massachusetts, Amherst, in organizational behavior and administrative theory. Posner is a member of the Academy of Management, American Psychological Association, Beta Gamma Sigma, Organization Behavior Teaching Society, and the Engineering Management Society. He is currently president of the Western Academy of Management, serves on the board of directors for two companies, and is a frequent conference speaker.

The Leadership Challenge

PART ONE

Knowing What Leadership Is Really About

> Leadership appears to be the art of getting others to want to do something that you are convinced should be done.
>
> ——*Vance Packard,*
> The Pyramid Climbers

How do you get other people to want to follow you? How do you get other people, by free will and free choice, to move forward together on a common purpose? Just how do you get others to want to do things?

By studying the times when leaders performed at their personal best, we were able to identify five practices common to most extraordinary leadership achievements. When leaders do their best, they challenge, inspire, enable, model, and encourage.

Asking leaders about their personal best is only half the story. Leadership is a relationship between leader and followers. A complete picture of leadership can be developed only if we ask followers what they look for or admire in a leader. Our research shows that the majority of us want leaders who are honest, competent, forward-looking, and inspiring. In short, we want leaders who are credible and who have a clear sense of direction.

In the next two chapters, we provide an overview of the findings from our major empirical studies about "When Leaders Are at Their Best" (Chapter One) and "What Followers Expect of Leaders" (Chapter Two). After reading these chapters, you will have a better idea of what characteristics define leaders—from both a leader's perspective and his or her subordinates'.

1

1

When Leaders Are at Their Best: Five Practices and Ten Commitments

> I think good people deserve good leadership.
> ——*Debi Coleman, Vice-President*
> *and Chief Financial Officer,*
> *Apple Computer*

After twenty-five years in the packaged goods industry, Tom Melohn quit. He quit to become "head sweeper"—that's what it says on his resumé—of North American Tool and Die. Translate "head sweeper" to mean co-owner, president, and chief executive officer of that San Leandro, California, manufacturing company.

When Melohn and his partner, Garner Beckett, took over NATD, the company was a poor performer in an industry being attacked by offshore competitors. In a period of eight years under Melohn's leadership, NATD increased its sales by a factor of 5, increased its pretax profits by 750 percent, reduced annual turnover from 27 percent to 4 percent, and decreased the reject rate from 5 percent to a tenth of a percent. By year eight, NATD had opened its second plant—Melohn calls it "Plant 20" to give people a sense that the company is growing—and received its ninth "vendor of the year" award.

To what does Melohn attribute this extraordinary turnaround? Certainly not to his skills as a machinist. He was a self-described "peddler"—his last position before NATD was senior vice-president of marketing—and claims he cannot even hammer a nail or screw the license plates onto his car. Nor was it his business education. He holds a master's degree in history from Princeton University, and he claims he has never read a book on business. Nor was it his industry experience. Remember, he was a peddler in packaged goods.

And it wasn't geographical advantage in distribution, proprietary products, or new equipment. NATD is in a region filled with lots of small job shops, it makes parts to the specifications of its customers, and its equipment is old.

So what is the magic?

"We set three objectives for NATD," says Melohn. "First, we planned to grow the company profitably. Second, to share the wealth among employees. And third, and equally critical, it was important to have fun—not just the two owners, but all our employees.

"And that is the key. To have fun. Yes, the numbers are important; they are our report card. Yet the real reason for our success is deceptively simple. It's our employees—our major asset. To see them grow, personally, professionally, financially—to share with them the excitement of building our company. The psychic income alone is enormous."[1]

The strategy for increasing company profits came from the customers. Melohn and his partner went out and interviewed about fifty buyers and twenty-five engineers. They asked them what they needed, what they wanted from a job shop. The answers were always the same: quality, service, price.

So quality became the NATD hallmark. But at NATD, quality doesn't start in quality control. "It's too late there," says Melohn. "They're just the traffic cop. . . . Nope, at NATD quality must be in each employee's head and heart or we're dead." You'll find Melohn on the shop floor preaching the gospel of quality every day at NATD.

At NATD, the owners also share the wealth. They have a company employee stock ownership plan. The employee stock is free, and the owners have waived their rights to participate. They also recognize employees with cash awards for contributing to the goal of "no rejects."

"Another action area that reinforces our belief in the importance of our employees is called caring. Simply stated," says

Melohn, "at NATD we care about our people. We care a great deal. Not just as employees, but as human beings, as friends. And we try to help them in any way we can." From sending flowers, to buying doughnuts, to loaning company trucks, to monthly "Super Person" awards, Melohn shows how much he cares.

"The only way to achieve these goals, we decided, was to create an atmosphere of complete trust between us, the owners, and all our employees." But Melohn adds "one admonition: you've got to really mean it when you say you want such an atmosphere. You truly have to believe it. Then you've got to work at improving relations every day in every situation. Otherwise, your employees will sense the hypocrisy, and all will be for naught."

Apple Computer, Inc., is one of North American Tool and Die's customers. At the time of our interviews, the person in charge of the operation to which NATD sells was Debi Coleman. Coleman was the vice-president of worldwide manufacturing for Apple, the only female vice-president of manufacturing in a Fortune 500 company. (In 1987 Coleman was appointed chief financial officer for Apple.)

Coleman began her business career at Texas Instruments. After earning her M.B.A. degree at Stanford, she joined Hewlett-Packard. But Apple Computer offered boundless opportunity, and she joined them, starting as a finance manager for the Macintosh project. In the brief period of five years, she held five other jobs, as Macintosh project controller, Macintosh division controller, product group controller, Macintosh division operations manager, and finally vice-president of worldwide manufacturing.

Manufacturing is not the usual choice for a Stanford M.B.A., but Coleman always wanted to work in the factory. "I don't think you should ever manage something that you don't care passionately about," says Coleman. "The move I made from finance to manufacturing was just not intuitively obvious to people, except if you knew how passionately I cared about manufacturing."

Some of the accomplishments of which Coleman is the proudest occurred while she was Macintosh division operations manager. One of her tasks was to improve the performance of the Fremont manufacturing plant—one of the most innovative personal computer factories in the world.

Under her leadership as factory manager, the throughput yield in the factory went from a first-pass cumulative yield of about 30 percent to one of 70 percent in nine months. Incoming acceptance on materials went from 80 percent to 96–99 percent. They got over thirty inventory turns a year.

A lot of solid manufacturing processes contributed to these results. The Fremont facility was conceived as an integrated factory—everything under one roof, with one management team. They also operated with just-in-time inventory management, bar code serialization to monitor work in progress, unique vendor partnerships, and a host of other impressive innovations.

While all those manufacturing innovations were important, they weren't the only things that made the Mac factory a highly productive and reliable facility. First, says Coleman, "I really can't claim credit for all these things." She attributes them to the people who work there.

So what was her contribution? "One of them was a total willingness to listen to everybody about what was going on." Another was "spending time on the floor . . . five hours a day." And then there were the numerous little things Debi did. She refurbished the bathrooms off the production floor, had the factory floor cleaned around the clock, sealed and waxed the floor, painted the factory walls white, set up an Apple values committee, and for the first two months held catered supper meetings with production folks every Tuesday and Thursday.

Details, details, details. Coleman works very hard at the details. Why work so hard? "I think good people deserve good leadership. The people I manage deserve the best leader in the world. If you could see them, you would understand why somebody would want to work sixty hours a week to make those people more successful."

Tom Melohn and Debi Coleman each seized the opportunity to lead. They chose a pioneering path and led their organizations to new summits of excellence. Melohn and Coleman are exceptional, to be sure, but their stories are not.

We have found such achievements to be commonplace. We have discovered that there are thousands of success stories in business. Getting extraordinary things done in organizations is not restricted to a select few stars or a select few companies. It is som thing the vast majority of managers are capable of doing in t re.

at can we learn from Tom Melohn, Debi Coleman, and th ls of others who have told us their stories? What does it ta other people, by the force of their own free wills, despit al risk and hard work, to want to climb to the summit.

Th r studies, we have discovered that the ordinary executives w nced others to join them on pioneering journeys followed of a three-phase strategy. We refer to it as the VIP—visio nent-persistence—model of leadership.

When peop hed their personal best leadership experiences, they told c vhen they imagined exciting, highly attractive futures for zanizations. They had *visions* and dreams of what could had absolute and total personal belief, and they were con their abilities to make extraordinary things happen.

These leaders recogni rand dreams do not become significant realities through t s of a single leader. They knew that scores of people wer ceded to create, produce, sell, and sponsor the vision. The *involvement* of many others is key to making it all the way to the top.

Our sample of leaders acted on their wise understanding that new tomorrows are not realized without hard work and *persistence*. The personal best projects were distinguished by the fact that all of them required relentless effort, steadfastness, competence, planning, attention to detail, and encouragement.

Five Leadership Practices Common to Successful Leaders

As we looked deeper into this dynamic process, through the case analyses and survey questionnaires, we uncovered five fundamental practices that enabled these leaders to get extraordinary things done. When they were at their personal best, our leaders:

1. Challenged the process.
2. Inspired a shared vision.
3. Enabled others to act.
4. Modeled the way.
5. Encouraged the heart.

These practices are not the private property of the leaders we studied. They are available to anyone who wants to accept the leadership challenge.

Challenging the Process. Leadership is an active, not a passive process. While many leaders attributed their success to "luck" or "being in the right place at the right time," none of them sat idly by or waited for fate to smile upon them. Although the distinctive competencies of a person may fit the needs of the moment, those who lead others to greatness seek challenge. All the cases we collected about leadership personal bests involved some kind of challenge. The challenge may have been an innovative new product, a reorganization, or a turnaround, but the majority of the cases involved a change from the status quo. They involved *challenging the process.*

Leaders are pioneers—people who are willing to step out into the unknown. They are people who are willing to take risks, to innovate and experiment in order to find new and better ways of doing things. But leaders need not always be the creators or originators of new products or work processes. In fact, it is just as likely that they are not. Product innovations tend to come from customers, vendors, and line employees. Process innovations tend to come from the people doing the work.

The leader's primary contribution is in the recognition of good ideas, the support of those ideas, and the willingness to challenge the system in order to get new products, processes, and services adopted. In this sense, it might be more accurate to call them early adopters of innovation.

Innovation, according to Robert Metcalfe, chairperson of 3COM, "requires gambling and risk taking. We tell our folks to make at least ten mistakes a day. If they're not making ten mistakes a day, they're not trying hard enough."[2] And Olle Bovin, a manager at Hewlett-Packard in Europe, claims, "You have to be brave enough to fail as a leader." If this seems like foolish advice, recall the times you have tried to play a new game or a new sport. Did you get it absolutely perfect the first time you played it? Probably not. Experimentation, innovation, and change all involve risk and failure.

It would be ridiculous to state that those who fail over and over again eventually succeed as leaders. Success in business is not a process of simply buying enough lottery tickets. The key that unlocks the door to opportunity is learning. Warren Bennis and Burt Nanus, authors of *Leaders,* tell us that the ninety successful leaders they studied regard almost "every false step as a learning opportunity, and not the end of the world."[3] Leaders are learners. They learn from their mistakes as well as their successes.

Inspiring a Shared Vision. Robert Swiggett, chairperson of Kollmorgen Corporation, offers a straightforward view about the job of a leader. It is, he says, "to create a vision." Every organization, every social movement begins with a dream. The dream or vision is the force that invents the future.

Leaders spend considerable effort gazing across the horizon of time, imagining what it will be like when they have arrived at their final destinations. Some call it vision; others describe it as a purpose, mission, goal, even personal agenda. Regardless of what we call it, there is a desire to make something happen, to change the way things are, to create something that no one else has ever created before.

In some ways, leaders live their lives backwards. They see pictures in their minds' eyes of what the results will look like even before they have started their projects, much as an architect draws a blueprint or an engineer builds a model. Their clear image of the future pulls them forward. But visions seen only by leaders are insufficient to create an organized movement or a significant change in a company. A person with no followers is *not* a leader, and people will not become followers until they accept a vision as their own. You cannot command commitment, you can only inspire it.

Leaders *inspire a shared vision.* They breathe life into what are the hopes and dreams of others and enable them to see the

exciting possibilities that the future holds. Leaders get others to
buy into their dreams by showing how all will be served by a
common purpose.

To enlist people in a vision, a leader must "know your
followers and speak their language," according to Beverly Ann
Scott, organization development manager at McKesson. People
must believe that you understand their needs and have their interests at heart. Only through an intimate knowledge of their
dreams, their hopes, their aspirations, their visions, their values
is the leader able to enlist their support.

There is an old Texas saying that "you can't light a fire
with a wet match." Leaders cannot ignite the flame of passion in
their followers if they themselves do not express enthusiasm for
the compelling vision of their group. Leaders communicate their
passion through vivid language and an expressive style.

Person after person in our study reported that they were
incredibly enthusiastic about their personal best projects. Their
own enthusiasm was catching; it spread from leader to followers.
The leader's own belief in and enthusiasm for the vision are the
spark that ignites the flame of inspiration.

Enabling Others to Act. Leaders do not achieve success by themselves. When we asked Bill Flanagan, vice-president of manufacturing at Amdahl Corporation, to tell us his personal best, he
replied that he couldn't, "because it wasn't my personal best. It
was our personal best. It wasn't me. It was us."

After reviewing over 500 personal best cases, we have developed a simple one-word test to detect whether someone is on the
road to becoming a leader. That word is *we*.

Exemplary leaders enlist the support and assistance of all
those who must make the project work. They involve, in some
way, those who must live with the results, and they make it possible for others to do good work. They encourage collaboration,
build teams, and empower others. *They enable others to act.* In
91 percent of the cases we analyzed, leaders proudly discussed
how teamwork and collaboration were essential. Additionally,
our data on others' perceptions of leaders indicate that this is the
most significant of all the five practices.

When Versatec needed a table for its conference room,

instead of buying one, Renn Zaphiropoulos, president and chief executive officer, invited the managers over to his house to build one. In his garage one Saturday, they built a twenty-one-foot-long teakwood conference table, hauled it to the company on a flatbed truck, and carried it up two flights of stairs to the conference room. This off-line camaraderie illustrates the family feeling that typically develops among highly committed, productive teams.

This sense of teamwork goes far beyond the leader and his or her immediate subordinates. It includes peers, superiors, customers, suppliers—all those who must support the vision. Rosabeth Moss Kanter, a Harvard professor, confirms this in her research on successful innovations inside large corporations. In her book *The Change Masters,* she reports, "The few projects in my study that disintegrated did so because the manager failed to build a coalition of supporters and collaborators."[4] The effect of enabling others to act is to make them feel strong, capable, and committed. Those in the organization who must produce the results feel a sense of ownership. They feel empowered, and when people feel empowered, they are more likely to use their energies to produce extraordinary results.

Modeling the Way. At a recent faculty convocation at Santa Clara University, the president, Reverend William J. Rewak, S.J., spoke eloquently about the changes anticipated for the campus. After he showed slides of the planned new buildings and gardens, he said: "Vision needs management, electricity, and concrete." Grand dreams, he reminded us, cannot become significant realities with élan alone. Leaders also must have detailed plans. They must steer projects along the course, measure performance, raise funds, and take corrective action. Many conventional management practices are certainly useful. Yet there is an even more demanding leadership task if a person is to direct the course of action. The leader must *model the way.*

Irwin Federman, president and chief executive officer of Monolithic Memories, puts it this way: "Your job gives you authority. Your behavior earns you respect."[5] While managers appraise their subordinates, subordinates also appraise their managers. The test they use is a simple one: Does my leader practice what he or she preaches? Ninety-five percent of our leaders

reported that they modeled the way through planning and leading by example.

In order to lead by example, leaders must first be clear
about their business beliefs. Managers may speak eloquently
about vision and values, but if their behavior is not consistent
with their stated beliefs, people ultimately will lose respect for
them. It may be best to take the advice of Frank J. Ruck, Jr.,
former president of Employee Transfer Company and current
president of Thermal Designs, Inc., who says of his leadership
style: "I began by becoming a role model that exemplifies the
organizational and management values I believe are important."[6]

Being a role model means paying attention to what you
believe is important. It means showing others through your
behavior that you live your values. Tom Melohn believes he
should "share whatever wealth was created" at NATD. So each
year, employees are given shares of NATD stock. And that stock
is newly issued.

Tom Peters, coauthor of *In Search of Excellence* and *Passion for Excellence,* summarizes this practice superbly when he
says, "The only magic is brute consistence, persistence, and attention to detail."[7] Leaders act in ways that are consistent with their
beliefs, they are persistent in pursuit of their visions, and they are
always vigilant about the little things that make a big difference.

Encouraging the Heart. Each spring at Versatec, about 2,000 non-
managerial personnel come together to receive annual bonuses.
Recently, Zaphiropoulos arrived at the celebration dressed in a
satin costume and riding atop an elephant, accompanying the
Stanford Marching Band. Zaphiropoulos likes to say, "If you are
going to give someone a check, don't just mail it. Have a celebration."

The climb to the top is arduous and long. People become
exhausted, frustrated, and disenchanted. They often are tempted
to give up. Leaders must *encourage the heart* of their followers to
carry on. With elephants and music and a share of the gain,
Zaphiropoulos gives heart to his people so that they will continue the journey.

Of course, it is not necessary to be that dramatic to offer
encouragement. Simple things can create similar reactions. Phil

Turner, plant manager of the Wire and Cable Division of Raychem Corporation, occasionally will put on a clown costume and give out balloons. He enjoys celebrating milestones and the employees get a good laugh from Turner's playful acts. Sue Cook, former manager of employee development at Apple Computer and now a consultant with the Tom Peters Group, is a master of celebration. She gives out stickers, T-shirts, buttons, and every other conceivable award when people achieve a milestone. Mervyn's top management send note cards that have "I heard something good about you" printed at the top. They are sent not just to other officers but to clerks, buyers, trainers, and other line employees.

People do not start their work each day with a desire to lose. It is part of the leader's job to show them that they can win. In the cases we collected, there were numerous examples of individual recognition and group celebration. The marching bands, the bells, the T-shirts, the note cards, the personal thank-yous are the visible signs of encouragement to keep on winning. If people smell a charlatan making noisy pretenses, they will turn away. But genuine acts of caring draw people forward.

There is one other aspect of encouragement that came through in the cases we examined: the encouragement that leaders give themselves. When we asked George Gananian, owner of Star Graphics, why he worked so hard, he said, "I love to turn the key in the door and put on the coffee pot." Love of their products, their people, their customers, their work—this may just be the best-kept secret of exemplary leadership.

The Ten Commitments of Leadership

Our research has shown us that leadership is an observable, learnable set of practices. Leadership is not something mystical and ethereal that cannot be understood by ordinary people. It is a myth that only a lucky few can ever decipher the leadership code. We have discovered hundreds of people who have led others to get extraordinary things done in organizations. There are thousands, perhaps millions, more. The belief that leadership cannot be learned is a far more powerful deterrent to development than is the nature of the leadership process itself.

We found the following behavioral commitments in the personal best leadership cases:

Challenging the Process
   1. Search for Opportunities
   2. Experiment and Take Risks

Inspiring a Shared Vision
   3. Envision the Future
   4. Enlist Others

Enabling Others to Act
   5. Foster Collaboration
   6. Strengthen Others

Modeling the Way
   7. Set the Example
   8. Plan Small Wins

Encouraging the Heart
   9. Recognize Individual Contribution
   10. Celebrate Accomplishments

We will fully explore each of these commitments in Chapters Three through Twelve. But before we do that, let us see what followers expect of leaders.

2

What Followers Expect
of Their Leaders:
Knowing the Other Half
of the Story

> To be persuasive we must be believable; to be believable we must be credible; to be credible, we must be truthful.
> ——*Edward R. Murrow, Journalist and News Commentator*

Challenging the process, inspiring a shared vision, enabling others to act, modeling the way, and encouraging the heart: these are the practices that leaders use to get extraordinary things done in organizations. These are the ways that leaders get others to want to contribute their best to the organization. But what we have described so far is only half the story. As we have asserted, leadership is not only about leaders; it is also about followers. Followers determine whether someone possesses leadership qualities. Upper management cannot confer leadership on someone they select to manage a unit. Over time, those who would be followers will determine whether that person should be—and will be—recognized as a leader. Leadership is in the eye of the follower.

To balance our portrait of leadership, we investigated the expectations that followers have of leaders, to determine the extent to which their perceptions of leadership matched what leaders themselves said they did.

Leader Characteristics That Followers Admire

To begin the investigation, along with professor Warren Schmidt we surveyed nearly 1,500 managers from around the country in a study sponsored by the American Management Association.[1] We asked the following open-ended question: "What values (personal traits or characteristics) do you look for and admire in your superiors?" More than 225 different values, traits, and characteristics were identified. Subsequent content analysis by several independent judges reduced these items into fifteen categories. The most frequent responses, in order of mention, were (1) integrity (is truthful, is trustworthy, has character, has convictions), (2) competence (is capable, is productive, is efficient), and (3) leadership (is inspiring, is decisive, provides direction).

In a follow-up study sponsored by the Federal Executive Institute Alumni Association, we surveyed 800 senior executives in the federal government.[2] Responding to the categories generated in the previous study, public-sector executives rated integrity, competence, and leadership as the three characteristics most admired in their superiors.

In a subsequent study, we elaborated on several categories and added a few new characteristics not included in the previous two studies. In a two-year series of executive seminars conducted at Santa Clara University and several corporate locations, over 2,600 top-level managers completed a checklist of superior leader characteristics. The results from these surveys, shown in Table 1, are striking in their regularity. It appears that there are several essential tests that a person must pass before we are willing to grant him or her the title *leader*. According to our research, the majority of us admire leaders who are:

- Honest
- Competent
- Forward-looking
- Inspiring

An internal study at AT&T has produced results that support our findings. Boyd Clarke and Ron Crossland of AT&T's Cincinnati-based Sales and Marketing Education Center have administered an internal AT&T version of our modified checklist of characteristics of admired leaders as part of their leadership research. Their findings show striking similarity to the findings among the general management population. The top five characteristics selected by AT&T employees were: (1) honest, (2) competent, (3) inspiring, (4) courageous, and (5) forward-looking.[3] Considering all the hurdles AT&T has overcome in recent years, it seems predictable that "courageous" would rank slightly higher on their results than on the national survey.

You will note the similarity between some of these characteristics and the practices described by successful leaders in Chapter One. We will examine the relationship among leaders' practices and these attributes at the end of this chapter. At this point, we will examine four characteristics in greater detail.

Honesty. In every survey we conducted, honesty was selected more often than any other leadership characteristic. When you think

Table 1. Characteristics of Superior Leaders.

Characteristic	U.S. Managers (N = 2,615)	
	Ranking	*Percentage of Managers Selecting*
Honest	1	83
Competent	2	67
Forward-looking	3	62
Inspiring	4	58
Intelligent	5	43
Fair-minded	6	40
Broad-minded	7	37
Straightforward	8	34
Imaginative	9	34
Dependable	10	33
Supportive	11	32
Courageous	12	27
Caring	13	26
Cooperative	14	25
Mature	15	23
Ambitious	16	21
Determined	17	20
Self-controlled	18	13
Loyal	19	11
Independent	20	10

about it, honesty is absolutely essential to leadership. After all, if we are to willingly follow someone, whether it be into battle or into the boardroom, we first want to assure ourselves that the person is worthy of our trust. We want to know that he or she is being truthful, ethical, and principled. We want to be fully confident in the integrity of our leaders. That over 80 percent of American managers want their leaders to be honest is extremely encouraging. The unfortunate news is that fewer than half of American citizens think that business executives are honest. According to a *New York Times*/CBS poll conducted in the spring of 1985, only 32 percent of the public believes that most corporate executives are honest;[4] 55 percent think that most are not honest. There is clearly a gap between what we admire and what the public thinks it is getting.

Just how do followers measure such subjective characteristics? In our discussions with respondents, we found that it was the leader's *behavior* that provided the evidence. In other words, whatever leaders say about their own integrity, followers wait to be shown. The only way we can know for sure whether someone is honest is to observe how he or she behaves. Leaders are considered honest by followers if they do what they say they are going to do. Agreements not followed through, false promises, deceptions, and cover-ups are all examples of indicators that a leader is not honest. On the other hand, if leaders keep their word and behave in a straightforward manner, we consider them honest.

Consistency between word and deed is another way we judge someone to be honest. If a leader espouses one set of values but personally practices another, we find that person to be duplicitous. If the leader practices what he or she preaches, then we are more willing to entrust that individual with our careers, our security, and sometimes even our lives. Honesty is also related to values and ethics. We appreciate people who take a stand on important principles. We resolutely refuse to follow those who lack confidence in their own beliefs. Confusion over where the leader stands creates stress; not knowing the leader's beliefs contributes to conflict, indecision, and political rivalry. We simply do not trust people who will not tell us their values, ethics, and standards.

Another element of trustworthiness is highlighted by the results of a related study of leadership practices that we conducted. In that study, we found that of all the behaviors describing leadership, the most important item was the leader's display of trust in others. Irwin Federman, president and chief executive officer (CEO) of semiconductor manufacturer Monolithic Memories, says it best: "Trust is a risk game. The leader must ante up first."[5] If leaders want to be seen as trustworthy, they must first give evidence of their own trust in us.

Competence. The leadership attribute chosen next most frequently is competence. To enlist in another's cause, we must believe that that person knows what she or he is doing. We must see the person as capable and effective. If we doubt the leader's abilities, we are unlikely to enlist in the crusade.

Leadership competence does not necessarily refer to the leader's technical abilities in the core technology of the business. For managers, there is, of course, the rather universal expectation that the person be able to get things done for the business unit. Having a winning track record is the surest way to be considered competent. Expertise in leadership skills themselves is another dimension of competence. The abilities to challenge, inspire, enable, model, and encourage—the skills that we discussed in the previous chapter—must be demonstrated if leaders are to be seen as capable.

The type of competence that followers look for seems to vary with the leader's position and the condition of the company. For example, the higher the rank of the leader, the more people demand to see demonstrated abilities in strategic planning and policy making. If a company desperately needs to clarify its distinctive skills and market position, a CEO with savvy in competitive marketing may be perceived as a fine leader. But at the line functional level, where subordinates expect guidance in technical areas, these same managerial abilities will not be enough.

We have come to refer to the kind of competence needed by leaders as value-added competence. Functional competence may be necessary, but it is insufficient. The leader must bring some added value to the position. Tom Melohn, whom we looked at in the last chapter, is a good case in point. As a former consumer marketing executive, Melohn knows nothing about how to run a drill press or a stamping machine. Yet, in the eight years since he and his partner bought the company, NATD has excelled in every measure in its industry. If Melohn brings no industry, company, or technical expertise to NATD, what has enabled him to lead the firm to its astounding results? Our answer: he added to the firm what it most needed at the time—the abilities to motivate and to sell. Melohn entrusted the skilled craftspeople with the work they knew well, and, for his own part, he applied the selling skills he had learned from a quarter century in marketing consumer products. He also recognized and rewarded the NATD "gang" for their accomplishments, increasing their financial and emotional sense of ownership in the firm.

Being Forward-Looking. Over half of our respondents selected being forward-looking as one of their most sought-after leadership traits. We expect our leaders to have a sense of direction and a concern for the future of the organization. This expectation directly corresponds to the ability to envision the future that leaders described in their personal best cases. But whether we call it vision, dream, calling, goal, or personal agenda, the message is clear: admired leaders must know where they are going.

Two surveys that we did on top executives reinforce the importance of clarity of purpose and direction. In one study, 284 senior executives rated "developing a strategic planning and forecasting capability" as their most critical concern. These same senior managers, when asked to select the most important characteristics in a CEO, ranked "a leadership style of honesty and integrity" first and "a long-term vision and direction for the company" second.[6]

It is important to note that by *forward-looking*, people do not mean the magical power of a prescient visionary. The reality is far more down to earth: it is the ability to set or select a desirable destination toward which the organization should head. The vision of a leader is the magnetic north that sets the compass course of the company. Followers ask that a leader have a well-defined orientation toward the future. We want to know what the company will look like, feel like, be like when it arrives at its goal in six months or six years. We want to have it described to us in rich detail so that we will know when we have arrived and so that we can select the proper route for getting there.

Inspiration. We also expect our leaders to be enthusiastic, energetic, and positive about the future. We expect them to be inspiring—a bit of the cheerleader, as a matter of fact. It is not enough for a leader to have a dream about the future. He or she must be able to communicate the vision in ways that encourage us to sign on for the duration. As Apple Computer manager Dave Patterson put it, "The leader is the evangelist for the dream." Again, followers seem to align with leaders. Recall that in the personal best cases, inspiring a shared vision was a common practice.

In his book *Working,* Studs Terkel quotes Nora Watson, an editor: "I think most of us are looking for a calling, not a job. Most of us, like the assembly line worker, have jobs that are too small for our spirit. Jobs are not big enough for people."[7] Her words underscore how important it is to find some greater sense of purpose and worth in our day-to-day working life. While the enthusiasm, energy, and positive attitude of a good leader may not change the nature of work on the assembly line, they certainly can make the work more enjoyable.

Not everyone agrees with this. Some react with discomfort to the idea that being inspiring is an essential leadership quality. One chief executive officer of a large corporation even told us, "I don't trust people who are inspiring." No doubt this is a response to past crusaders who led their followers to death or destruction. Other executives are skeptical of their ability to inspire others. Both are making a terrible mistake. In the final analysis, it is essential that leaders inspire our confidence in the validity of the goal. Enthusiasm and excitement signal the leader's personal commitment to pursuing that dream. If a leader displays no passion for a cause, why should others?

Putting It All Together: Credibility

Honest. Competent. Forward-looking. Inspiring. Taken singularly, these terms may not be altogether surprising descriptions of leadership attributes. But together, these characteristics comprise what communications experts refer to as "credibility."

In assessing the believability of sources of communication—people in such roles as newscasters and salespeople, as well as managers—researchers typically evaluate them on three criteria: their perceived trustworthiness, expertise, and dynamism. Those who rate more highly on these dimensions are considered to be more credible sources of information.

These three characteristics are strikingly similar to honesty, competence, and inspiration—three of the four most frequently selected items in our survey. What we found—quite unexpectedly—in our investigation of admired leadership qualities is that, more than anything, we want leaders who are credible. Above all else, we must be able to believe in our leaders. We must believe that their word can be trusted, that they will do what they say, that they have the knowledge and skill to lead, and that they are personally excited and enthusiastic about the direction in which we are headed.

In a revealing study, Charles O'Reilly of the University of California, Berkeley, investigated the credibility of the top management groups of three companies. Using the criteria of trustworthiness, expertise, and dynamism, O'Reilly measured how credible the employees perceived their top managements to be. He then examined the relationship between top management credibility and employee commitment on the basis of shared values—what he called "moral involvement." He found that "When employees perceive management to be trustworthy and to have a coherent philosophy, they also report higher levels of identification and value congruence."[8] O'Reilly concludes from this study that when top management is perceived to have high credibility and a strong philosophy, employees are more likely to:

- Be proud to tell others they are part of the organization.
- Talk up the organization with friends.
- See their own values as similar to those of the organization.
- Feel a sense of ownership for the organization.

But when top management is perceived to have low credibility, employees are more likely to believe that other company employees:

- Produce only when watched.
- Are motivated primarily by money.

- Say good things about the organization at work, but feel differently in private.
- Would consider looking for another job if the organization were experiencing tough times.[9]

O'Reilly's study offers clear reasons for organizational leaders to take seriously how their employees perceive their credibility. The loyalty and commitment of employees may depend upon it. But there is a difference between newscasters and leaders. While we demand that both be credible in order for us to accept what they are saying, we demand something more of leaders. We demand that they be forward-looking: that they have a sense of direction, a vision for the future. We expect newscasters to be independent when reporting what is happening today; we expect leaders to have a point of view and to be firm about the destination of our national or organizational journey. We want journalists to be cool and objective; we want leaders to articulate the exciting possibilities. While leaders are supposed to make the news, journalists are only supposed to report it.

A study by the Times Mirror Company serves to illustrate this point.[10] In late 1985, they investigated public attitudes toward the news media. Among the questions they asked the sample of 4,000 Americans was how they would rate the believability of a number of news organizations and media figures. The most believable media organization was the *Wall Street Journal*. It received an 87 percent believability rating. The most highly rated news anchor was Walter Cronkite, with a 92 percent believability rating. In that same study, the Times Mirror Company also asked people to rate the believability of the president of the United States, Ronald Reagan. Reagan was at the time the most likable and approved second-term president in the history of polling, with an approval rating of 68 percent. He received an identical believability rating of 68 percent. On this score, Reagan did not fare as well as Walter Cronkite, Peter Jennings, David Brinkley, Dan Rather, John Chancellor, and nine other news people. He did slightly better than Jack Anderson and Phil Donahue.

In commenting on these ratings, the Times Mirror Company said: "Yet President Reagan was seen then as less believable than all the major anchors and major news organizations that appear in this study. . . . One qualification is in order. President Reagan is not in the non-partisan news business. He is in partisan politics. Rather, Jennings and Brokaw are very credible, but they are in the believability business, not in partisan politics."[11]

What this study makes evident is that when a leader takes a position on issues—when he or she has a clear point of view and a partisan sense of where the country or the organization ought to be headed—that individual will be seen as less believable than someone who takes no stand.

What are the implications for leaders? First, we place leaders in an awkward situation. We demand that they be credible, but we also contribute to undermining their credibility by expecting them to focus on a clear direction for the future. Leaders must learn how to balance their own desire to achieve important ends with the followers' needs to believe that the leader has their best interests at heart.

Second, because of this fact, leaders must be ever diligent in guarding their credibility. Their ability to take strong stands—to challenge the status quo, to point us in new directions—depends upon their being perceived as highly credible. No one will want to go the leader's way if they doubt that person's trustworthiness, expertise, or dynamism.

Again, Reagan makes a good case in point. While his believability and approval rating was 68 percent as late as October 1986, by December 1986 only 56 percent believed he was honest and open, according to a *Newsweek*/Gallup poll.[12] His approval rating fell to 47 percent in December 1986. Why the sharp and sudden decline? Many in the public believed that Reagan was not being candid and forthcoming about his role in the secret arms deal with Iran and diversion of funds to the Nicaraguan Contras. He was no longer perceived to be as credible as he had been previously.

Only history will tell the full impact on Reagan of this affair. But it is clear evidence of the importance of honesty in the believability rating of a leader. While Reagan is in politics and business executives are in less visibly partisan pursuits, executives can draw a lesson from this: without credibility, you will find it difficult to govern.

Credibility is one of the hardest attributes to earn. And it is the most fragile of human qualities. It is earned minute by minute, hour by hour, month by month, year by year. But it can be lost in very short order if not attended to. We are willing to forgive a few minor transgressions, a slip of the tongue, a misspoken word, a careless act. But there comes a time when enough is enough. And when leaders have used up all their credibility, they will find that it is nearly impossible to earn it back.

The Essence of Leadership

It is clear that the majority of us can agree on what we want from our leaders. We want them to be credible, and we want them to have a sense of direction. If someone is to lead us, that person must be able to stand before us and confidently express an attractive image of the future, and we must be able to believe that he or she has the ability to take us there.

There are many striking relationships between what leaders say they do when at their personal best and what followers say they admire and look up to in their leaders. Clearly, the leadership practice of inspiring a common vision involves being forward-looking and inspiring. By challenging the process, leaders enhance the perception that they are dynamic. The practice of modeling the way includes the clarification of a set of values and being an example of those values to others. This consistent living out of values is a behavioral way of demonstrating honesty or trustworthiness. We trust leaders when their deeds and words match. Trust is also a major element of enabling others to act. In their descriptions of their personal bests, leaders said that they trusted others, which fostered others' trust in them. Likewise, encouraging the heart—the recognition and celebration of significant accomplishments—contributes to perceptions of being just, fair, and sincere.

The quality of competence or expertise is more difficult to ascertain from leaders' descriptions of their personal bests. They did not talk about this directly. We can infer that since they were talking about a time when they did their best, they were also talking about a time when they felt competent. Competence is determined by one's track record. If we succeed at something over time, we can assume some expertise in that area. The cases in our research are examples of competent performance.

When leaders follow the practices described in their personal bests, they attract others to what they represent. In a certain sense, they manage their credibility. They are conscious of how their behavior shapes the impressions others have of them, and so they take charge of how others come to see them. So long as this is done with sincerity and integrity—and not with the unethical manipulation of the con artist—leaders earn credibility in the eyes of their followers. It is this credibility that establishes the foundation upon which dreams for the future can be built.

We began this section of the book with a statement made by Vance Packard twenty-five years ago in his book *The Pyramid Climbers*. He offered one of the most straightforward definitions of leadership we have found: "In essence leadership appears to be the art of getting others to want to do something you are convinced should be done."[13] Two words in this definition stand out as most significant: *to want*. Without *to want* in the definition, the meaning of leadership is significantly altered. Choice, internal motivation, and inner desire disappear. Leadership then implies force or something less than voluntary involvement.

It is a fairly easy task to get people to do something. Promise them a favorable review, a promotion, or a bonus if they perform exceptionally well. Or if incentives don't work, threaten to report them, demote them, fire them, or punish them in some other way. With these extrinsic rewards and pressures, we can get most people to do things. Managers have been proving this for years. But what of those who have no bonuses to give, no promotions to offer, and no performance reviews to write? What of those who cannot pay any compensation and yet ask us to contribute our time, our resources, our services, our energies, even our lives? What of those who must rely upon our willingness, our internal motivation, to give of ourselves for some just cause? Do they not lead?

To get a feel for the true essence of leadership, assume that everyone who works for you is a volunteer. Assume that they are there because they want to be, not because they have to be. What would need to exist for them to want to enlist in such an organization? What would you need to do under those conditions if you wanted people to perform at high levels? What would you need to do if you wanted them to remain loyal to your organization?

If there is a clear distinction between the process of managing and the process of leading, it is in the distinction between getting others to do and getting others to want to do. Managers, we believe, get other people to do, but leaders get other people to want to do. Leaders do this by first of all being credible. That is the foundation of all leadership. They establish this credibility by their actions—by challenging, inspiring, enabling, modeling, and encouraging. In the next ten chapters of this book, we will describe how leaders engage in each of these practices. We will support these practices with our own research and that of other leadership scholars. In addition, we will offer you suggestions on how you can put these to use in your everyday work.

PART TWO

Challenging the Process

The ability to participate in a challenge and to
make it a shared challenge is an incredible task
for a leader.

—*Patricia M. Carrigan,*
Plant Manager,
General Motors

Challenge is the opportunity for greatness. People do their best
when there's the chance to change the ways things are. Maintaining the status quo breeds mediocrity. Leaders seek and accept
challenging opportunities to test their abilities. They motivate
others to exceed their limits. They look for innovative ways to
improve the organization. Leaders do their best when there is a
tough assignment or quest for change.

Most innovations do not come from leaders. They come
from customers and people who do the work. Leaders listen to
the advice and counsel of others. They know that good ideas
enter the mind through the ears, not the mouth.

Leaders experiment and take risks. Since risk taking
involves mistakes and failure, leaders learn to accept the inevitable disappointments. They treat them as learning opportunities.
In the next two chapters, we will see how leaders:

- Search for Opportunities.
- Experiment and Take Risks.

3

Search for Opportunities:
Confronting and Changing
the Status Quo

Leadership requires changing the "business-as-usual" environment.

——Joe J. Sparagna, Vice-President,
Elsin Corporation

Take out a piece of paper and draw a line down the middle. Now think about the people you consider leaders. They can be either contemporary or historical ones. Think about the men and women who you believe have led their organizations, communities, states, nations, and the world. Write their names in the left-hand column.

In the right-hand column opposite each name, record the events or actions with which you identify these individuals. When you think of each of these people, with what situations do you associate them?

Take out another piece of paper. Again, draw a line down the center. This time, make a list of all those people you think of as managers. Opposite their names, make note of the events or actions with which you identify them. What situations come to mind when you think of managers?

Now review the two lists. What does an analysis of the leadership situations reveal to you? Is there any pattern? What do they have in common? What does an analysis of the management situations reveal to you? Is there a pattern there? And what, if any, differences are there between the lists of management and leadership events?

Here is what we predict you will find:

If some of the leaders on your list are business people, you have associated them with the turnaround of failing companies, the start-up of entrepreneurial ventures, the development of new lines of products or services, or other business transformations. For those on your list who are leaders in government, the military, the arts, the community, or the church, we would predict a similar kind of association. Most likely, you identify these leaders with creation of new institutions, resolution of serious crises, winning of wars, revolutionary movements, protests for improving social conditions, political change, innovation, or some other social transformation.

And the management situations? We would predict that they would be actions such as cutting costs, improving efficiency, establishing stability, making things run smoothly, or other measures to control organization processes.

When we think of leaders, we recall times of turbulence, conflict, innovation, and change. When we think of managers, we recall times of stability, harmony, maintenance, and constancy.

We need leaders, and we need managers. Both are essential to making social systems work. But each plays distinctively different roles. And the unique role of the leader is to take us on journeys to places we have never been before.

Throughout this book, we use the metaphor of the journey as the most appropriate metaphor for discussing the tasks of leaders. That is because the root origin of the word *lead* is a word meaning "to go."[1] This root origin denotes travel from one place to another. Leaders can be said to be those who "go first." They are those who step out to show others the direction in which to head. They begin the quest for a new order.

In this sense, leaders are pioneers. They are people who venture into unexplored territory. They guide us to new and often unfamiliar destinations. People who take the lead are the foot soldiers in the campaigns for change.

By comparison, the root origin of *manage* is a word meaning "hand."[2] Managing seems to connote "handling" things. Managers tend to focus on control and maintenance of the status quo. A major difference between management and leadership can be found in the root meanings of the two words, the difference between what it means to handle things and what it means to go places. The unique reason for having leaders—their differentiating function—is to move us forward. Leaders get us going someplace.

Now, the path out of crisis and into peace, or out of the familiar and into the novel, is full of ghostly unknowns. It is often through the wilderness. It is often blocked by the barriers of convention. The study of leadership is the study of how men and women guide us through empty and frightening expanses of uncharted territory.

The appropriate place to begin our detailed discussion of leadership practices is with the leaders' *search for opportunities*. Leaders look for ways to radically alter the status quo, for ways to create something totally new, for revolutionary new processes, for ways to beat the system. Whether leaders are selected for projects or initiate them, they always search for opportunities to do what has never been done.

The Challenge of Change

The first thing that struck us as we analyzed the personal best cases was that they were about significant change. Regardless of function, regardless of industry, regardless of level, the leaders in our study talked about times when they led adventures into new territory. They told us how they turned around losing operations, started up new plants, installed untested procedures, or greatly improved the results of poorly performing units. And these were not the usual 10, 25, or even 50 percent improvements in products and processes seen in many organizations. The cases involved times when the magnitude of changes was in the *hundreds* of percent. The personal best leadership cases were about firsts, about radical departures from the past, about doing things that had never been done before, about going to places no one else had yet discovered.

It may not seem so startling that the majority of our leadership cases were about innovation and change. It is probably what comes to your mind when you think about the time you did your best as a leader. But you see, we did not ask people to tell us about change; we asked them to tell us about their personal best leadership experiences. We asked them to tell us about an event or series of events that they believed to be their individual standard of excellence—their record-setting leadership performance. They could discuss any leadership experience they chose, past or present, unofficial or official, in any organization and functional area.

What participants chose to talk about were times of change. They did not choose to write about stability and the status quo. The attitude of Joe J. Sparagna, vice-president of Elsin Corporation, was typical: "Leadership requires changing the 'business-as-usual' environment." Patricia M. Carrigan was one who did just that.

In July 1982, Patricia M. Carrigan faced a significant challenge of change. That month she became the first female assembly plant manager in the history of General Motors. Educated as a clinical psychologist, until then she had spent more years in public education than in the auto industry. The task before her was awesome—the turnaround of the Lakewood assembly plant in Atlanta.

Lakewood had a long history of labor-management conflicts. For example, on September 14, 1970, the Lakewood plant was shut down, in one of General Motors's longest strikes—136 days. At issue were more than 5,500 grievances and 1,100 cases of protested discipline. One grievance in particular attracted media attention: an employee had demanded compensation for a shoeshine, alleging that his foot had been stepped on by a security officer.

Soon after Carrigan began her tenure at Lakewood, the plant was again hit by trouble, this time from declining car sales. It was shut down for a year and a half. "The fact that the plant was out of production so long that its workers scattered to other plants across the country gave strong impetus to change," says Carrigan.

Two years after the plant reopened under her efforts, Carrigan departed for a new assignment at the General Motors plant in Bay City, Michigan. In those short two years, Lakewood became an entirely different place. Its successes were evidence of a phenomenal change, perhaps the most extraordinary of any plant anywhere. Here are a few of those as described by Carrigan:

> In May of that year (1984), Lakewood became the first plant in GM history to attain a widely accepted corporate standard for high quality in the first published audit after start-up and the first to repeat that performance just after the second shift started up.
>
> Grievances have remained at or near zero, and discipline incidents have declined by 82 percent since the plant has operated on two shifts. There have been no cases of protested discipline since the plant reopened.
>
> Despite the addition of heavy daily and Saturday overtime since production resumed, absenteeism declined from 25 percent to 9 percent, saving more than $8 million.
>
> Sickness and accident costs were cut by two-thirds. A jointly established five-year goal for reduction in sick-leave costs was attained in the first year, netting a $1.3 million credit for 1984 and lower rates for 1985.[3]

These results are testimony to the unprecedented cooperation between management and labor at Lakewood. Jointly, they accomplished what few have ever been able to do, in any industry. They completely transformed an organization, and they made it work.

Getting these results did not just happen. It required a totally new approach to working together. The strategy had three main ingredients. First, a two-week pre–start-up training class for all employees was jointly structured and presented by labor and management. The training presented detailed business information as well as jointly developed plans for improving plant business performance. That same training was then conducted for all new employees after start-up. Hourly and salaried people served as facilitators.

Second, labor and management jointly encouraged greater participation in the business by Lakewood employees. By October of 1985, there were 133 planning/problem-solving work groups functioning on a voluntary basis, involving over 90 percent of the work force.

Third, an extensive ongoing training program was established for Lakewood employees at "Lakewood University"—eight portable classrooms housed in an unused part of the plant. At the time of Carrigan's departure, labor and management had jointly enhanced the skills of over 3,000 people in a total of over 360,000 hours of training.

All of these incredible actions flowed directly from the jointly developed plant philosophy. The essence of it is contained in these four principles:

> To change, take risks, accept responsibility, and be accountable for our actions.
>
> To respect all people, promoting unity, trust, pride, and dedication to our mission.
>
> To achieve a high quality of work life through involvement of all our people in an environment of openness and fairness in which everyone is treated with dignity, honesty, and respect.
>
> To promote good communications among all employees by operating in an open atmosphere with freedom to share ideas and speak one's mind without fear of reprisal.[4]

Carrigan gives credit for these achievements to the "partnership with people." But the employees at the plant recognized her contribution as well. When she left, the union local honored her with a plaque. The last three sentences describe Carrigan's impact: "Therefore be it resolved that we, the members of Local 34, honor Pat M. Carrigan for her leadership, courage, risk-taking, and honesty. Therefore, be it further resolved that Pat M. Carrigan, through the exhibiting of these qualities as a people person, has played a vital role in the creation of a new way of life at the Lakewood plant. Therefore, be it resolved that the members of Local 34 will always warmly remember Pat M. Carrigan as one of us."[5]

Perhaps more than anything else, leadership is about the "creation of a new way of life." And to make that happen, leaders must foster change, take risks, and accept the responsibility for making it happen. But Carrigan goes beyond that. "The challenge," she says, "is posed by what's out there and by our need to survive. The ability to participate in that challenge and to make it a shared challenge in the organization is an incredible task for a leader. The question is, 'How are you going to do that?' If you're going to expect an organization to take some risks, you have to show some willingness to do that too."[6]

Carrigan, and the other leaders in our study, accepted the challenge presented by the shifts in their industries or the new demands of the marketplace. They found opportunities to get extraordinary things done. They showed the willingness to take risks for the sake of changing the business-as-usual environment.

Agents of Change. When we reviewed the literature for this book, one very useful reference was *The Change Masters* by Rosabeth Moss Kanter, a Harvard Business School professor. In her research, Kanter investigated the human resource practices and organizational designs of innovation-producing organizations. She wanted to know what fostered and what hindered innovation in the American corporation.

Our study and Kanter's were done quite independently of each other at different periods in time. Our purposes were also different. We were studying leadership, and Kanter was studying innovation. Yet when we compared Kanter's cases with ours, we were struck by their similarity. In some cases, Kanter's innovators and our leaders talked about nearly identical projects, yet they were in completely separate organizations in vastly different regions of the country. We arrived at a similar conclusion in analyzing our respective cases: leadership is inextricably connected with the process of innovation, of bringing new ideas, methods, or solutions into use. To Kanter, innovation means change, and "Change requires leadership, after all, a 'prime mover' to push for implementation of strategic decisions"[7] Both of our sets of cases are evidence of that.

Similarly, James MacGregor Burns, professor of government at Williams College and author of *Leadership*, concludes his probing analysis of the subject by saying: "The ultimate test of practical leadership is the realization of intended, real change that meets people's enduring needs."[8] We would agree. The real result of the work of Carrigan, or any of the other leaders with whom we talked, was that the organization was substantively improved. There was a real difference that could be seen, felt, and measured. It wasn't just that a new system was installed, but that a new system was in use and making things better for everyone. It wasn't just that there was a reorganization, but that the new structure made a difference. It was not just a creative solution for the organization's problems but the implementation of that solution.

Initiation of Change. Leaders must be change agents and innovators. But they need not be entrepreneurs, if we mean by that term those who actually initiate and assume the risk for a new enterprise. Neither must they be "intrapreneurs"—entrepreneurs inside a corporation. In fact, we maintain that the majority of leadership in this world is neither entrepreneurial nor intrapreneurial.

In our research, we asked people to tell us who initiated the projects that they selected as their personal bests. We assumed that in the majority of the cases, they themselves would have been the sources of the ideas, the entrepreneurs or the intrapreneurs. What we found, instead, was that more than half the cases were initiated by someone other than the leaders, usually the leader's immediate superior.

Some to whom we have reported this finding see it as discouraging news. It is taken as demonstrating a lack of initiative on the part of our managerial personnel. We see it otherwise. If we examine our own careers as managers, we realize that much, if not most, of what we do is assigned. Many of us do not get to start everything we do from scratch. We do not always get to hire all our people, choose all our colleagues, decide on all the products and services. That's just the reality of business.

We were actually encouraged to find a substantial number of examples of exceptional leadership in situations that were not self-initiated. It would cause us to be terribly pessimistic if the only times people reported doing their best were when they got to be the founder and CEO. That would rule out a whole lot of people and the majority of business opportunities. Carrigan, for example, was selected to be plant manager. She did not found General Motors or start the plant. But when she arrived at Lakewood, she took it upon herself to excel. She enabled others to achieve what had never before been done in the automotive industry.

Or take the case of Lary Evans. He wasn't one of the founders of Tandem Computers, but he did achieve some extraordinary results there. When we talked to him, he was vice-president of manufacturing. (He has since moved on to become vice-president of manufacturing at Sequent Computer.) When we asked him to tell us about his personal best leadership experience, he selected the one on which he was working at the time. He and his team had as their objective to reduce the time it took to manufacture a Tandem Non-Stop (TM) computer. At the time that Evans was brought into the vice-presidency, he told us, the manufacturing build time was twenty-six weeks—from the time the first component part arrived at the company until the tested product was shipped to the customer. When we talked to Evans, about nine months into the process, the manufacturing build time had been reduced to ten weeks. Evans said that by the end of eighteen months it would be down to six. In one year, a full twenty weeks were shaved off the time it took to manufacture a computer, which is an extraordinary accomplishment in anyone's book. We asked Evans how he and his team were able to do it, and he said: "Well, the first thing you've got to do is challenge the process all the time."

Whether one is an entrepreneur, an intrapreneur, a manager, or an individual contributor, the leadership attitude is what makes the difference. That attitude is characterized by a posture of challenging the process—of wanting to change the business-as-usual environment.

There are three important lessons from our finding that not all personal best leadership experiences are self-initiated. First, people who become leaders do not always seek the challenges they face. Challenges also seek leaders.

Second, opportunities to challenge the status quo and introduce change open the doors to doing one's best. Challenge is the motivating environment for excellence.

Third, challenging opportunities often bring forth skills and abilities that people do not know they have. Given the opportunity and the support, ordinary managers can get extraordinary things done in organizations.

The Conditions That Foster Leadership

We had never seen a recruiting poster for leaders—not until Reno Taini and Randi DuBois gave us one. Taini and DuBois are founders of Pro-Action, an organization that conducts challenging educational adventures for students and executives. One of their clients is Operation Raleigh. Taini and DuBois assist Operation Raleigh in selecting members and in guiding expeditions. At the top of the Operation Raleigh recruiting poster is printed in big, bold letters: "Venturers Wanted!" Below the headline is a photograph of a group of people neck deep in a river with, believe it or not, smiles on their faces. The recruiting copy reads:

Join the Voyage of Discovery

For 1500 young Americans between the ages of 17 and 24, it will be the adventure of a lifetime. Underwater archaeology on sunken ships, aerial walkways in tropical rainforests, medical relief for remote tribal villages—innovative, exciting, worthwhile projects.

Beginning in late 1984, Operation Raleigh will take four years to circle the globe in support of scientific research, community aid, and challenging exploration.

The selected applicants will join fellow venturers from many nations for three-month periods. They will work alongside an expert expedition staff under rigorous conditions in over 40 countries worldwide.

Science and service are the themes and leadership development is a primary goal. It is the pioneer spirit of Sir Walter's day rekindled, and you are invited to apply.[9]

We think the Operation Raleigh recruiting poster is the most descriptive statement we have ever seen of the conditions that develop leadership abilities. Leadership opportunities are indeed voyages of discovery and adventures of a lifetime. They are challenging explorations under rigorous conditions. It does require a pioneering spirit to lead. These are the conditions that foster leadership.

Our clue to this came when we reviewed the answers to this item on our personal best questionnaire: "What five or six words would you use to best describe the character (the feel, the spirit, the nature, the quality) of your personal best leadership experience?" The answers read like the recruiting poster for Operation Raleigh. They suggested a highly spirited outlook, one that viewed the white waters of change as a personal challenge. Here is a sampling of responses:

David Arkless described the spirit of his international diplomacy mission for Hewlett-Packard, S.A.: "challenging, tough work, fun, daunting, unusual, uplifting." Julie Marshall talked about starting up a store for Nordstrom: "demanding, exciting, stimulating, stressful, whole-hearted, fun." Gayle Hamilton wrote about her new budget system project at Pacific Gas and Electric: "challenging, frustrating, tedious, influential, growing." When Gale Kingsbury led a project to improve financial systems at Tektronix, he found it "energizing, rewarding, motivating, strengthening, exciting, challenging." And Phil Lemay of Amdahl, when he was president of Industrial Services Techniques, Inc., in Montreal, found the experience "exciting, motivating, unique experience, satisfaction, something special, pride." All of these descriptions are vibrant and full of life. They resonate. They pulse and throb. The personal bests were times when people felt fully alive.

In analyzing the character of personal bests, the most frequently used words were *challenging, rewarding,* and *exciting.* Words signifying *intensity*—dedication, intense, commitment, determination—and *inspiration*—inspiring, uplifting, motivating, energizing—also appeared regularly. *Unique, important, proud,* and *empowering* got a fair share. Fully 95 percent of the cases were described in these terms. But leadership bests can also be filled with stress. Of the 95 percent who said their projects were exciting, 20 percent of the managers we studied also described their cases as frustrating, and 15 percent said that they aroused fear or anxiety. Yet the vast majority of these same individuals also used the more positive descriptors. Rather than being debilitated by the stress of the experience, they were challenged and energized by it. So stress can be associated with doing one's best. But that stress is a healthy stress. It gets people moving. It is what stress researcher Hans Selye describes as "eustress," or positive stress.

It is also instructive to observe how people chose *not* to

describe their personal bests. In no single instance in any of the cases did anyone use the word *boring*. Neither did anyone ever use *dull, unsatisfying, ordinary, indifferent, impassive, apathetic,* or *routine*. Humdrum situations are not associated with award-winning performances. Fundamentally, we associate doing our best with experiences that ignite enthusiasm in us. When it comes to excelling as leaders, the memorable times are filled with excitement. They are experiences that arouse feelings of passion. Starting a new organization, turning around a losing operation, installing a new system, greatly improving the social condition, enhancing the quality of our lives are all uplifting human endeavors.

Whether it is overcoming adversity or creating something unique and new, adventure is the context most conducive to doing our best as leaders. Enterprising situations contribute to a sense of personal achievement and self-worth. Boring tasks do not promote leadership or high performance.

When you enter the office of Renn Zaphiropoulos, president and chief executive officer of Versatec, Inc., your eyes catch this framed quotation: "Do not follow where the path may lead. Go instead where there is no path and leave a trail." This gives you an early clue to the business philosophy of Zaphiropoulos. He clearly believes in challenge, in blazing new trails, in setting a new course, and you would expect him to be the entrepreneur that he is. In 1969, Zaphiropoulos, along with four engineers, left Varian Associates to found Versatec. It is now the largest producer of electrostatic printers and plotters in the country.

Zaphiropoulos selected the development of the ECP-42 color plotter as the most recent example of a personal best leadership experience. "We were on a four-year bonus plan with Xerox," he explained. (In 1975 Versatec decided to sell the company to Xerox, but management remained with Zaphiropoulos and Versatec.) The subsidiary was to be paid "only if the predicted cumulative profit for four years turned out to be true. . . . But if you delivered 10 percent more, your shares doubled." And if the company did 10 percent more than that, then the shares multiplied again.

The last year in the four-year bonus plan for Versatec was 1983. But the situation did not appear promising. Zaphiropoulos told his managers, " 'Guys, the way the industry is going, things don't look as if we're going to make all this money. We need something to do that.' Bill Lloyd (one of the other founders and vice-president of research and development) said, 'Well, look, the color machine that we planned to develop for 1985, instead of taking two and a half years to do it, let's do it in five months.' So I said, 'That's a good idea.' We went on and made a plan to really do that. They accelerated the program, and they started acting in a very inspired way. At the end of 1982 we announced the machine, which made a lot of money in 1983. . . . So that saved the long-range plan."

And what did Zaphiropoulos do as the CEO to enable them to help the development group to meet the plan? "Instead of telling them I thought they were crazy, I said, 'That's a wonderful idea. What do you need?' . . . The thing was that there were some very brilliant ideas early that made the game playable. It wasn't shooting for the moon. See, people are motivated to play the game which is neither too easy nor too difficult. This, by hindsight, was just the right kind of level of challenge, and they met the challenge. It was one of the great ones."

Zaphiropoulos contends that challenge is part of most high-achieving efforts. "I believe nobody does anything without stress," he says. "The question is, 'How big should the stress be?' . . . People like interesting games to play. And there are certain things which motivate them to do that and certain things that de-motivate people; they give up. A game which is a repeat is not interesting. But if you somehow bring out a game that really gets people going, you can do all kinds of stuff."

Like other successful leaders, Zaphiropoulos searches for opportunities for people to exceed their previous levels of performance. He regularly sets the bar higher. And like other successful leaders, he knows that the challenge cannot be so great as to be discouraging. This awareness of the human need for challenge and the sensitivity to the human need to succeed at that challenge are among the critical skills of any leader.

The Intrinsically Motivating Environment

There is an old management cliché that goes: "What gets rewarded gets done." So the business world offers a lot of extrinsic rewards to get people to perform. Money, stock options, bonuses, perks, prestige, and position are some of the incentives of business. Zaphiropoulos, however, goes beyond the use of incentives. He attempts to structure work as a game.

Carrigan's success at the Lakewood plant did not involve a huge financial payoff for the employees involved. In some ways, her situation involved survival of the organization. So why did she and the Lakewood people go so far beyond survival expectations? Why did they set such incredible goals for themselves? Why, for that matter, do people do things for nothing? Why do they volunteer to put out fires, raise money for worthy causes, or help a child in need? Why do people join Mother Teresa in caring for the poorest of the poor? Why do they risk their careers to start a new business or risk their security to change the social condition? Why do they sign up for Operation Raleigh, or the Peace Corps, or Hands Across America? Why, heaven forbid, would anyone find satisfaction in anything that did not pay a lot of money or provide a lot of prestige? If extrinsic rewards explained all our behavior, then we would be hard pressed to find an explanation for any of these actions.

We believe that intrinsic motivation must be present if people are to do their best. And contrary to the hierarchical theory of motivation, we believe that it is possible to excel even when one is fighting for survival. So we would like to contribute another management axiom to the literature, one that helps explain why people seek to excel:

What *is* rewarding gets done.

But, if external rewards and punishments are successful, why should business leaders concern themselves with these intrinsic rewards? After all, people in business are not volunteers. They are getting paid.

It is precisely because people are getting paid, because people are eligible for bonuses and other awards, that a leader ought to be concerned. If work comes to be seen solely as a source of money and never as a source of satisfaction, then employers will totally ignore other human needs at work—needs such as learning, self-worth, pride, competence, and serving others. Employers will come to see workers' enjoyment of their tasks as totally irrelevant, and they will structure work in a strictly utilitarian fashion. The results will be—in fact, have already been—disastrous for many organizations. By employing only the hands of workers, and not their heads and hearts, organizations lose precious return on their investments in people.

We should also be concerned if employees must justify their employment in a particular organization as solely economic. If they gain only financial rewards and meet only security needs in their organizations, they will never contribute more than the minimum. They will also feel alienated and will leave when another, equally or better paying job becomes available. Research shows that monetary rewards have actually decreased people's desire to perform a task. Pay and other external rewards can significantly lower intrinsic motivation and can create dependence upon expensive reward systems.[10]

The absolute dedication to extrinsic motivators severely limits an organization's ability to excel. It constrains managers' abilities to use the full potential of employees. It wastes human talent and drains away organizational resources. Certainly we should pay people fairly and provide equitable benefits. This is definitely not an argument for exploitation. However, reliance upon external incentives and pressures constrains people. It does not liberate them to perform their best. It also constrains managers from ever learning how to get others to want to do what needs to be done. And if you do not learn how to get people to want, you will never learn how to lead.

As we observed earlier, the words used most frequently to describe the spirit of the personal bests were *challenging, rewarding,* and *exciting.* People truly enjoyed their best experiences. There was something about them that was intrinsically valuable. The work itself seemed to be a strong source of motivation. What makes something intrinsically motivating—a reward in itself? And what can we learn from this that might make us better leaders?

University of Chicago professor Mihaly Csikszentmihalyi conducted an inventive study to explore the nature of activities that contain rewards within themselves.[11] He studied such activities as rock climbing, dance, chess, and high school basketball.

But since none of these were so-called productive pursuits, he bridged the gap between leisure and work by adding to his study composers of music, surgeons, and teachers. He wanted to know what made these activities and jobs enjoyable. Csikszentmihalyi discovered that the primary reasons that the people he studied enjoyed their chosen activities were the enjoyment of the experience and the use of their skills. All these reasons are purely intrinsic. They sound tautological, but the fact of the matter is that we enjoy doing something because the doing of it is enjoyable. Those reasons that were most extrinsic in Csikszentmihalyi's study—"power, prestige, glamor"—ranked last.

What is it about the structure of these activities that produces the intrinsic motivation? Csikszentmihalyi found a surprisingly consistent answer. "Whatever the specific structure of an autotelic activity is like, it seems that its most basic requirement is to provide a clear set of challenges."[12] The challenges that rank highest in Csikszentmihalyi's study are "designing and discovering something new," "exploring a strange place," and "solving a mathematical problem."[13] These are not the only challenges in life, but they do suggest that the key to intrinsic motivation is getting involved in something that requires us to look at the situation in new ways.

Whether it is doing our best as leaders or enjoying what we do, answering the summons of adventure lifts our spirits. There is something about being invited to do better than we have ever done before that compels us to reach deep down inside and bring forth the warrior within.

A word of caution, however. Too much challenge and change can be frightening. It can immobilize. According to Csikszentmihalyi, activities that are too demanding for a person's capabilities can produce anxiety. The key to structuring activities for maximum intrinsic motivation is to find the proper balance between the opportunities for action and the person's skills.

The lessons for leadership are clear. First, for leaders to perform at their personal bests, they must experience the project itself as enjoyable and challenging. They must feel that it is one that calls upon them to use all of their skills and talents to the fullest. Second, if leaders wish to get the best from others, they must search for opportunities for people to create or to outdo themselves. Leaders must find opportunities for people to solve problems, make discoveries, explore new ground, reach a difficult goal, or figure out how to deal with an external threat. And they must make it fun. Third, leaders must know the skills of their people. In order to find the proper balance between action opportunities and individual skills, leaders must know what others can do and what they find personally challenging. It is not just what challenges the leader that is important. It is what challenges everyone and is within their capabilities to perform.

The Paradox of Routines

We have argued, on the basis of the personal best cases, that the opportunity to "change the business-as-usual environment" is the fertile soil for leadership. The challenge of creating a new way of life is intrinsically motivating to leaders and followers alike. Routines, on the other hand, can be the enemies of change. They can stifle the very adventure that leaders seek to create.

Warren Bennis, now a professor at the University of Southern California and coauthor of *Leaders*, described how routines prevented change when he was president of the University of Cincinnati: "My moment of truth came toward the end of my first ten months. It was one of those nights in the office. The clock was moving toward four in the morning, and I was still not through with the incredible mass of paper stacked before me. I was bone weary and soul weary, and I found myself muttering, 'Either I can't manage this place, or it's unmanageable.' I reached for my calendar and ran my eyes down each hour, half-hour, quarter-hour to see where my time had gone that day, the day before, the month before. . . . My discovery was this: I had become the victim of a vast, amorphous, unwitting, unconscious conspiracy to prevent me from doing anything whatever to change the university's status quo."[14] Bennis coined a phrase to describe this phenomenon. "This discovery, or rediscovery, had led to what might be called Bennis's First Law of Academic Pseudodynamics, to wit: Routine work drives out nonroutine work, or: how to smother to death all creative planning, all fundamental change in the university—or any institution."[15]

Every executive we know can relate to Bennis's dilemma.

It seems that situations and people conspire to make leaders into bureaucrats. The means by which organizations do this is through established routines—all those memorandums, all those telephone calls, all those reports, meetings, plans, speeches, letters, and so on. Bennis, by his own example, found himself caught up in the routine and the trivial. "But I have invested endless time in a matter only vaguely related to the prime purposes of our university,"[16] said Bennis at the time.

So leaders must challenge the process precisely because any system will unconsciously conspire to maintain the status quo and prevent change. But leaders live with a paradox when fighting against the routines of organizational life. On the one hand, they must destroy routines. Routines get us into ruts. Routines dull our senses. Routines stifle our creativity, constrict our thinking, remove us from stimulation, destroy our ability to compete. Once-useful routines sap the vitality out of an organization and cause it to atrophy. Yet some routines are essential to establishing a definable, consistent, measurable, and efficient operation. We get annoyed when we can't figure out who reports to whom. We get confused when our employers keep changing the strategy. We get absolutely livid when our boss takes us off one project and puts us on another just when we were beginning to get the hang of it. There are no economies in always changing. Constant changes in direction and in the ways things are done are confusing to employees, vendors, and customers.

Routines and routine work are among those things we can't live with and we can't live without. Established procedures annoy us, and yet we are glad we have them when we expect the trains to run on time. Repetitious work is definitely tedious. Yet if we never did anything the same way twice, we would never make any money. The critical issue for leaders is not routines or no routines, but which routines. Those few essential routines that serve the key values of the organization should be worshiped. Those that do not should be rooted out. Those routines that help the organization to change—routines such as customer satisfaction surveys—should be promoted. Those that are excuses—the "we never do it that way around here" routines—should be exposed for the injury they do to the welfare of the organization and its people.

If organizations and societies are to make progress, then, leaders must be able to detect when routines are becoming dysfunctional. They must be able to see when routines are smothering creative planning and blocking necessary advancement.

Russell L. Ackoff, professor at the University of Pennsylvania's Wharton School, offers one way out of this dilemma. "If I could add only one subject to business-school curricula," writes Ackoff, "it would be on how to beat the system. Beating the system means making a well-designed system work poorly or a poorly designed system work well."[17] Sharon Kneeland, human resources manager for Coherent General, is one of those who takes Ackoff's medicine for fostering change. At one of our workshops a while back, she said that one of the things she learned from her personal best leadership experience was: "It is easier to ask forgiveness than permission." Kneeland is an old hand at beating the system, and she knows that sometimes leaders just have to do it now and confess later. Leaders may be rule makers, but they are also rule breakers.

Commitment Number 1: Search Out Challenging Opportunities to Change, Grow, Innovate, and Improve

In this chapter, we have observed how closely associated are leadership, change, and innovation. When people talk about their personal best leadership experiences, they talk about the challenge of change. When we look at the research on innovation, we see the presence of leaders. When we review the events involving people we consider to be leaders, we find that we associate them with major social transformations. Leaders always seem to be present whenever there is a search for opportunities to introduce the new and untried.

The quest for change is an adventure. It tests our skills and abilities. It brings forth talents that have been dormant. It is the training ground for leadership. And while the challenge of change is tough, it is also enjoyable. For leaders to get the best from themselves and others, they must find the task intrinsically motivating. Extrinsic rewards are insufficient. When it comes to getting extraordinary things done in organizations, what is rewarding gets done. Here are some suggestions on how you can search for opportunities in your leadership role:

1. *Treat every job as an adventure.* Even if you have been in your job for years, treat today as if it were your first day. Ask yourself, "If I were just starting this job, what would I do?" Chances are you would do some things differently. Begin doing those things now.

Think of your leadership assignment as an exciting adventure through unexplored wilderness. Think of your subordinates and colleagues as pioneers. Set your sights on discovering some new territories together. Identify those projects you have always wanted to undertake but never have. Ask your team members to do the same. Pick one major project per quarter. Implement one smaller improvement every three weeks. Figure out how to do all of this within the budget you now have, or the money you will save or earn when your project succeeds. If you still need more money, just like any adventurer, go out and raise it from your supporters.

Your new projects do not have to be ones that change the world. They can be anything that gets your organization moving on the road to ever greater heights. Remember how, early in her tenure as plant manager of Apple Computer's Macintosh factory, Debi Coleman initiated cleaning the floors, painting the walls white, and fixing up the employee washroom—mundane stuff, but it hadn't been done before, and the employees responded to it.

2. *Treat every new assignment as a turnaround, even if it isn't.* Chances are your present organization may need to hire a turnaround artist if you do not stay alert to ways to constantly improve the organization. The talent and resources for excellence are there, dormant in your organization. All you have to do is unlock them. There is no magic to making a previously poorly performing unit a high-performing one. Often the critical difference is a leader who sees within the existing group untapped energy and skill and who assumes that excellence can be achieved. It is that old pioneering spirit reawakened.

Ask for a tough assignment. Ask your superiors to give you an opportunity to take on that losing operation. Challenge calls forth leadership. There is no better way for you to test your own limits than to voluntarily place yourself in difficult jobs. Joe

Sparagna of Elsin got to be a vice-president that way. He actively promoted a new and difficult project, got the support of key management, built a team, won the proposal, and got the promotion.

3. *Question the status quo.* Right now, make a list of all the practices in your organization that fit the description: "That's the way we have always done it around here." For each one, ask yourself: "How useful is this for becoming the best we can become? How useful is this for stimulating creativity and innovation?" If your answer is "absolutely essential," then keep it. If not, find a way to change it. Review all the policies and procedures. For each one, ask yourself the same question and take the same action. Vow to eliminate every stupid rule and every needless routine within the next month.

Clearly, some standard practices and some policies are critical to productivity and quality assurance. On the other hand, many are simply matters of tradition. Take executive parking spaces, for instance. Better use could be made of them for customers, guests, and the employee of the month.

Hold a meeting with employees and ask them what really bugs them about the organization. Ask them what gets in the way of doing the very best job possible. Promise to look into everything and get back to them with answers in two weeks. Commit yourself to removing three frequently mentioned organizational roadblocks that stand in the way of getting extraordinary things done.

4. *Go out and find something that is broken.* There is an old cliché that says, "If it ain't broke, don't fix it." Nothing could stifle innovation more than accepting that attitude. There is always something that needs fixing in every organization. Go find the things that need fixing in yours.

Wander around the plant, the store, the branch, or the office. Look for things that do not seem right. Ask questions. Probe. When Phil Turner moved from facilities manager to plant manager of the Wire and Cable Division of Raychem Corporation, he spent a lot of time just getting accustomed to the sounds and smells of the place. At first he could not tell one sound from another. It seemed like indistinguishable noise. But soon he was able to hear the special music of each machine, much as a conductor gets to know the instruments in an orchestra.

One of the things that Turner discovered in his wanderings was that the machines that spool the wire were not running at full speed. When he asked why, he was told that it was because people did not know how to fix them. They were afraid that if the machines were run at capacity, they would wear down. Turner went quickly into action and began an employee training program that not only got the machines up but also enabled the operators to fix them if they ever broke again.

A new assignment is a perfect opportunity to use your naive understanding of the operation to your advantage. Everyone tolerates your dumb questions. By constantly asking people, "Why do we do this, and why do we do that?" you will uncover some needed improvements in the organization.

5. *Add adventure to every job.* Leaders are not the only ones who do their best when challenged. All of us do. For people to excel, they must find what they do intrinsically motivating— rewarding in and of itself. Challenge, as we have learned in this chapter, is the key ingredient in activities that are enjoyable. Look for ways to add challenge to the jobs of people in your unit.

You can do this by asking people to join you in solving problems or by asking them for creative ideas, or by delegating more than just the routine jobs, such as filling out forms. The magic of quality circles is challenge. People who had never been asked for the time of day are now given the problem-solving tools and the opportunity to contribute.

However, be sure to find out what motivates each of your team members. Different people find different things challenging. Get to know their skill levels. What might be a stretch for one person is too easy for another. This means that you will have to spend some time with each person.

6. *Break free of the routine.* We all get to be creatures of habit. We take the same routes to work, we eat at the same restaurants, we talk to the same people. Make a list of your daily routines. Ask yourself: "Which ones help me find opportunities for improvement in this organization, and which ones hinder me?" Keep the helpers, and get rid of the hindrances. If you have a difficult time dumping some of those hindrances, just ask yourself, "What is the worst thing that can happen if I do?" Usually you will find that the pain is worth the gain in creativity and productivity.

Each day, break one useless old habit, and start a whole new one. See if it helps. Call some new people. Read a new book. Visit a new place. Actively search for something new. Worlds we have never even dreamed about suddenly become open to us when we make ourselves available to them.

7. *Make the adventure fun.* If you are not having fun doing what you are doing, chances are you are not doing the best you can do. And the same is true for others. We are not talking about a laugh-a-minute party here. Every moment cannot be fun, but the overall experience can be. There is absolutely no reason why every employee cannot be given the opportunity to solve a problem, explore a new area, create a new process, learn a new operation. Just for the fun of it, make a list of all the activities that are fun for you. Ask your colleagues at work to do the same. Now, pick one and figure out a way to integrate it into the work of your organization.

Of course, we must keep in mind that projects that are fun, exciting, and challenging can also be risky. In the next chapter we will examine how leaders thrive on the risks involved in their experiments and innovations.

4

Experiment and Take Risks:
Learning from Mistakes
and Successes

When people don't make mistakes, I'm uncom-
fortable. They're not reaching out, growing.
——*Frank J. Ruck, Jr., President,*
Thermal Design, Inc.

The search for opportunities beyond tradition is an exploration
of the new. It requires individual creativity and organizational
innovation. That means that a leader must have an openness to
ideas and a willingness to listen. It means that leaders must try
untested approaches and accept the risks that accompany all
experiments.

In this chapter, we will explore the sources of innovative
ideas and the importance of keeping lines of communication
open. We will see leaders turn mistakes and failures into learning
opportunities. We will also discover how the right attitude can
turn a difficult change into a learning opportunity. But first we
must solve the "nine dot problem."

At an Apple Computer leadership workshop, president and
chief executive officer John Sculley stood before a group of about
thirty upper middle managers and drew a nine dot puzzle con-
sisting of three rows of three dots each. He asked the participants
to draw these nine dots on their paper, place a pen or pencil on
one of the dots, and then cover all nine dots with four straight
lines without lifting the pen or pencil from the paper. Some of

the attempts looked like that shown in Figure 1. Sculley allowed
a few frustrating minutes for people to work on the problem.
Then he drew the solution (shown in Figure 2 at the end of this
chapter).

What becomes immediately evident is that we tend to construct an imaginary square in our heads when attempting to
solve the puzzle. It is this imaginary box—a self-imposed constraint—that makes it impossible to solve the problem. Only
when we remove these constraints can we hope to find ways to
connect all nine dots with four straight lines.

Sculley's use of this problem demonstrated to Apple managers that solutions to the problems that Apple was facing in its
marketplace could not be found within the imaginary box.
Instead, the solutions were outside the assumed boundaries. After
offering this simple illustration, Sculley went on to question the
assumptions on which Apple was conducting its business. He
urged Apple managers to look beyond their current market opportunities and explore untapped avenues. Only by freeing themselves from the conventional Apple wisdom could the managers
move into newer, more profitable areas.

This is one example of creative self-appraisal. It illustrates
how a leader can intervene in a nonroutine way to steer an organization in a new direction. Sometimes leaders must take it upon

Figure 1. An Attempt to Solve the Nine Dot Problem.

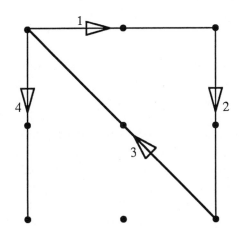

themselves to shatter the existing mold that gives shape to the organization in order to awaken creativity. For example, Jack Telnack, Ford Motor Company's chief design executive for North America, wanted to strengthen the company's design approval process. As a way of initiating the improvement, he asked his designers to identify all the ways in which they hindered the process. Then he invited people from outside of his group to add their criticisms to the list. With the help of Michael Doyle and other consultants from Interaction Associates, Telnack and his organization were able to use this list in making the design approval process significantly more efficient and effective.[1] The designs that have emerged from Telnack's shop have already won two *Motor Trend* Car of the Year awards. More are likely to be on the way.

The "nine dot problem" is also a metaphor for the self-imposed constraints of rules, routines, and assumptions that we mentioned at the close of the last chapter. Standard operating procedures are the habits of organizations. Even the loosest of organizations adopts practices that become second nature. These cultural norms operate in subtle but powerful ways to box us in and restrict our thinking. These norms are especially potent barriers in times when innovation is required.

Creative solutions to difficult business problems require identifying or, better yet, avoiding these self-imposed limitations. We need to look outside the existing way of doing things if we are to be innovative. Innovation is critical to an organization's health. Without constant innovation in products, services, and work processes, an organization will atrophy. Innovation is the nourishment of organizational development.

A Lesson from Innovation: Communicate

Leaders can benefit from understanding one major lesson that emerges from the extensive research studies on innovation. It is essential to keep the communication channels open if new products, processes, and services are to flow into the organization. Communication pathways are the veins and arteries of new ideas.

Leaders can expect demand for change to come from both inside and outside the organization. Customers are the source of demand for product and service innovation. Process innovation will most likely come from outside the ranks of management. The people doing the work are the source of most process ideas. But organizational members are likely to cut themselves off from critical information sources over time. Maybe it is because they are too busy. Maybe it is because they think that they have heard it all before. Maybe it is because the company cuts the travel, phone, and conference budgets. Whatever the reason, unless external communication is encouraged and supported, people are going to interact with outsiders less and less over time.

If leaders are going to detect demands for change, they must use their *outsight*. They must stay sensitive to the external realities. They must go out and talk to their constituents, be they customers, employees, stockholders, vendors, bosses, or just interested parties. They must listen and stay in touch.

External and Internal Communication. James M. Utterback of Massachusetts Institute of Technology is one of this country's leading authorities on innovation. He has studied thousands of innovations in both processes and products. Utterback has found that "Market forces appear to be the primary influence on innovation. From 60 to 80 percent of important innovations in a large number of fields have been in response to market demands and needs."[2] Other researchers reach similar conclusions. Very few innovations emerge from someone in the organization saying "Aha, maybe we can find a user for this technical idea."[3]

Modesto Maidique, director of the University of Miami Innovation and Entrepreneurship Institute, and Billie Jo Zirger, Stanford University research associate, studied the introduction of 224 new electronics products, half successes and half failures. The key success factor, they found, was the development team's interaction with the customer.[4] They also reported that it was not only external communication that made the difference. Internal communication was also a critical factor in the successful introduction of new products.

The results of research by Ralph Katz and Tom Allen of the MIT Sloan School give additional evidence to support these claims. Katz and Allen conducted a field study of research and development teams over a number of years. Among other things, they examined the relationship between the length of time that

people had been working together in a particular project area—
what they called "group longevity"—and the level of communication of project groups at various stages of their lives. Three
areas of interpersonal oral communication were examined for
each team: (1) intraproject communication, (2) organizational
communication, and (3) professional communication. Each
team's technical performance was also measured by department
managers and laboratory directors.[5] What they found was that
the project groups with the highest longevity index reported
lower levels of communications in all three areas. "Members of
these groups, therefore, were significantly more isolated from
external sources of new ideas and technological advances and
from information within other organizational divisions, especially marketing and manufacturing."[6] When the relationship
between communication and technical performance was examined, it was found that the lower-performing groups were those
who had been together for longer than five years. The best-per-
forming groups were those who had been together for between
one-and-a-half and five years.

Research and development teams who have been together
too long (that is, for more than five years) cut themselves off from
precious sources of information. This isolation results in lower
technical performance. There just are not enough good new ideas
floating around the lab when people don't listen to the world
outside. The higher-performing groups, on the other hand, have
significantly more communication with people outside their labs.
These connections may be with organizational units such as marketing and manufacturing or with outside professional associations. Even more significantly, the low-performing teams cut
themselves off from the kind of information they needed the most.
"This suggests that it is not a reduction in project communication per se that leads to less effective project performance," concludes Katz, "but rather it is an isolation from sources that can
provide the most critical kinds of evaluation, information, and
new ideas."[7] If we extend the implications of this research beyond
the research lab, we can understand how some work groups and
organizations become myopic and unimaginative. It isn't that
the people themselves are dull or slow-witted. It is that they have
become too familiar with their routines and too isolated from

outside influences. To infuse fresh ideas into an organization, a leader needs to shake it up periodically. That can be done by adding new members, sending existing ones off on a tour, or holding a seminar. Whatever the technique, the leader must be on the alert for hardening of the communication arteries.

"Outsight" and Insight. On one recent visit to the coast of northern California, we came across some important advice for leaders. In each room in the Mendocino Hotel, there was a pamphlet describing the local sites along the Pacific Ocean. At the top of the pamphlet in bold letters was a warning: "Never turn your back on the ocean." It went on to say how, when we are standing along the coast, we may want to turn around to look inland, to catch a view of the town. But we were told not to take our eyes from the ocean. Why? Because a rogue wave may come along when our backs are turned and sweep us out to sea. Many an unsuspecting traveler has been a victim of the rogue wave. This is good advice for leaders as well as for travelers. When we take our eyes off the external realities, turning inward to admire the beauty of our own organizations, we may be swept away by the swirling waters of change.

So it is with innovation. If creative ideas come from outside our own group, then innovation requires the use of outsight. Outsight is the power of perceiving external realities. It is the sibling of insight—the ability to apprehend the inner nature of things. The awareness and understanding of these outside forces comes through openness. It is by keeping the doors open to the passage of ideas and information that we become knowledgeable of what goes on around us. Leaders must destroy confining barriers. Those who enclose themselves, who shut the doors to the world outside, will never be able to detect change. And, worse, they may be overtaken by it. Over and over again, those we interviewed told us that leaders keep their eyes and ears open. They permit passage of new ideas into the system. They remain free from concealment and expose themselves to a broader view of things. Ann Bowers, president of the business consulting firm, Enterprise 2000, and former corporate human resources executive, put it this way: "People who get extraordinary things done are always out and about."

Leaders remove the protective covering in which organizations often seal themselves. Leaders are willing to hear, consider, and accept ideas from sources outside the company. As Irwin Federman, president and chief executive officer of Monolithic Memories, remarked: "Leaders listen, take advice, lose arguments, and follow."[8] At first, Federman's comment seems counter to our traditional assumptions about leadership. Our initial reaction is that leaders are supposed to tell other people what to do, give advice, win arguments, and lead. But Federman knows that if leaders were to behave like that, their organizations would never succeed.

Innovation requires even more listening and communication than does routine work. When guiding a change, leaders must establish more relationships, connect with more sources of information, and get out and walk around more frequently. It is only through human contact that change and innovation can be effectively led. It does not happen from the fifty-second floor of the headquarters building. Leaders stay in touch. They stay in touch with trends in the marketplace. They stay in touch with the ideas and advice of others. They stay in touch with social, political, technological, economic, and artistic changes. It is only by staying in touch with the world around them that leaders can ever expect to change the business-as-usual environment.

The Importance of Taking Risks

Risk is inherent in every successful innovation. Whenever leaders experiment with innovative ways of doing things, they put themselves and others at risk. Walter B. Wriston, former chairperson and CEO of Citibank, is particularly sensitive about how our society views risk. He writes, "While the constitutional framework set limits on power, the driving force of our society is the conviction that risk-taking and individual responsibility are the ways to advance our mutual fortunes. . . . Today, however, the idea is abroad in the land that the descendants of these bold adventurers (those who wrote the Constitution) should all be sheltered from risk and uncertainty as part of our national heritage. . . . Emerson's counsel—'always do what you are afraid to do'—is now rejected as too upsetting, and one should steer the safe, noncontroversial course."[9]

If we want to lead efforts to improve the way things are, we must be willing to take risks. Studies on innovative research and development teams, for example, show that the work climate for success is characterized by two things: an equitable reward system that recognizes excellence and a willingness to take risks and experiment with innovative ideas.[10] One of the most glaring differences between the leader and the bureaucrat is the leader's inclination to encourage risk taking, to encourage others to step out into the unknown and not play it safe. There is no simple test for determining what an acceptable level of risk is. One person's risk is another's routine activity. Some mountain climbers we know are absolutely terrified of speaking in public, while many accomplished public speakers fear heights.

We must each determine our own level of comfort with trying new things by measuring our own skill against the required tasks. Tasks that are too easy to achieve do not motivate, while tasks that are far beyond our normal capabilities can depress us. Leaders get to know the skills and motivating tasks of their followers. They also set goals that are higher than current levels, but not so high that people will only feel frustration. Leaders raise the bar gradually and offer coaching and training to build skills to get over each new level.

Risk as a Self-Imposed Constraint. Reno Taini and Randi DuBois know about risk. Their organization, Pro-Action, sponsors executive development programs involving, among other things, outdoor challenges. Through their programs, people learn about trust, risk taking, group problem solving, and teamwork. Their unique approach to learning has been featured on television news magazines, the "Ripley's Believe It or Not" television program, and a new film.

In 1966, Taini began experimenting with the use of outdoor adventures in educating high school students. He was a field biologist, and he felt that classroom learning was insufficient to give kids a true sense of the wonders of nature. So he began taking them on field trips. He called it the Wilderness School. His students climbed mountains, crossed deserts, and rafted white waters. Taini also took his students into the urban wilderness— the places in the inner city where students confront the challenges of poverty and homelessness. They served holiday meals to seniors and gathered litter from the public streets.

In the process, Taini found that not only did they learn about nature, humanity, and survival, they also experienced themselves firsthand. "Valid challenges of shared adventure are the catalysts I use initially to produce a positive change in self-concepts, to develop communication and human relations skills, and to ignite students to learning," he says. Such creative contributions to the field of teaching and the development of students won Taini the award of California Teacher of the Year in 1981.

In 1976, Taini began working with DuBois, a recreation specialist, to take the Wilderness School into the larger community. It began as a volunteer project. Many of the parents and friends of the students wanted to have the same adventure as the kids. So they created the Ropes Course on five acres in La Honda, California. It's a maze of ropes, cables, tires, logs, trees, platforms, ladders, and other gear and ideas collected from everything from ships to fire stations. Taini, DuBois, and their staff have served over 30,000 people. Executives from some of the country's largest corporations have learned about trust and risk taking through this unusually powerful form of education. They have also worked with Vietnam veterans in wheelchairs and abused women with emotional scars. Children as young as five and adults as old as seventy have experienced the thrill of shared adventure and the quest for self-discovery.

Taini and DuBois invite people who go through their program to do things most have never done before, to experiment with themselves, to test their self-imposed limitations. For example, they invite people to walk a cable stretched thirty-five feet above the ground between two trees, or leap for a ring from a platform at thirty feet. Each event is rigged for maximum safety, and no one has ever been injured in any of these events. We use these events in our leadership development programs to provide leaders with the opportunity to personally experience what it feels like to try something new. For most participants, it is the first time they have ever walked a tightrope or climbed a fifteen-foot-high wall. One of the lessons that emerges from these physical activities is that our fear and apprehension are greater barriers to success than the actual difficulty or danger of the experiment itself.

DuBois puts it this way: "Consistently we observe that the weakest muscle in the body is the one between the ears. Self-imposed limitations and beliefs hold most people back. When individuals feel the surge of adrenalin and the thump of their hearts growing louder they frequently interpret that feeling as fear. We encourage them to explore and push on their perceived limits. By translating that feeling into excitement, they then discover the elation of victory over crippling doubts and the tie backs to their workplace are enormous." The key to DuBois and Taini's success in building Pro-Action is venturing beyond the limitations that people normally place around themselves. They saw teaching field biology as an outdoor adventure and recreation as an opportunity for personal growth. Now they lead a creative enterprise that enables others to experience victory over doubt.

Encouraging People to Risk Failure. The risks involved in the Ropes Course are like the risks leaders must take when involved in mastering change: making a mistake—failing. To be sure, failure can be costly. For the manager who leads a failed project, it could be a stalled career, or even a lost job. For an entrepreneurial leader, it could mean the loss of personal assets. For mountain climbers and other outdoor adventurers, lives are at risk.

According to the people with whom we spoke, however, it is absolutely essential that we take those risks. Over and over again, people told how important failure was to their success. It may seem ironic, but many echoed the words of Mike Markkula, vice-chairperson of Apple Computer: "I believe the overall quality of work improves when you give people a chance to fail." Maidique goes even further than that. He claims that the results of his innovation research demonstrate that "Success does not breed success. It breeds failure. It is failure which breeds success."[11] If that advice seems patently absurd, examine the careers of many famous winners. Babe Ruth struck out 1,330 times. In between his strike-outs, he hit 714 home runs. R. H. Macy failed in retailing seven times before his store in New York became a success. Edison tried thousands of filaments before finding the right one for the light bulb. At precisely 8:01 P.M. on September 11, 1985, baseball star Pete Rose smacked his 4,192nd career hit. That was good enough to surpass Ty Cobb and put Rose in the record books for "most hits, career." But Rose also deserves another baseball record: most outs—9,518 of them.

We all know from personal experience the role that failure plays in success. Earlier, we asked you to recall the times when you tried to learn a new game or a new sport. It might have been skiing, tennis, bridge, hockey, roller skating, or any of a dozen other enjoyable activities. When you think back, did you get it perfect the very first day you played? Not likely. We understand from our own life experiences that nothing is ever done perfectly the first time we try it—not in sports, not in games, not in school, and most certainly not in business.

Actually, there was someone who reported to us that he did get it perfectly the first time he played a new sport. It was Urban E. Hilger, Jr., president, Dalmo-Victor division of the Singer Company. Naturally curious, we asked Hilger to tell us about that experience. We wanted to know his secret of success. So he told us this story: "It was the first day of skiing classes. I skiied all day long, and I didn't fall down once. I was so elated; I felt so good. So I skiied up to the ski instructor and I told him of my great day. You know what the ski instructor said? He told me, 'Personally, Urban, I think you had a lousy day.' I was stunned. 'What do you mean, lousy day?' I asked. 'I thought the objective was to stand up on these boards, not fall down.' The ski instructor looked me straight in the eye and replied: 'Urban, if you're not falling, you're not learning.'" Hilger's ski instructor understood that if you can stand up on your skis all day long the first time out, then you are only doing what is easy. You are not pushing yourself to try anything new or difficult. If your objective is to stay upright, you are not going to improve yourself, because, when you try to do something you do not know how to do, you will fall down. It is guaranteed, as anyone who has ever learned to ski knows very well.

The point of this discussion is not to promote failure for failure's sake. We do not advocate for a moment that failure ought to be the objective of any business. Instead, we advocate learning. Leaders do not look for someone to blame when mistakes are made in the name of innovation. Instead, they ask: "What can be learned from the experience?" The two very finest teachers of business are named *trial* and *error*.

There is no simple test for determining the appropriate level of risk in a venture. We must weigh costs and benefits, potential losses versus gains. We must factor in the present skills of the team members and the demands of the task. But even if we could compute risk to the fifth decimal place, every innovation still exposes us to some peril. Perhaps the healthiest thing we can do is determine whether what we can learn is worth the cost. And as we shall see in the next section of this chapter, our ability to grow and learn under stressful, risk-abundant situations is highly dependent on how we view change.

The Hardiness Factor: Surviving the Stress of Change

We have already discussed how uncertainty and risk are part of the price we pay for innovation. But how do we learn to accept the inevitable failures and accompanying stress of innovation?

Many of us associate stress with illness. We have been led to believe that if we experience serious stressful events in our lives, we will become ill. If we were to adopt this point of view, we might as well sit back in our overstuffed easy chairs, plop ourselves in front of the television set, and never venture into the world. The reports of illness resulting from stress are misleading. Not all stress contributes to severe illness, not even the most strenuous. After all, many people have experienced life-threatening, even torturous circumstances and not fallen ill. It all depends on how we cope with them. And some stress can even energize us. The personal bests are clear examples of difficult, stressful projects that generated enthusiasm and enjoyment.

Approaching Stress Positively. University of Chicago researchers Suzanne C. Kobasa and Salvatore R. Maddi have taken a different approach to the study of stress.[12] Kobasa was intrigued by people who experienced high degrees of stress yet had relatively low degrees of illness. She hypothesized that these individuals would show a distinctive attitude toward stress when compared to the people who experienced both high stress and high illness. For the answers to her questions, Kobasa turned to Illinois Bell, where she studied groups of executives. These executives encountered the normal stressful life events of other middle and upper managers. But in addition, at the time of the study, Illinois Bell, like all the Bell operating companies, was going through the enormous upheaval brought on by the prospect of deregulation. Theoretically, Illinois Bell executives were certainly at risk of stress-related illnesses.

In a longitudinal study that began in 1975 and ended in 1982, data were collected on illnesses that occurred between 1972 and 1982. Kobasa and her colleagues found that, indeed, while some executives had high stress scores and high illness scores, another group of executives with equally high stress scores were below average on incidents of illness. She selected about 100 from each group for a more detailed analysis. As the researchers had predicted, there was a clear attitudinal difference between the high-stress/low-illness group and the high-stress/high-illness group. That difference was what they called "psychological hardiness."

Specifically, high-stress/low-illness executives were more *committed* to the various parts of their lives. They felt a greater sense of *control* over the things that happened in their lives. And they experienced more positive *challenge*. The high-stress/high-illness executives were more alienated, felt more powerless, and saw change as more of a threat than a challenge. Furthermore, the researchers found that psychological hardiness was more important as a source of resistance to stress than were personal constitution, health practices, or social support. The big three of commitment, control, and challenge combined to block the strain of stress and the resulting illness. Maddi and Kobasa describe how this coping process works:

People strong in commitment find it easy to be interested in whatever they are doing and can involve themselves in it wholeheartedly. They are rarely at a loss for things to do. They always seem to make maximum effort cheerfully and zestfully. In contrast, alienated people find things boring or meaningless and hang back from involvement in the tasks they have to do. They are often at a loss for leisure activities. Although they are seldom strongly involved, they often appear taxed. People strong in control believe and act as if they can influence the events taking place around them. They always reflect on how to turn situations to advantage and never take things at face value. In contrast, people who feel powerless believe and act as if they are passive victims of forces beyond their control. They have little sense of resource or initiative and prepare themselves for the worst. People strong in a sense of challenge consider it natural for things to change and anticipate the changes as a useful stimulus to development. They see life as strenuous but exciting. In contrast, people who feel threatened think it is natural for things to remain stable, and they fear the possibility of change because it seems to disrupt comfort and security.[13]

People with a hardy attitude, then, take the stress of life in stride. When they encounter a stressful event—whether positive or negative—(1) they consider it interesting, (2) they feel that they can influence the outcome, and (3) they see it as an opportunity for development. This optimistic appraisal of events increases their capacity to take decisive steps to alter the situation. Instead of avoiding the problem, they choose action to confront—and control—it. Hardiness contributes to a person's ability to cope with stress by transforming stressful events into manageable or desirable situations, rather than regressing and avoiding the issue.

Fostering Hardiness. How do we develop the hardy personality? Is it wired in our genes? Do we get it from our parents? Do we learn it in school? Does it depend upon the neighborhood we live in? Just how do we come to have the attitudes of commitment, control, and challenge?

According to Maddi and Kobasa, the family atmosphere is the most important breeding ground for a hardy attitude. When there is a varied environment, many tasks involving moderate difficulty, and family support, then hardiness flourishes. And it is not related to our socioeconomic background. But we should not resign ourselves to a life of illness or unresolved stress if we did not grow up in the right environment. Maddi and Kobasa state: "We think that hardiness can be learned at any time in life and, therefore, that people are not damned by an unfortunate childhood."[14] It may be more difficult to overcome a habitual pattern of avoidance, but it is possible to learn to cope assertively with stressful events. Counseling is one way, but organizations can also help their employees cope more effectively. In a sense, organizations can simulate the conditions that nurture an attitude of hardiness. They can do three things to create a climate that develops hardiness:

- To build commitment, offer more rewards than punishments.
- To build a sense of control, choose tasks that are challenging but within the person's skill level.
- To build an attitude of challenge, encourage people to see change as full of possibilities.

There are two important implications for leaders from this work on hardiness. First, people cannot lead if they are not psychologically hardy. People will not follow others who avoid stressful events and who will not take decisive action. Second, even if leaders are personally very hardy, they cannot enlist and retain others if they do not create an atmosphere that promotes psychological hardiness. People will not remain long with a cause that distresses them. They need to feel that same sense of commitment, control, and challenge. They need to believe that the project is important and worthy. They need to feel that they can influence decisions and outcomes. They need to experience the journey ahead not as a threat but as an adventurous challenge. They need to believe that they can overcome adversity if they are to accept the challenge of change. Leaders must create the conditions that make all of that possible.

This was the case in the personal best examples we collected. These were stressful events in the lives of our leaders. They involved significant personal and organizational changes. Certainly they were as stressful as those that the Illinois Bell executives faced. Yet fully 95 percent of the cases were described in terms consistent with the conditions for psychological hardiness. The personal best cases indicated commitment rather than alienation, control rather than powerlessness, and challenge rather than threat. The people in our study discarded all those cases that aroused feelings of alienation, powerlessness, and threat. Instead, they chose those that aroused the opposite feelings.

While our cases are a highly biased sample of only the best of times, we believe that it is instructive to know that we associate doing our best with feelings of meaningfulness, mastery, and stimulation. It is useful to know that we are biased in the direction of hardiness when thinking about our best. It is helpful to know that we do not produce excellence when we feel uninvolved, insignificant, and threatened. Furthermore, feelings of commitment, control, and challenge give us internal cues for recognizing when we are excelling and when we are only getting through the day. They tell leaders what signs to look for when assessing the capacity of their groups to get extraordinary things done. They give us guidelines to use when creating an environment for success.

And there is more good news. The personal best cases signify that the vast majority of us can feel in charge of change at least some of the time. They tell us that the vast majority of us know what success feels like. They tell us that we have an intuitive sense of what makes us strong and what makes us weak. The challenge is to apply these lessons more rigorously to our daily lives at work. Leaders have a responsibility to create an environment that breeds hardiness and motivation on a regular, not an occasional, basis.

Excelling During Uncertain Times

Hardiness is a prerequisite for mastering risk and the challenge of change. Both leaders and followers need to feel personally capable of successfully making the transition from the old to the new. A hardy attitude enables people to better cope with the risks and the failures of innovation. In the process of transformation, however, people and their organizations live with a high degree of ambiguity. Innovation creates hassles in our lives. It upsets the stability we have worked hard to establish. It throws off our equilibrium.

So there is another important leadership competency needed to guide people through turbulent waters—the ability to make decisions under conditions of extreme uncertainty. Leaders are not just masters of change, they are also masters of uncertainty. Uncertainty creates the necessary condition for leadership. Whenever either ends or means are agreed upon, someone other than a leader can better solve the problem. But when confusion over ends and means abounds, leadership is needed. Uncertainty is the source of the favorable winds for leadership.[15]

Changing jobs or moving across town can be a real nuisance. But creating a whole new way of life in a corporation thrusts us into unfamiliar situations where we do not know how to function. That anxiety of not knowing what to do or where to go can cause a great deal of turbulence in our lives. The intense anxiety of major change and the need for positive leadership were dramatically illustrated to us a few years ago when taxpayers across the country revolted. Fed up with the upward spiral of taxes, citizens decided to take matters into their own hands. They passed initiatives in many states to limit government's authority to raise property taxes. Since property taxes were the major source of local revenues, tax limitations severely restricted the capacity of county agencies to provide health, education, and welfare services.

We observed firsthand the effect this had on the dedicated civil servants who had been providing these services. Along with our colleague Paul Mico, we had the opportunity to help several agencies deal with the effects of California's Proposition 13, which reduced property taxes in that state. In one series of meetings, we asked county health department employees to divide into three groups: those who knew that they would still have a job if Proposition 13 passed, those who knew that they would have to leave, and those who were uncertain about what would happen to them. Each group was asked to discuss how they felt about the situation and how they were personally and professionally coping with it.

The reactions of the different groups were most revealing. They demonstrate how people respond to uncertainty. The group of people who knew that they would have to leave had resigned themselves and were making other plans. The group who knew that they would stay felt a little guilty, but they were otherwise accepting. The people in the uncertain group—those who did not know what would happen to them—exhibited the most stress and hostility. They felt stuck, unresolved about whether to stay or leave, and angry for being in the situation. For the uncertains, the old rules had broken down, and there were no new rules in place. They were unclear about their own personal goals. They were uncertain about the goals of the county. They had little or no experience in dealing with the situation, so it was difficult to predict the effects of various alternatives. They were immobilized. They were unable to decide what to do. These were people who had lost their sense of identity.

It is one thing for taxpayers to want a change—to foster innovation, if you will—but another to offer a positive new direction. This the citizens and their tax-cutting champions did not do. They tore something apart but offered nothing in its place. Responsible leaders, on the other hand, cannot afford to behave so capriciously. They know that not only must they "change the business-as-usual environment," they also must help people through the uncertainties of the change. When we face such situations, what is the appropriate course to take? What is the role of leader when the known ways of dealing with things seem no longer relevant?

As we have seen in this section, leaders have a hardy attitude about change. They see it as an opportunity to innovate. They venture outside the constraints of normal routine and experiment with creative and risky solutions. So their first act during times of adversity is to create a climate in which organizational members can also accept the challenge of change. To create purposeful movement out of uncertainty, leaders must also guide and channel the often frenetic human motion of change toward some end. When things seem to be falling apart, leaders must show us the exciting new world we can create from the pieces. Out of the uncertainty and chaos of change, leaders rise up and articulate a new image of the future that pulls the organization together. In the next section of this book, we will discuss at length how leaders do this—how they *inspire a shared vision* of the future and enlist others in it. In subsequent chapters, we will discuss how leaders mobilize others to make the new vision a reality.

Commitment Number 2: Experiment, Take Risks, and Learn from the Accompanying Mistakes

Leaders are experimenters. They experiment with new approaches to old problems. But we block innovation and creativity by imposing constraints on our own thinking. A major leadership task involves identifying and removing these self-imposed constraints. Leaders find ways to get outside the imaginary boundaries of organizational convention. Studies of product and process innovations teach us that most ideas for improvement come from people other than leaders. So leaders use their outsight—their ability to perceive external realities—to discover these useful ideas for themselves. Innovation is always risky. Whenever we try something new, there is always the chance that we may make a mistake. Wise leaders recognize this necessary fact of the innovative life. Instead of punishing failure, they encourage it. Instead of trying to fix blame for mistakes, they learn from them.

Innovation and change are also stressful. But the stress of change need not be harmful. With an attitude of hardiness, leaders can take charge of change and turn it into an adventure. Here are some ways you can establish a climate in which people can take charge of change and turn uncertainty into an opportunity to experiment, take risks, and learn from the accompanying mistakes:

1. *Institutionalize processes for collecting innovative ideas.* In the last two chapters, we have railed against unnecessary bureaucratic routines. However, we urge you to keep all the formal and informal mechanisms for gathering feedback and ideas for improvement. If external and internal communication are keys to innovation, then one of your top priorities ought to be finding more ways to gather suggestions from customers, employees, suppliers, and other stakeholders.

Processes for collecting suggestions are abundant. There are focus groups, advisory boards, suggestion boxes, breakfast meetings, brainstorming sessions, customer evaluation forms, mystery shoppers, mystery guests, visits to competitors, and scores more. Each is a way to open the eyes and ears to the world outside the boundaries of the organization. They are ways you can become a net importer of new ideas. It helps if you can be creative about these processes and make them fun for employees and customers. Stew Leonard's Dairy, for example, gathers employees' ideas through the One Idea Club. As many as fifteen employees pile into a van and visit another store, with the goal of each employee bringing back at least one implementable idea. For the Good Idea Club, employees put creative ideas in a suggestion box. Rewards of $10 to $100 are given to employees whose ideas are accepted. There is also a suggestion box for customers, which daily is stuffed to capacity.

Another technique used in organization development is

organizational mirroring. A concerned organization invites one or more outside groups to meet with it face to face and give it feedback on how it helps and hinders others' performance. Jack Telnack, chief design executive for Ford Motor Company, used a version of organizational mirroring in improving the design approval process.

2. *Put idea gathering on your own agenda.* Whatever method you use, you must make gathering new ideas a personal priority. Most weekly staff meetings, for instance, are status reports on the present. If you are serious about promoting innovation and getting others to listen to people outside the unit, make sure that you devote 25 percent of every weekly staff meeting to listening to ideas for improving process technologies and developing new products or services. Invite people from other departments to offer their suggestions on how your unit can improve. Invite customers to staff meetings.

Actively search out people in your organization who are championing an innovation. Even if you do not personally agree with all the innovations, make sure that everyone knows that you support the creative thinking that is going on. Make idea gathering a part of your daily, weekly, and monthly schedule. Call three customers who have not purchased anything from you in a while and ask them why. Call three customers who have made recent purchases and ask them why. Ride a route with one of your sales or delivery people. Work the counter and ask customers what they like and don't like about your business. Shop at a competitor's store. Better yet, anonymously shop for your own product and see what the sales people in the store say about it. Call your company and see how the phones are answered.

If you want to receive the weak as well as the strong signals from the folks on the line or the customers in the marketplace, always keep your antenna up. You never can tell where new ideas will come from. Raymond H. DeMoulin, general manager of the professional photography division of Eastman Kodak Company, got one in a Tokyo fish market. He noticed that a photographer who could use only one hand was having trouble getting the lid off a film container and finally had to use his teeth. DeMoulin made a mental note of the incident, and when he got back to the States, he had a more flexible lid developed.[16]

The point is: spend time outside your organization consciously looking for new things to try, like the folks in the One Idea Club at Stew Leonard's. Come back from each scouting trip with at least one new idea to implement. Tell people that you got it while wandering around and that you encourage them to do the same. Be highly visible in your role as chief listener.

3. *Set up little experiments.* If you are uncertain about the effect of some of these new ideas, experiment with them first. Consumer product companies do this all the time. They try out new products in select locations before launching them in all markets. A word of caution: do not wait until you have a perfect product or process before trying it out. If you wait until everything is perfect, you will never launch a new product or make an improvement. The window of opportunity can close very quickly. As Tom Peters and Bob Waterman, coauthors of *In Search of Excellence,* are fond of saying, "Do it. Fix it. Try it." It is always better to conduct tests at the early stages of innovation than to wait until millions of dollars have been spent and possibly wasted.

A rigorous evaluation of your process innovations can be very instructive as well. Select a few beta, or second, test sites after alpha, or first, tests have been completed. Usually beta tests are done at customer locations. Establish ways of quantifying the outcomes, select comparison groups, conduct pretests with your experimental and control groups, run the experiment, and measure the results. While the costs of research evaluation are often as much as the cost of the intervention itself, the learnings are usually worth the expense. In one evaluation research project in which we were involved, we studied the impact of management team building on eight participating teams. We found that those teams participating in the study, the experimental groups, did better than the equivalent teams who did not participate, the comparison groups. We also found that some of the experimental groups did better than others. Further investigation led us to the discovery of "organizational readiness." That is, some teams were better prepared than others to accept innovation. Knowing that ahead of time now enables us and others to do a more effective job of management team development.

4. *Renew your teams.* We all know that even the best teams get stale after a while. Teams seem to go through life cycles, just

as products do. After a while, teams need to be refreshed. Never let them get disconnected from outside information. Make sure members get to attend professional conferences, participate in training programs, and visit colleagues in other parts of the organization. It is tempting to slash the meeting, training, and travel budgets when times get tough, but beware. You could pay the price of falling further behind the competition. Staying ahead of the competition means staying ahead in your knowledge of the technology and the market.

It is useful to add a new member or two to the group every couple of years. Rotate some people out and rotate others in. New people, especially those who have not been socialized into your way of doing things, can help you get a new perspective on the situation. If you cannot move people in or out and you have a long-tenured group to lead, then be very directive in your insistence that they go out and locate a measurable number of process or product enhancements. Force them to interact with others, and send them as much information as you can about new developments in the field. Put everybody through a creativity course. Give everyone the knowledge, skills, and tools they need to contribute to the generation of new ideas. Also, put everyone through a listening course. No great idea ever entered the mind through an open mouth.

5. *Honor your risk takers.* Tom Peters suggests that every company create an innovators' Hall of Fame. He urges you to include every business function, from research and development to marketing, inventors of big and small innovations, and even those whose role is simply to support innovation. Put a glass case in a prominent place in the hall for employees and visitors to see. Fill it with trophies, plaques, pictures, and the paraphernalia of innovation. We have one in our business school at Santa Clara University. Students, parents, administrators, executives, guests, and faculty all stop to read it. The contributors stop by, too. It is a great boost to morale and a helpful reminder.

When John Couch was at Apple Computer, one of his jobs was managing the Lisa personal computer project. After the project had been completed, Couch took out a full-page advertisement in the local paper, thanking by name everyone who had worked on the Lisa.

Make sure to reward good tries, not just the successes. Well-intentioned efforts that do not work out are just as important as the winners. Many, if not most, innovations fail. If people are going to continue to contribute new ideas, they need to see that failure does not result in being cast out to Siberia.

6. *Analyze every failure, as well as every success.* Many, many important lessons are learned from failure. (We frequently suggest to participants in our training programs that they write a case on their "personal worst" leadership experience.) While it is tempting to let the past memories fade, the lessons are too precious to go unrecorded.

At the completion of a project, or at periodic intervals during it, take the team off site on a retreat and do a review. Build the agenda around four questions: What did we do well? What did we do poorly? What did we learn from this? How can we do better the next time? Make sure that everyone contributes. Record all the ideas visibly on chart paper. Type all the notes and make them available to everyone. Take immediate action when you return. At the start of the next project, begin with a review of these lessons.

7. *Model risk taking.* Encourage others to take risk by doing it yourself. To promote innovation and shake his executive team out of its conservatism, one chairperson we know did a belly dance in public. Then he got his executive team to do the same.

We have been part of several programs in which the leader was an active participant in challenging physical tasks, such as the Ropes Course that we described earlier in this chapter. Often in these activities, the formal leaders would have to step aside and let one of their subordinates guide the activity. Rather than sitting on the sidelines and watching, the leaders made themselves vulnerable by trying and often failing in front of all the others.

We find that programs such as Outward Bound are extremely valuable experiences for learning about risk taking, teamwork, and trust. Outward Bound is a training and development organization specializing in the use of challenging outdoor adventures as the medium for learning about leadership, teamwork, self-confidence, and survival. Randi DuBois and Reno Taini lead executives on expeditions as another way of helping them learn to stretch themselves. Whether you choose to participate in an organized expedition or to do something as simple as make a sales call on a tough customer, showing others that you are willing to risk is essential to getting others to do the same.

8. *Foster hardiness.* Leaders and their teams benefit from working in a climate of psychological hardiness, especially during times of stressful change. Leaders must foster a sense of commitment, control, and challenge if people are to feel healthy and hardy as they participate in the introduction of innovations that have an effect on their work lives.

To maintain commitment to change, leaders should make every effort to maximize opportunities for free choice and public support. Employee suggestion programs and quality circles are ways to increase choice. It is better to get people to sign up for a change in public than in private. Signatures on documents and verbal pledges in public are common ways we make commitments visible.

Innovation and change must be perceived as opportunities rather than threats if people are to feel strong and efficacious. Leaders should do everything they can to communicate the positive aims of the change and its benefits to individuals and the organization. They should keep channels of communication open and go overboard to inform everyone of all plans. Innovation is a breeding ground for rumor, so leaders should overcommunicate. A rumor-control center might even be necessary if the change is especially traumatic. Retreats, staff meetings, workshops, teleconferences, and other methods of facilitating communication are useful in reducing the level of threat that a change might produce.

Also critical to our psychological hardiness is the belief that what we have committed ourselves to is worthy of our best efforts. We want to believe that we are dedicating ourselves to the creation of a noble and meaningful future. The leader has a responsibility to show how accepting the present challenge will actually help shape a better tomorrow. So we now turn to a discussion of the leadership practice of *inspiring a shared vision.*

Figure 2. The Nine Dot Problem: Solved.

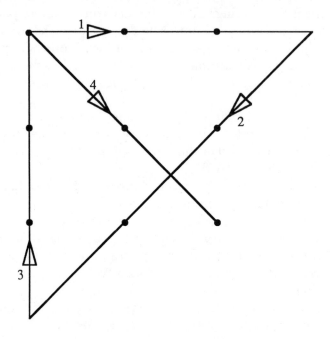

PART THREE

Inspiring a Shared Vision

To manage is to lead, and to lead others requires that one enlist the emotions of others to share a vision as their own.

———*Henry M. Boettinger, retired director of corporate planning, AT&T*

There is no freeway to the future. No paved highway from here to tomorrow. There is only wilderness. Only uncertain terrain. There are no roadmaps. No signposts. So pioneering leaders rely upon a compass and a dream.

Leaders look forward to the future. They hold in their minds visions and ideals of what can be. They have a sense of what is uniquely possible if all work together for a common purpose. They are positive about the future, and they passionately believe that people can make a difference.

But visions seen only by the leaders are insufficient to create organized movement. They must get others to see the exciting future possibilities. Leaders breathe life into visions. They communicate their hopes and dreams so that others clearly understand and accept them as their own. They show others how their values and interests will be served by the long-term vision of the future. Leaders are expressive, and they attract followers through warmth and friendship. With strong appeals and quiet persuasion, they develop enthusiastic supporters. In this section we will explore how leaders:

- Envision the Future.
- Enlist Others.

79

5

Envision the Future:
Imagining Ideal Scenarios

The leader's job is to create a vision.
——*Robert L. Swiggett,*
Chairperson,
Kollmorgen Corporation

At first glance, there seems to be little relationship between Arlene
Blum's desire to get a team of women atop Annapurna and Phil
Turner's view of the work of the men and women of Raychem's
facilities department. What can possibly be less similar than
climbing a mountain and fixing a toilet?

At 3:29 P.M. on October 15, 1978, a team of ten women
accomplished something that no other group had ever done. The
American Women's Himalayan Expedition was the first American climbing team to reach the summit of Annapurna I, the
tenth-highest mountain in the world. Arlene Blum was the leader
of the expedition. Her stirring account of that adventure, *Annapurna: A Woman's Place,* is a highly acclaimed adventure story.
But why would someone, whether man or woman, want to do
something like that?

"For us, the answer was much more than 'because it is
there,'" says Blum. "We all had experienced the exhilaration,
the joy, and the warm camaraderie of the heights, and now we
were on our way to an ultimate objective for a climber—the
world's tenth-highest peak. But as women, we faced a challenge
even greater than the mountain. We had to believe in ourselves
enough to make the attempt in spite of social convention and

two hundred years of climbing history in which women were usually relegated to the sidelines."[1] Blum talks about how women had been told for years that they were not strong enough to carry heavy loads, that they didn't have the leadership experience and emotional stability necessary to climb the highest mountains. After a climb of Mount McKinley in 1970, her personal faith in the abilities of women climbers was confirmed.

"Our expedition would give ten women the chance to attempt one of the world's highest and most challenging peaks, as well as the experience necessary to plan future Himalayan climbs. If we succeeded, we would be the first Americans to climb Annapurna and the first American women to reach eight thousand meters (26,200 feet)."[2]

When we interviewed Phil Turner, he was facilities manager for Raychem Corporation. (He was later promoted to plant manager for Raychem's Wire and Cable Division.) We had the chance to sit in with him one day when he was talking with his supervisors. Turner was describing the daily life of the people who work in facilities. A typical "day in the life" might begin with this phone call: "Phil, the toilet is overflowing in the men's room. Would you send somebody over to fix it?" Or "Phil, the air conditioner is broken in our building. It feels like it's 110 degrees in this place. Would you send someone over to fix it?" Or "Phil, the paint's peeling off the walls in our plant. Send somebody over to fix it." Or "Phil, when are the plans for the new plant going to be done? We're already six months behind schedule."

Turner related to his managers how one could get the impression that the people who work for Raychem were ungrateful, how it might seem that they didn't appreciate the hard work of the good folks in facilities. "But," Turner said, "I don't think that's what they are trying to tell us at all. I think what they are trying to tell us is that they care about their space. I have a vision for this department. I got the insight from Bob Saldich [senior vice-president of Raychem]. The other day, Bob came by my office. The door was open and he walked in. He put his hand on my shoulder and said, 'Phil, I want to thank you for planting those flowers outside my office window. They make me feel good.' So I think our job is to make people feel good," declared Phil.

"Our job is to lift people's spirits through beauty, cleanliness, and functionality, enthusiasm, good cheer, and excellence." And from the United Way campaign of that year, Turner borrowed the hot air balloon and made it the symbol of the facilities operation.

The Importance of Having a Vision

These two leaders, Blum and Turner, saw what others had not seen. They both imagined something for their groups that went far beyond the ordinary, far beyond what others thought possible. For Blum, it was proving that women are capable of doing things that others thought impossible. For Turner, it was showing that there is a special purpose to the work that others thought ordinary. Both Blum and Turner, and hundreds of other leaders in our study, shared the characteristic of "envisioning the future," of gazing across the horizon of time and imagining that greater things were ahead. They foresaw something out there, vague as it might appear from the distance, that others did not. They imagined that extraordinary feats were possible, or that the ordinary could be transformed into something noble.

When Turner told us about his personal best, he said, "I established in my own mind a vision of what we were about." Joe Nevin, Management Information System director at Apple Computer, describes leaders as "painters of the vision and architects of the journey." Major General John Stanford, commander of the U.S. Army's Military Traffic Management Command, said, "I am head of the future department for this organization."

Mark Leslie, an entrepreneur, represents that viewpoint with this statement: "The vision I believe is the key element. If there is no vision, there is no business."[3] All businesses or projects, big and small, begin in the mind's eye. They begin with imagination and with the belief that what is merely an image can one day be made real.

Until recently, *vision* was not part of the management lexicon. We might have heard it uttered by human potential psychologists, but it did not pass over the lips of business people and management scholars. *Purpose* was an acceptable term, but not *vision*. Current scholarly work on leadership has made us aware of the importance of leadership vision. Warren Bennis and Burt Nanus, for example, have looked into the lives of ninety leaders and found that one of their key strategies was "attention through vision." Bennis and Nanus assert: "To choose a direction, a leader must first have developed a mental image of a possible and desirable future state of the organization. This image, which we call a vision, may be as vague as a dream or as precise as a goal or mission statement. The critical point is that a vision articulates a view of a realistic, credible, attractive future for the organization, a condition that is better in some important ways than what now exists."[4]

It is not just academics who have brought leadership vision out of the dark shadows. A few years ago, the magazine *Esquire* devoted an entire issue to "50 Who Had Made the Difference." Lee Eisenberg, contributing editor, wrote the following in his introduction to the section on nine "visionaries": "While their contemporaries groped at the present to feel a pulse, or considered the past to discern the course that led to the moment, these nine squinted through the veil of the future. Not that they were mystics. They were much more worldly than that. For most of them, reality was pure and simple; what set them apart was the conviction that a greater reality lay a number of years down the pike."[5] Vision is even mentioned in corporate advertisements. Shearson/Lehman Brothers ran an ad that read: "Vision is having an acute sense of the possible. It is seeing what others don't see. And when those with similar vision are drawn together, something extraordinary occurs."[6]

Not everyone we interviewed, however, used the term *vision* in describing leadership practices. We will never forget our encounter with Andrew S. Grove, president and CEO of Intel Corporation. We had been interviewing entrepreneurs and leaders about their personal best, and some of them had talked about their dreams and visions for their new ventures. Then we sat next to Grove at lunch one day. We told him about our findings and asked, "What was your vision when you started Intel?" He replied very sternly, "I did not have a vision." Embarrassed, and feeling that all our hard work had been for nothing, we asked less boldly, "Well, what did you have when you started Intel?" "I had a personal agenda," he stated bluntly.

Grove's straightforward response set us straight on one thing. It doesn't matter what label you put on the behavior; the intention is the same. What Grove made clear, by both his tone and his words, was that when he and Robert Noyce and Gordon Moore cofounded Intel Corporation, they wanted to *do* something. They wanted to do something significant. They wanted to accomplish something that no one else had yet achieved. They wanted to build an organization that would be the best in the world at what it did.

No matter what it is called—personal agenda, purpose, legacy, dream, goal, or vision—the intent is the same. Leaders must be forward-looking and have a clear sense of the direction that they want their organizations to take.[7] To begin your own thinking about your vision, ask yourself this question: "Am I in this job to do something, or am I in this job for something to do?" Our guess is that you will answer: "To do something, of course." If that is your answer, now write your response to this question: "What is the something that you want to do?" When you get through the easy answers and come to those that have the greatest personal meaning, then you know that you are on the right track.

The Meaning of Vision

We prefer to use the term *vision* not because it is fashionable but because it is the most descriptive term for the ability that leaders discussed with us. We prefer *vision*, first of all, because it is a "see" word. It evokes images and pictures. Visual metaphors are very common when we are talking about the long-range plans of an organization. Second, *vision* suggests a future orientation—a vision is an image of the future. Third, *vision* connotes a standard of excellence, an ideal. It implies a choice of values. Fourth, it also has the quality of uniqueness. Therefore, we define a vision as *an ideal and unique image of the future.*

Think about it in another way. Suppose you suddenly feel a strong inner desire to go on a challenging expedition to a place to which you have never been. It is a desire that you can't shake, something that you think about day and night. You wake up thinking about it. You go to bed thinking about it. It becomes an obsession.

At first, your desire for challenge is quite vague. There is not yet a specific destination in mind. But soon you feel a need to decide on the kind of challenging journey that you want for yourself. You look at some alternatives: trekking through the mountains, sailing an ocean, hiking across a desert, going on a safari. Whether from conscious thought or meditation, you discover what appeals to you the most: you decide to take a trek through a mountain in the Himalayas.

Next, you consult a travel guide, study maps, look at photographs. You talk to people who have climbed the Himalayas before. You read adventure stories by those who have done it before. You begin to get a real sense of the place—the weather, the dress, the customs, the food, the travel conditions—all those impressions that clarify your understanding of your destination. Not wanting your trip to be just like all the others you have heard about, you decide that you will make this something special. You decide that your expedition will be unique, one that no one else has ever undertaken—you want to be the first to do it your way. You want it to be particularly exceptional—perhaps even one the *National Geographic* would want to cover.

Then, you might set a date. Your destination being the Himalayas, your trip requires considerably more preparation time than a day's drive to the nearest beach. The planning will also be much more elaborate, requiring more complex thinking. A trek in the Himalayas is not something that is usually done alone. So you determine who else might share your desire for challenge and how they would benefit from the experience. You recruit some colleagues, selling them on the benefits of high adventure. Then the planning begins in earnest.

Creating a vision for your organization is similar in many ways to these initial stages of planning an expedition. It begins with a vague desire to do something that would challenge yourself and others. As the desire grows in intensity, you realize that it isn't a passing fancy but something that you are determined to do. The strength of this internal energy forces you to clarify what it is that you really want to do. The end result becomes clearer and clearer. You begin to get a sense of what you want the organization to look like, feel like, and be like when you and others have completed the journey. An image of the future begins to take shape in your mind. You may even write it down or draw a model of it.

Because you want what you create to be unique, you differentiate your organization from all the others that produce the same product or provide the same service. Yours is a distinctive vision. It is also ideal. After all, you want to set a new standard of perfection, beauty, or excellence. You want yours to be a model for others. It is an ideal and unique image of the future.

Visions for organizations, as well as visions for journeys, are more complex than this, of course. And we do not necessarily follow such a sequential process for clarifying our visions. This is especially true if no one has ever achieved them before. The pioneers in any endeavor have no maps to study, no guidebooks to read, no pictures to view. They can only imagine all the possibilities. As it was with the first voyage of Columbus, the explorer can only dream. Without any previous experience for guidance, the first ones to explore may find that their dreams were only fantasies, or that the visions were much more difficult to attain than originally imagined. On the other hand, the lack of previous experience makes it easier in that pioneers can make up the kind of future that they wish to create or discover. Alan Kay, a senior fellow at Apple Computer, is fond of saying, "The best way to create the future is to invent it." Evidence of inventing the future can be found in any account of bold new adventures. Those who set out in search of America were not realistic by any means. But that did not deter them from making the journey; in fact, it helped. Their dreams of the new world fueled their enthusiasm and better enabled them to persuade others that many interests would be served.

Let's take a closer look at these four attributes of vision—future orientation, image, ideal, and uniqueness. We will discuss another attribute—the collective nature of visions—in the next chapter.

Future Orientation: Looking Forward. Visions are statements of destination, of the ends of our labor. Therefore, all visions are future oriented. It may take three years from the time we decide to climb a mountain until we actually reach the summit. It may take four to six years before a new car is ready for production. It may take a decade to build a company. A vision is a point on the horizon that will be reached only at some date in the future, a statement of what will be created years or decades ahead. To create visions, leaders must become preoccupied with the future. They must be able to project themselves ahead in time.

In Chapter Two, we looked at what followers wanted of their leaders. One of those attributes was the ability to be "forward-looking." In a study that we conducted of the skills needed by CEOs, we found that "having a long-term vision or direction for the firm" was the second most important criterion, after "honesty and integrity." Elliot Jacques, a management scholar and researcher in England, has this to say about the executive's ability to think ahead: "I have found that 'executive vision,' or the ability to view scenarios in terms of extended planning horizons, is an integral part of the upper management psyche. Some top executives, for example, are capable of planning in 20-year time spans."[8]

Different tasks require different spans of time to complete. The leader of a research and development team that has a vision of designing the world's fastest supercomputer may think ten years ahead. The leader of a manufacturing group who wants a factory that produces the highest-quality product in the industry may think three years ahead. Time spans also vary according to the planner's position. Line managers may look ahead only two or three years. The CEO may have a ten- or twenty-year vision for the company. As a rule of thumb, we believe that leaders should set for themselves the goal of developing their abilities to envision the future at least three to five years ahead.

Whether we are looking at vision from the perspective of the follower, of the executive, or of the management scholar, there is strong agreement that leaders must occupy themselves with thinking about the future. The result of that thinking ahead is what we call "vision."

Image: Seeing the Future. We often hear managers talk about foresight, clarity of purpose, future scenarios, forecasts, focus, points of view, perspectives on the issue. These are all visual references. In his book *Hey, Wait a Minute,* John Madden writes about a conversation he had with Vince Lombardi about the differences between a good coach and a bad coach. Lombardi answered, "The best coaches know what the end result looks like, whether it's an offensive play, a defensive play, a defensive coverage, or just some area of the organization. If you don't know what the end result is supposed to look like, you can't get there. All the teams basically do the same things. We all have drafts, we all have training camps, we all have practices. But the bad coaches don't know what the hell they want. The good coaches do."[9] What holds true for good coaches also holds true for good leaders.

It is striking how our language reveals the visual nature of our thoughts about the future state of affairs. When we invent the future, we try to get a mental picture of what things will be like long before we have begun the journey. Visions are our windows on the world of tomorrow. When we are talking about going places where we have never been before, whether to the top of an unclimbed mountain or to the pinnacle of an entirely new industry, we imagine what they would be like. We dream about the possibilities. Those who are more auditory by nature talk about a "calling." All of us make efforts to see into the future—not in some mystical sense, but in a cognitive sense. We do it every time we plan a trip for the summer or put a little money in the bank for our retirement. While some of us may have greater telescopic sight than others, it is a more common skill than we assume.

Visions, then, are conceptualizations. They are images in the mind. They are impressions and abstractions. They become real as leaders express those images in more concrete terms to their constituents. Just as architects make drawings and engineers build models, leaders find ways of giving expression to their hopes for the future.

Ideal: A Sense of the Possible. "Most companies select goals that are too short term," asserts Robert H. Hayes of the Harvard Business School. "It is impossible for a company to create a truly sustainable competitive advantage—one that is highly difficult for its competitors to copy—in just five to ten years (the time frame that most companies use). Goals that can be achieved within five years are usually either too easy or based on buying and selling something. Anything that a company can buy or sell, however, is probably available for purchase or sale by its competitors as well."[10] Hayes goes on to say, "Short-term goals also work to back companies into a mode of thinking that is based on forecasts (What do we think is going to happen?) rather than on visions (What do we want to happen?)"[11]

Visions are about possibilities, about desired futures. They are ideals, standards of excellence. As such, they are expressions of optimism and hope. A mode of thinking based on visions opens us up to considering possibilities, not simply probabilities. Probabilities must be based upon evidence strong enough to establish presumption. Possibilities need not. All new ventures begin with possibility thinking, not probability thinking. After all, the probability is that most new businesses will fail. If entrepreneurs took this view, however, they would never start a new business. Instead, they operate from the assumption that anything is possible. Like entrepreneurs, pioneering leaders also assume that anything is possible. It is this belief that sustains them through the difficult times.

It is instructive to recall that the personal best cases we collected were about possibilities. They were about improving upon the existing situation or even creating an entirely new state of existence. There was a dissatisfaction with the status quo and a belief that something better was attainable. Personal best leadership experiences are examples of possibility thinking. They represent the choice of an ideal. Ideals reveal our higher-order value preferences. They represent our ultimate economic, technological, political, social, and aesthetic priorities. The ideals of world peace, freedom, justice, a comfortable life, happiness, self-respect, and the like are among the ultimate strivings of our existence—the ones that we seek to attain over the long term. They are statements of the idealized purpose that all our practical actions will enable us to attain.

Uniqueness: Pride in Being Different. Visions are unique. They set us apart from everyone else. They tell insiders and outsiders what is different about our group or our company. They communicate what makes us singular and unequaled. Visions must differentiate us from others if we are to attract and retain employees, customers, and investors. There is no advantage in working for, buying from, or investing in an organization that does exactly the same thing as the one across the street or down the hall. Only when people understand how we are truly distinctive, how we stand out in the crowd, will they want to sign up with us.

Being unique also fosters pride. It boosts the self-respect and self-esteem of everyone associated with the organization. The prouder we are of the place we shop, the products or services we buy, or the place we work, the more loyal we are likely to be. One of the best ways to discover the uniqueness in your organization's vision is to begin by asking why your customers, internal or external, would want to buy your particular service or product. One of our favorite answers is this simple yet eloquent statement from Podesta Baldocchi, a florist: "We do not sell flowers. We sell beauty." While customers of a florist do exchange money for a dozen roses, what they are really buying is something more than that. They want to beautify their homes, or express their love for others, or brighten the day. It doesn't take vision to sell a flower on a street corner, but it does take vision to sell beauty.

Uniqueness is also the way smaller units within large organizations can have their own vision while still being encompassed by the corporate vision. While every unit within a corporation or public agency must be aligned with the overall organizational vision, it still can express its distinctiveness within the larger purpose. Every function and every department can differentiate itself from the others by finding its most distinguishing aspects. Each can be proud of its ideal and unique image of its future while still working toward the common future of the larger organization.

Maureen Saltzer Brotherton has brought all of these elements together. To our knowledge, she is the youngest general manager of a daily newspaper in the country (*The Valley Times* in Pleasanton, California). Prior to this job, Brotherton had orchestrated the profitable start-up of a tabloid weekly with a circulation of 6,500 (and in the newspaper business profitable start-ups are an uncommon occurrence). "We had an opportunity to create something out of nothing," Brotherton explained, "and I got the staff to believe in themselves and the project and to see that others believed in their ability as well."

Brotherton has a unique and ideal image about the future of her organization and what the people in this organization can accomplish. Here are a few excerpts from what she told people at *The Valley Times* when they had reached a significant circulation milestone:

I want to see us truly *be* the winning team. Be the First Choice, the *only* good local choice. Be the heartbeat of the Valley.

When we win, our *readers* win—they'll get *more* of everything, because we will have the space to give it to them. When we win, our *advertisers* win—they'll get results, because we will have the loyal readers to bring them those results. When we win, our *carriers* and *circulation staff* win—because routes will be lucrative enough that we will have a carrier waiting list in *every* district. When we win, our *editorial staff* wins—because they'll have space for *all* their meaningful, in-depth, and exciting stories. Our *photographers* will have room to truly showcase their art. When we win, our *salespeople* win—because these business emissaries will have happy customers, and more customers. When we win, we will even find the time to thank those who usually go thankless, our *support staffs*. When we win, we will *be* the pulse of the Valley—with the image, market share and financial rewards that come to *winners*.

And, we *will* win. We *will* be the Valley's heartbeat. But only because of *you*. Because we already have a multitalented and caring editorial staff. We already have photographers who turn news photos into those frozen meaningful moments. We already have a sales staff who know how to get results for their customers—and who are backed up by our creative artists. We will win because we already have a circulation department who not only gets the paper out but who can sell it, too. And we already have support staff who go that extra mile.

You already offer so much. And, you can offer more to hurry us on the way: Sell that extra ad, get all the papers out on the customers' porches, scramble for those award-winning photos and stories. Keep on scooping the *Herald*. Most of all, help each other on the way. I'll be there with you, every step of that way—listening to your frustrations, acting on your requests, backing up your needs with concrete support, keeping your paths as clear as I possibly can.

Together, we are the winning team that will make *The Valley Times* the heartbeat of the Valley.

We have found in our research that a clear vision is a powerful force. It has a significant influence on followers. When leaders clearly articulated their vision for the organization, people reported significantly higher levels of job satisfaction, commitment, loyalty, esprit de corps, clarity of direction, pride, and productivity. It is quite evident that clearly articulated visions make a difference.

The Sources of Vision

Intuition is the wellspring of vision. In fact, by definition, intuition and vision are directly connected. Intuition has as its root the Latin word meaning "to look at." Intuition, like vision, is a "see" word. It has to do with our abilities to picture and to imagine.

Despite the fact that vision and intuition are identified by leaders as important, they have not been subjects of serious study in business. "But there will be little headway in the field of management if managers and researchers continue to search for the key to managing in the lightness of ordered analysis. Too much will stay unexplained in the darkness of intuition,"[12] wrote management scholar Henry Mintzberg in the *Harvard Business Review*. This assertion is based upon his research on the nature of managerial work. Mintzberg summarizes his findings: "One fact recurs repeatedly in all of this research: the key managerial processes are enormously complex and mysterious (to me as a researcher, as well as to the managers who carry them out), drawing on the vaguest of information and using the least articulated of mental processes. These processes seem to be more relational and holistic than ordered and sequential, and more intuitive than intellectual; they seem to be most characteristic of right-hemispheric activity.[13]

Envisioning and intuiting are not logical activities. They do not lend themselves to easy study and observation. They are extremely difficult to explain and quantify. So we have either ignored them or not taken them seriously. Even so, in recent studies, senior executives have reported that their intuition has been a guide in most of their important decisions.[14] And yet, while the use of intuition is commonplace among executives, they are very reluctant to talk about it.[15] Hard-bitten senior managers see it as too soft and mystical to openly acknowledge.

They appear to be afraid that their executive colleagues, all of whom also use intuition, will think that they are weird. Intuition is like that big elephant in the middle of the room—everybody can see it, but since it isn't supposed to be there, no one will talk about it.

Experience Is the Best Teacher. H. Ross Perot, the founder of EDS, defined intuition this way: "It means knowing your business. It means being able to bring to bear on a situation everything you've seen, felt, tasted, and experienced in an industry."[16] Intuition, seen from Perot's perspective, is the bringing together of knowledge and experience to produce new insights. But the knowledge that executives deem important, as Perot implies, is not the formal knowledge that we acquire in school. It is knowledge gained through hands-on experience in the company and the industry.

One of our studies confirms this. When we asked senior managers to rate the criteria that they used in selecting a CEO, they ranked "knowledge of how the company operates" third and "knowledge of the industry" seventh on a list of twenty-three competencies. Yet "academic training in business" and "knowledge of management science" were rated sixteenth and seventeenth.[17] Direct experience with the organization and the industry is the source of knowledge on how the organization and industry operate. Intuition, insight, and vision come from the knowledge that we acquire through direct experience and store in our subconscious.

Intuition, then, is not some mystical process. Rather, it is a clearly understandable phenomenon. As we acquire experience in an organization and an industry, we acquire information about what happens, how things happen, and who makes things happen. The longer we spend in an organization and an industry, and the more varied our experiences, the broader and deeper our understanding is likely to be. Often, when presented with an unfamiliar problem, we consciously (or unconsciously) draw upon those experiences to help us solve problems. We select relevant information, make relevant comparisons, and integrate experience with the current situation. For the experienced leader, all of this may happen in a matter of seconds. But it is the years of

direct contact with a variety of problems and situations that prepare the leader for unique insight. Listening, reading, smelling,
feeling, and tasting the business improve our vision.

The research reported by Omar A. El Sawy in *Temporal
Perspective and Managerial Attention* extends our understanding
of the relevance of past experience in planning for the future.[18]
El Sawy studied thirty-four chief executive officers, dividing
them into two equal groups. Among the tests that he administered to the two subgroups was the Vista Test. In one part of
this test, the CEOs were asked to look ahead into their personal
futures—to "think of things that might (or will) happen to you
in the future." In the second part, they were asked to look into
their personal pasts—to "think of the things that have happened
to you in the past." In each case, they were asked to list ten
events and to date each event. In the case of the future events,
they wrote down their "best estimates of exactly when the event
will start" and, in the case of the past events, "their best estimates of exactly when the event started." They also weighted
each event according to its degree of importance to them at the
present time.

One group listed the past events first, and the other group
listed the future events first. El Sawy then compared the length of
the past and future time horizons for the two groups. The CEOs
who listed their past events first had significantly longer future
time horizons—a maximum of 9.18 years, as compared with only
5.11 years for the group that listed future events first. There were
no differences between the two groups in the past time horizons;
the maximum was about twenty years for each group. El Sawy
refers to this as "the Janus precedence effect."

Of several plausible explanations for the Janus precedence
effect, the one that El Sawy feels that his research supports is
what he calls the "one-way mirror hypothesis." This hypothesis
states, "We make sense of our world retrospectively, and all understanding originates in reflection and looking backward. . . . We
construct the future by some kind of extrapolation, in which the
past is prologue, and the approach to the future is backward-
looking."[19] It appears that when we first gaze into our past, we
elongate our future. We also enrich the future and give it detail
as we recall the richness of our past experiences.

El Sawy's research does not rigorously ascertain which approach (past first or future first) yields a better estimate of the "true" future. He did not follow executives over time to see which group was more accurate in its predictions. However, it does show us that there are ways to improve upon our abilities to see farther into the future. One way is to reflect upon our past. So long as our memories or records of the events are accurate, and so long as we draw from those relevant experiences, the past can be a very important source of information about what will interest us in the future.

If being forward-looking is a skill needed by leaders—as our and others' research clearly indicates—then being backward-looking may enhance that ability. That is, when drawing upon our experience and recalling our past, we may be better able to envision the future.

Applying his findings to corporate rather than personal planning, El Sawy comments, "The Janus precedence effect suggests that in strategic planning sessions, if we want to plan for the distant future, and we want the participants to elongate their time horizons in their image of future, let them talk about history first. Let them look into the past and deliberate about it, before looking into the future."[20]

Applying Past Knowledge to the Present. While knowledge and experience are the resources of intuition, they are not by themselves enough to produce an ideal image of the future. Visions do not leap out of our past wholly formed. Nor is our future merely a straight-line projection from the past. Like all raw materials, knowledge and experience must first be extracted, refined, and processed before they produce usable ideas.

Our hunch is that, while the past is the prologue, the present is the opportunity. The past gives us the knowledge and experience from which to draw. The present offers the chance to apply it. The past is the source of light. The present is the opening in the door through which the light is able to shine. The essential executive action, then, is opening the door. Opportunity often knocks but never waits long. If we keep shut the doors of opportunity, the light can never shine on us. Opening the door is what many people describe as "trusting your intuition."

Don Bennett, a Seattle businessperson and the first amputee with one leg and crutches to climb Mount Rainier's 14,410-foot volcanic summit, describes how he came up with the idea for the Amputee Soccer League this way: "Where did it come from? Well, when I got off the mountain I was in top shape. The best shape I had ever been in my life. And so right away because I'm doing one thing on the positive, my mind is thinking, 'What can I do to stay in shape?' So where does it come from? I think there is a bolt of lightning in the middle of the night. All I had was the inspiration. I didn't know that much about soccer. I didn't know there were even two sizes of soccer balls. . . . So the next thing with the inspiration is 'get out and start doing something.' The doing part of it is picking up a phone, calling a few friends, and saying 'Why don't you meet me over on Mercer Island. I've got an idea here. I really feel it.' So when they come over, I pull out a soccer ball. They already have their crutches, and we start kicking it. . . . Then things start happening."

Bennett's description of the process that he went through in starting the unique soccer team is typical of others in our study. There was a moment of inspiration—a bolt of lightning—and then action—not planning, but action to test out the idea. As Bennett said, "You've got to kick the ball around to get a feel for it. To see if you like it. . . . The inspirations come with kicking the ball."

And what gets the action started? "You have to feel strong about it," says Bennett. Peter McKay, owner of a seminar business in Australia, said about his personal best, "It took absolute and total personal belief." First you convince yourself. Unless you are first persuaded that your "bolt of lightning" has value, you will not act on it. If you say, "Oh, no one would ever buy that," you will be right. They won't buy it, because you aren't likely to sell. As we will see in the next chapter, people will not follow those who lack conviction for their own ideals.

Visions are reflections of our fundamental beliefs and assumptions about human nature, technology, economics, science, politics, arts, and ethics. Two leaders may have identical experiences and identical opportunities and yet have completely different visions of the organization's future. The reason for their divergence may be their fundamentally different premises. They may have very different visions of the way the world works.[21] Our fundamental beliefs about the potential of our workers, our technology, our economy, our ethics and morals, and our quality of life will all influence what we foresee for our groups and organizations. Those who see unlimited potential in each will have a very different vision of the future from that of those who see limitations and constraints. Before an opportunity can be seized, the leader must assume that something will come of the seizing. So where do visions come from? They flow from the reservoir of our knowledge and experience. They mix with our conviction. They are filtered through our assumptions. They take form when we open the doors of opportunity.

Sandra Kurtzig, founder and chairperson of ASK Computer Systems, said that when you start a company, "You have to have focus." The most important role of visions in organizational life is to give focus to human energy. Visions are like lenses. They focus unrefracted rays of light. They enable everyone concerned with an enterprise to see more clearly what is ahead of them.

Just recall the last time you watched a slide show. Imagine that the projector was out of focus. How would you feel if you had to watch blurred, vague, and indistinct images for the entire presentation? We have actually done this little experiment in some of our leadership programs. The reaction is predictable. People express frustration, impatience, confusion, anger, even nausea. They avoid the situation by looking away. When we ask them whose responsibility it is to focus the projector, the vote is unanimous: "The leader, the person with the focus button." Now some people will get up out of their chairs, walk over to the projector, and focus it themselves. It is gratifying that individuals in organizations are assertive enough to take control of any situation. But this act does not change how these people feel. They are still annoyed that the person with the button—the leader— would not focus the projector.

The leader's job is to focus the projector. No matter how much involvement other people have in shaping the vision, we expect that the leader will be able to articulate it. That is what we mean when we say we expect the leader to be forward-looking. We also refer to this as the Jigsaw Puzzle Principle: it is easier to put the puzzle together if you can see what is on the box cover. In any organization, people have different pieces of the organizational puzzle. Members may have detailed descriptions of their roles and responsibilities, but very often they lack information about the "big picture"—about the overall purpose or vision of the organization.

While people may be able to play the game, randomly sticking their pieces here and there in an attempt to make them fit, they may lack the essential information that will enable them to contribute to the whole. It is possible that after many random tries, the puzzle will eventually be assembled by the persistent few. It is more likely that many will become frustrated, lose interest, and quit the game. The leader's job is to paint the big picture, to give people a clear sense of what the puzzle will look like when everyone has put their pieces in place. Visions are the big picture.

As an illustration of the role of visions, Robert H. Hayes quotes this comment by William Bricker, chairman and CEO of Diamond Shamrock: "Why has our vision been narrowed? Why has our flexibility been constricted? To my mind there is one central reason: our strategies have become too rigid. . . . A detailed strategy [is] like a road map . . . [telling] us every turn we must take to get to our goal. . . . The entrepreneur, on the other hand, views strategic planning not as a road map but as a compass . . . and is always looking for the new road."[22] Hayes goes on to say, "This is a provocative analogy: when you are lost on a highway, a road map is very useful; but when you are lost in a swamp whose topography is constantly changing, a road map is of little help. A simple compass—which indicates the general direction to be taken and allows you to use your own ingenuity in overcoming various difficulties—is much more valuable."[23]

There is no freeway to the future, no paved highway from here to tomorrow. There is only wilderness, only uncertain terrain. There are no roadmaps, no signposts. Instead, the explorer relies upon a compass and a dream. The vision of an organization acts as its magnetic north. It possesses the extraordinary ability to attract human energy. It invites and draws others to it by the force of its own appeal.

Sharing the Vision

We had the occasion recently to conduct a series of leadership workshops with a large international manufacturing company. One part of the project involved viewing videotaped interviews of company employees in which they talked about the subject of leadership. Everyone was asked to respond to the question, "What is leadership?" One response from an assembly worker was particularly instructive. "One of the jobs of a leader," she said, "is to have a vision. But sometimes, top management sees an apple. When it gets to middle management, it's an orange. By the time it gets to us, it's a lemon."

Leadership vision is necessary but insufficient for an organization to move forward with purpose toward a common destination. As important, if not more so, is the ability to communicate that vision so that others come to see what the leader sees. Followers, in fact, have no idea what a leader's vision is until the leader describes it. The image that the followers develop in their minds is highly dependent upon the leader's ability to describe an apple so that it appears as an apple in the minds of others. Additionally, a shared vision is possible only if followers find the purpose appealing. Even when the leader is a master communicator, the followers won't bite from the apple if they prefer oranges. In the next chapter, we will discuss how leaders define a common purpose and then effectively communicate a vision so that others come to share it.

Commitment Number 3: Envision an Uplifting and Ennobling Future

We now recognize that leaders must create visions for their organizations. Whether you are leading a small department of 25, a large corporation of 25,000, or a nation of 250 million, visions set the agenda. They give direction and purpose to the enterprise. A vision is an ideal and unique image of a common future. It is a mental picture of what tomorrow will look like. It expresses our highest standards and values. It sets us apart and makes us feel special. It spans years of time and keeps us focused on the future. And for a vision to be attractive to more than an insignificant few, it must appeal to all of those who have a stake in it. Visions spring forth from our intuition. If necessity is the mother of invention, intuition is the mother of vision. Experience feeds our intuition and enhances our insight. Our past is prologue to our future, and leaders who are students of their own and the organization's history are better able to see into the future.

Organizational visions are influenced by our assumptions about people and the world in which we live. No matter how grand the opportunity, if a leader is not open to it, the vision will be constrained. Here are some things that you can do to enhance your own capacity to envision the future:

1. *Think first about your past.* In this chapter, we described the research of Omar El Sawy, who investigated the temporal perspective of chief executive officers. One of the things that he found was that the executives with the longer time horizons were the ones who wrote first about events in their past. Before you attempt to write your vision statement, we recommend that you write down significant past events. We especially like the "Life Line" exercise developed by Herb Shepard and Jack Hawley.[24] Here is an abbreviated version that you can use:

- On a blank piece of paper, draw your "lifeline." Start as far back as you can remember and stop at the present time.
- Draw your lifeline as a graph, with the peaks representing the highs in your life and the valleys representing the lows.
- Next to each peak, write a word or two identifying the peak experience. Do the same for the valleys.
- Now go back over each peak. For each peak, make a few notes on why this was a peak experience for you.
- Analyze your notes. What themes and patterns are revealed by the peaks in your life? What important personal strengths are revealed? What do these themes and patterns tell you about what you are likely to find personally compelling in the future?

We have done this exercise in our leadership workshops, and it can be extremely revealing and useful as you prepare to clarify your vision of the future. We have also applied the process to the organization rather than the individual. By looking over the history of their organizations, managers begin to see the organizational strengths and weaknesses, the patterns and themes, that have carried them to the present. They are then better informed about the foundation on which they are building the organizational future.

2. *Determine what you want.* Earlier, we suggested that you ask yourself this question: "Am I in this job to do something, or am I in this job for something to do?" Most probably your answer was: "To do something." If so, take out a sheet of paper and at the top write: "What I want to accomplish." Now make a list of all the things that you want to achieve. After you have done that, for each item ask yourself: "Why do I want this?" Keep on asking "why" until you run out of reasons. By doing this exercise, you are likely to discover those few higher-order values that are the idealized ends for which you strive. Here are a few other questions that you can use as catalysts in clarifying your vision:

- How would you like to change the world for yourself and your organization?
- If you could invent the future, what future would you invent for yourself and your organization?
- What mission in life absolutely obsesses you?
- What is your dream about your work?
- What is the distinctive role or skill of your organization (department, plant, project, company, agency, community)?
- About what do you have a burning passion?
- What work do you find absorbing, involving, enthralling? What will happen in ten years if you remain absorbed, involved, and enthralled in that work?
- What does your ideal organization look like?
- What is your personal agenda? What do you want to prove?

3. *Write an article about how you have made a difference.* Your responses to the questions above will give you some clues to what you would like to accomplish in your life and why. Now take it a step further. Imagine that it is the year 2000. Imagine that you have been selected to receive an award as one of the fifty

people who have made a difference in this century. Imagine that a national magazine has written an article about the difference that you have made to your organization, family, and community. Write that article.

When writing this article about your personal contributions, do not censor yourself. Allow yourself this opportunity to record your hopes and dreams, even if you find it somewhat embarrassing. The more comfortable you are in discussing your innermost wishes, the easier it will become to communicate a vision to others.

4. *Write a short vision statement.* Take all this information and write, in twenty-five words or fewer, your ideal and unique image of the future for you and for your organization. We recommend that it be short, because you ought to be able to tell it to others in about three to five minutes. Any longer than that, and others are likely to lose interest. Once you have written it, you might try drawing it. Or, if you can't draw, find a picture that resembles it or a symbol that can represent it. Pictures and symbols help in communicating it to others. Finally, we recommend that you create a short phrase of five to nine words that captures the essence of your vision. Phrases similar to Phil Turner's "We uplift people's spirits" and Podesta Baldocchi's "We do not sell flowers; we sell beauty" are what we have in mind. While your vision will be more involved and elaborate than a memorable phrase, these brief slogans are very useful in communication. They are not substitutes for a complete statement, but they do serve the purpose of helping others to remember the essential reason for the organization's existence.

5. *Act on your intuition.* Remember when Don Bennett came down from his climb of Mount Rainier and was inspired to start the Amputee Soccer League? Remember how he immediately called a few friends and asked them if they would like to join him in kicking the ball around? We recommend that you do the same. If you are inspired to do something, go try it. Go kick the ball around.

Visions often take a while to take shape in your mind. They take even longer to formulate into an articulate statement. Instead of struggling with words on paper, do something to act on your intuition. Then you will see whether you really are convinced that you are on the right track. You will also get to see whether others are as enthusiastic about it as you are. Visions, like objects in the distance, get clearer and clearer as we move toward them.

6. *Test your assumptions.* Our assumptions are mental screens. They expand or constrain what is possible. Remember the nine dot problem from Chapter Four. You might want to make a list of the assumptions underlying your vision. What do you assume to be true or untrue about your employees and your organization, about science and technology, about economics and politics, about the future itself? Ask a few close advisers to react to your assumptions. Do they agree or disagree? Ask people who you think might have different assumptions to respond to yours. Test your assumptions by trying an experiment or two.

7. *Become a futurist.* As Major General John Stanford told us, he sees himself as his organization's futures department. Make it your business to spend some time studying the future. John Naisbitt's book *Megatrends* is the most popular recent analysis of forces shaping the future. Alvin Toffler's *Future Shock* and *The Third Wave* and *American Demographics* magazine are also useful sources of information. There are dozens more. The University of Southern California's Center for Futures Research periodically publishes reports about likely events that are relevant to business. So does the Conference Board in New York and the World Futures Society in Washington, D.C. We recommend that you look into them.

Set up a futures research committee in your organization to study developing issues and potential changes in areas affecting your business. A few years ago, the American Life Insurance Council established the Trend Analysis Project. A team of more than 100 executives continually tracked more than sixty publications that represented new thoughts on trends in American society and abstracted the articles. A smaller team then pulled the abstracts into reports for use in planning and decision making. You could adapt this methodology, or a similar one, to your setting. Each of these is a way for you and your organization to develop your abilities to think long term.

8. *Use mental rehearsal.* Once you have clarified your vision, one of the most effective ways to help you realize it is

mental rehearsal, the act of mentally practicing a skill, sequence of skills, or attitude using mental imagery or kinesthetic feelings. It is used extensively in sports training to improve athletic performance. By visualizing yourself doing a move perfectly or reaching a desired goal, you increase your chances of making imagination become reality. Don Bennett told us that he imagined himself on the top of Mount Rainier a thousand times a day. Adapt this technique to your situation and imagine what it will be like when you and your organization attain your vision. Rehearse this scenario over and over again.

Affirmations are another practical technique. An affirmation is a positive assertion that something is already so. It is a way of making firm that which you imagine for the future. Sometimes it is called positive self-talk. An affirmation can be done in writing, silently, or spoken aloud. An affirmation is effective when it is written in the present tense, as if it already exists. It should be phrased positively in terms of what you want. It should be short and repeated over and over. Write several affirmations about the ideal and unique image of your organization that you can repeat to yourself.

These techniques, and others like them, help to create positive expectations about the future. They are not substitutes for personal conviction and a vision of substance, but they are extremely useful in keeping you focused on what you want to create. The more positive you feel about that future, the better you will be able to communicate positively with others. And that, as we shall see in the next chapter, is an integral part of enlisting others in your vision of the future.

6

Enlist Others:
Attracting People
to Common Purposes

*The executive must find a way to communicate
the vision in a way that attracts and excites
members of the organization.*
——David E. Berlew,
President,
*Situation Management
Systems, Inc.*

"Tonight I want to talk to you about creating and maintaining a corporate vision," began Robert L. Swiggett, chairperson and chief executive officer of Kollmorgen Corporation. He was giving a speech to participants in a leadership development program sponsored by Innovation Associates. He wanted those attending to get a sense of how the company saw itself. He began by asking people to use their imagination. As you read what Swiggett said, you might try to place yourself in that room listening to him.

Let's start out by putting our feet on the floor, both feet on the floor. Put your hands in your lap, sit up straight in your chairs, close your eyes, and take three deep breaths. I want you to visualize a very bright white light. Visualize that light about three feet in front of your forehead toward the ceiling. It's bright, it's white, and it's pure.
     Try to visualize the largest diamond you've ever seen coming in from the right. It's maybe three inches long. It's cut beautifully. The diamond moves over where the light is, and the

light is absorbed into the heart of that brilliantly cut three-inch diamond.

Visualize the diamond slowly rotating, and, every time one of the facets of the diamond lines up with your eyes, it scintillates . . . flashes . . . blue-white light coming out of the heart of that diamond. Think about the white light in a verbal sense. Think that it means number one. First. Absolutely first. Think about the diamond with the white light in the center that means first. I want to use that physical image to represent our vision of what we're trying to do in our company.[1]

Swiggett goes on to explain what he means by first.

How about first to market with the best technology? Now we have more facets on the diamond. Technology and marketing. But you can't sell much stock if you pitch like that. So how about first to the market with the best proprietary technology in growth markets? However, when we're talking to a special group in the company, that may not work. Why not first to the market with the best proprietary technology in growth markets, to get the largest market share, and maintain the best return on assets, to achieve the highest price-earnings ratio, fastest growth, and so on? And soon there are a thousand facets in the diamond. . . .

But, it all starts with the idea of being first. First with the best. And what we try to do in our business, in some way, is to measure everything we do against this big diamond in the sky, being the first with the best.[2]

Swiggett preaches this same message regularly to the people in his company. He does not always use a visualization exercise; sometimes it's a more straightforward presentation. Sometimes it's a discussion. He estimates that he spends at least one-fourth of his time talking to Kollmorgen employees about the company mission and culture. He refers to the formal meetings on company culture as Kollmorgen Kulture workshops.

How do we sell the idea throughout the organization? We have a thing called the "road show." We get this road show up and we go around and talk to about 100 people out of a 300-people division. We get together with them for two days and we talk about all this stuff. We talk about organization structure, we talk about the dynamics of systems, and we talk about these things with the intent of building a sort of emotional ideal about them.

Everybody sits in a sort of circle and we try to wander around so it's a non-classroom environment. We get people talking. It turned out to be absolutely inspiring because we got a lot of good ideas out of the people. We had to do this frequently and at various places to cover a large number of people in order to sell them this concept of being number one technically and in every other way.[3]

Using the metaphor of the "diamond in the sky" and the visualization exercise, Swiggett helps others to see the purpose of Kollmorgen. He enlists others in his vision of the company. He literally breathes life into the vision. He makes it scintillate, makes it glitter. He communicates what he hopes others will come to accept and support as their own.

Communicating a Common Vision

In the personal best cases that we collected, people frequently talked about the necessity to sell the vision to others. They talked about how they had to get others to buy into it. They reported that they had to communicate the purpose and convince others to support the vision. Matt Sanders III, formerly vice-president of Convergent Technologies and now part of a new start-up, says simply, "You have to teach others your vision." When leaders effectively communicate a vision—whether it is to a small group or a large organization—it has very potent effects. In one study we conducted, we asked managers to tell us the extent to which the senior executives in their organizations articulated what their vision of the company's future was all about. Those managers who felt that their senior executives effectively communicated the vision reported significantly higher levels of:

- Job satisfaction
- Commitment
- Loyalty
- Esprit de corps
- Clarity about the organization's values
- Pride in the organization
- Organizational productivity
- Encouragement to be productive

Clearly, teaching others your vision produces powerful results.

It is unfortunate, however, that managers do not make more use of this skill. We found in our research, for instance, that managers say that inspiring a shared vision is the most difficult of the five practices to learn. It is also the one that managers say is the most difficult to apply. When we ask people whether they consider themselves to be inspiring, only 10 percent say that they do. This common perception of ourselves as managers is in sharp contrast to how we perform when talking about our personal best leadership cases or about our ideal futures. When relating our hopes, dreams, and successes, we are always emotionally expressive. We lean forward in our chairs, our arms move about, our eyes light up, our voices sing with emotion, and smiles appear on our faces. We are enthusiastic, articulate, optimistic, and uplifting. In short, we are inspiring.

This apparent contradiction is most intriguing. We seem to see no connection between our animated, enthusiastic behavior when we are describing our dreams and the ability to lift others' spirits. What comes naturally when talking about deep desires for the future is not recognized as demonstrations of enlivening communication. We believe that this is because people have attributed something mystical to the process of inspiring a shared vision. They seem to see it as something supernatural, as a grace and charm that come from the gods. This mythology surrounding inspirational powers inhibits people far more than any lack of natural talent. When we examine even the most famous examples of exalting oratory, we can see that there is a basic structure to them that all of us can master.

On August 28, 1963, on the steps of the Lincoln Memorial in Washington, D.C., before a throng of 250,000, Martin Luther King, Jr., proclaimed his dream to the world. It was, he said that day, "a dream deeply rooted in the American dream." As he spoke, and as thousands clapped and shouted, a nation moved. That speech is one of the best contemporary examples of an inspiring public presentation. It is among the most instructive because of the speaker's skill, his success in moving his listeners. King's uplifting speech also illustrates how the ability to exert an enlivening influence is rooted as much in fundamental values, cultural traditions, and personal conviction as it is in rhetorical technique.

We play an audiotape of King's March on Washington address in all of our leadership development programs. As participants listen, we ask them to imagine that they are communication researchers studying how leaders enlist others. We ask them to listen to the content as well as to the delivery. We ask them to notice the use of various rhetorical techniques. We ask them to place themselves at the steps of the Lincoln Memorial and get a feel for how the audience reacted. Before you go further, you might want to read the words of King's "I Have a Dream" speech.

. . . I say to you today, my friends, that in spite of the difficulties and frustrations of the moment I still have a dream. It is a dream deeply rooted in the American dream.

I have a dream that one day this nation will rise up and live out the true meaning of its creed: "We hold these truths to be self-evident; that all men are created equal."

I have a dream that one day on the red hills of Georgia the sons of former slaves and the sons of former slaveowners will be able to sit down together at the table of brotherhood.

I have a dream that one day even the state of Mississippi, a desert state sweltering with the heat of injustice and oppression, will be transformed into an oasis of freedom and justice.

I have a dream that my four little children will one day live in a nation where they will not be judged by the color of their skin but by the content of their character.

I have a dream today.

I have a dream that one day the state of Alabama, whose governor's lips are presently dripping with the words of interposition and nullification, will be transformed into a situation where little black boys and black girls will be able to join hands with little white boys and white girls and walk together as sisters and brothers.

I have a dream today.

I have a dream that one day every valley shall be exalted, every hill and mountain shall be made low, the rough places will be made plains, and the crooked places will be made straight, and the glory of the Lord shall be revealed, and all flesh shall see it together.

This is our hope. This is the faith with which I return to the South. With this faith we will be able to transform the jangling discords of our nation into a beautiful symphony of brotherhood. With this faith we will be able to work together, to pray together, to struggle together, to go to jail together, to stand up for freedom together, knowing that we will be free one day.

This will be the day when all of God's children will be able to sing with new meaning, "My country 'tis of thee, sweet land of liberty, of thee I sing. Land where my fathers died, land of the pilgrim's pride, from every mountainside, let freedom ring."

And if America is to be a great nation this must become true. So let freedom ring from the prodigious hilltops of New Hampshire. Let freedom ring from the mighty mountains of New York. Let freedom ring from the heightening Alleghenies of Pennsylvania!

Let freedom ring from the snowcapped Rockies of Colorado!

Let freedom ring from the curvaceous peaks of California!

But not only that; let freedom ring from the Stone Mountain of Georgia!

Let freedom ring from every hill and molehill of Mississippi. From every mountainside, let freedom ring.

When we let freedom ring, when we let it ring from every village and every hamlet, from every state and every city, we will be able to speed up that day when all of God's children, black men and white men, Jews and Gentiles, Protestants and Catholics, will be able to join hands and sing in the words of that old Negro spiritual, "Free at last! Free at last! Thank God almighty, we are free at last!"[4]

Here are some of the things that people have noticed when listening to King's speech:

- "It was vivid. He used a lot of images and word pictures. You could see the examples."
- "People could relate to the examples. They were familiar to them. For example, the spirituals."
- "His references were credible, even to whites. It is hard to argue against the Constitution and the Bible."
- "He talked about traditional values of family, church, country."
- "He appealed to common beliefs."
- "He knew his audience."
- "He made geographical references to the places the people in the audience could relate to."
- "He included everybody; different parts of the country, all ages, both sexes, major religions."
- "He used a lot of repetition; for example, 'I have a dream,' 'Let freedom ring.'"

- "He said the same thing in different ways."
- "He began with a statement of the difficulties, and then stated his dream."
- "He was positive and hopeful."
- "He talked about hope for the future, but he also said they might have to suffer in order to get there. He didn't promise it would be easy."
- "There was a cadence and a rhythm to his voice."
- "He shifted from 'I' to 'we' halfway through."
- "He spoke with emotion and passion. It was deeply felt."
- "He was personally convinced of the dream."

One of the things that immediately becomes evident to everyone is the ease with which they are able to identify what makes King's speech so uplifting. It is easy to decipher the code. There is no mystery to its power. Then we take it a step further. We go down the list of observations, and we ask: Can you do more of this in presentations to your group? Can you:

- Use images and word pictures?
- Use examples that people can relate to?
- Talk about traditional values?
- Appeal to common beliefs?
- Get to know your audience?
- Use repetition?
- Be positive and hopeful?
- Shift from "I" to "we"?
- Speak with passion and emotion?
- Have personal conviction about the dream?

As we go through the list, participants in our leadership development programs respond with "Yes" to nearly every question. When the magic of inspiration is revealed, most say that they could do more than they now do to awaken the passion in others.

The analysis of King's speech also reveals that there is much more to enlisting others than rousing public oratory. Many leaders are just as effective, and far more comfortable, in bull sessions or fireside chats than in the pulpit. The essence of inspiration is not in the eloquence of speech. It is in the appeal of the message to the audience. Whether it is delivered to a crowd in the grandstands or one person in the office, there are three fundamental qualities of an inspirational presentation. In order to move others to share the vision, leaders (1) appeal to a common purpose, (2) communicate expressively, and (3) sincerely believe in what they are saying.

Discovering a Common Purpose

The first task in enlisting others is to find out what you and your constituents have in common. No matter how grand the dream of the individual visionary, if others do not see in it the possibility of realizing their own hopes and desires, they will not follow. It is incumbent upon the leader to show others how they too will be served by the long-term vision of the future.

In order to be able to speak for the common cause, leaders must get to know their followers. By knowing their followers, by listening to them, and by taking their advice, leaders are able to stand before others and say with assurance: "Here is what I heard you say that you want for yourselves. Here is how your own needs and interests will be served by enlisting in a common cause." Bill Hicks, our editor at Jossey-Bass, offers this insight: "Leaders tell us how we feel."

John Gardner, founding chairperson of Common Cause and a pre-eminent student of leadership, observes: "A loyal constituency is won when people, consciously or unconsciously, judge the leader to be capable of solving their problems and meeting their needs, when the leader is seen as symbolizing their norms, and when their image of the leader (whether or not it corresponds to reality) is congruent with their inner environment of myth and legend."[5]

Leaders are like mediums. They act as channels of expression between the down-to-earth followers and their otherworldly dreams. If a leader has a special gift, it is the ability to sense the purpose in others. So truly inspirational leadership is not really selling people some science fiction future. Rather, it is showing people how the vision can directly benefit them, how their specific needs can be satisfied. It is like holding up a mirror and reflecting back to them what they say that they most desire. When they see the reflection, they recognize it and are immediately attracted to it.

Harlan Cleveland, a former U.S. ambassador and respected university dean, recently made this observation: "Decision making proceeds not by 'recommendations up, orders down,' but by development of a shared sense of direction among those who must form the parade if there is going to be a parade."[6] Cleveland further illustrates his point with an excerpt from the satirist Russell Baker:

What does this country need today?
Leadership. . . . The country yearns for new leadership for a new era.

If led, will the country follow?
If given the right kind of leadership, the country will surely follow.

But what kind of leadership is the right kind?
The leadership that leads the country in the direction it wants to take.

And what specific direction does the country want to take?
Who knows? That's for the leader to figure out. If he is the right kind of leader, he will guess correctly. . . .

Am I wrong in concluding that it isn't leadership the country wants in a President but followership?[7]

Cleveland adds: "Russell Baker was not wrong. High policy—that is, major change in a society's sense of direction—is first shaped in an inchoate consensus reached by the people at large."[8] What is true for the society at large is also true for organizations. Corporate leaders know very well that what seed the vision are those imperfectly formed images in the marketing department about what the customers really wanted and those inarticulate mumblings from the manufacturing folks about the poor product quality, not crystal ball gazing in upper levels of the corporate stratosphere. The best leaders are the best followers. They pay attention to these weak signals and quickly respond to changes in the corporate course.

This notion of leaders as followers may take some getting used to. It flies in the face of the leaders-as-heroes myth perpetuated so long in comic books, novels, and movies. It also contradicts the newest myth of the entrepreneur as lone savior of the national economy. Yet, if we look closely, we see that even the entrepreneur is an astute listener and follower of others' desires. The entrepreneurial enterprise most appeals to those who want to be involved in something new and fresh, in an exciting and risky environment, in a climate free of corporate hassles. Those who don't want these things remain in more stable organizations. They don't take the chance. It's only when these little entrepreneurial ventures move out of the start-up garage and into the more mature organization that they begin to attract the more career-minded folks.

Leaders find that common thread that weaves together the fabric of human needs into a colorful tapestry. They seek out the brewing consensus among those they would lead. In order to do this, they develop a deep understanding of the collective yearnings. They listen carefully for quiet whisperings in dark corners. They attend to the subtle cues. They sniff the air to get the scent. They watch the faces. They get a sense of what people want, what they value, what they dream about. This is no trivial skill. It is not something to be taken lightly. It is to be prized. Sensitivity to others' needs is a truly precious human ability. But it is not a complex skill. Being sensitive to others simply requires a receptiveness to other people and a willingness to listen. It means spending time with them on the factory floor or in the showroom or warehouse or back room, not in the fifty-second-floor executive suite. It means being delicately aware of the attitudes and feelings of others and the nuances of their communication.

And what do leaders discover when they listen with sensitivity to the aspirations of others? What do they discover about the common values that link us together? A decade ago, psychologist David E. Berlew, now president of Situation Management Systems, Inc., speculated that what really excites people, what really provides meaning and generates enthusiasm, are these value-related opportunities:

• A chance to be tested, to make it on one's own.
• A chance to take part in a social experiment.

- A chance to do something well.
- A chance to do something good.
- A chance to change the way things are.[9]

Berlew's speculations about what workers might want from organizations seem to have been confirmed in a study conducted by psychologists Edward Lawler III and Patricia Renwick. They asked readers of *Psychology Today* to indicate those job aspects that they found most important to them and their current level of satisfaction with each. The top six reader-respondent rankings were, in order of importance:

1. The chance to do something that makes you feel good about yourself as a person.
2. The chance to accomplish something worthwhile.
3. The chance to learn new things.
4. The opportunity to develop new skills.
5. The amount of freedom that you have to do your job.
6. The chance to do the things that you do best.[10]

For those who are wondering where "the amount of pay you get" ranked, it was twelfth out of eighteen items.

These findings suggest that there is more to work than is commonly assumed. There is rich opportunity here for leaders to appeal to more than just the material rewards. Great leaders, like great companies and countries, create meaning, not just money. The values and interests of freedom, self-actualization, learning, community, excellence, uniqueness, service, and social responsibility are the ones that truly attract followers to a common cause.

"No matter how bewildering the times," writes Studs Terkel in *Working*, "no matter how dissembling the official language, those we call ordinary are aware of a sense of personal worth—or more often the lack of it—in the work they do."[11] Terkel ends his book with an interview with Tom Patrick, a Brooklyn fire fighter. Patrick shows us the depth of importance of meaningful, worthy work to human beings: "But the firemen, you actually see them produce. You see them put out a fire. You see them come out with babies in their hands. You see them give mouth-to-mouth when a guy is dying. . . . I can look back and say 'I helped put out a fire. I helped save somebody. It shows something I did on this earth.' "[12]

We believe that most of us, just like Patrick, want to know that we have done something on this earth. There is a deep human yearning to make a difference. We want to know that our life means something. We want to know that there is a purpose to our existence. Work can provide that purpose, and increasingly it is where men and women seek it. It is where we hope to gain much of our satisfaction from life. Work has become a place where we seek meaning and identity. In the United States, work has become as important as family to life satisfaction. In one study we found 50 percent of the U.S. managers surveyed said that their careers give them the most satisfaction in life.[13] Family was almost as important as work, and outside interests provided the rest of life satisfaction.

The results of this study are shown in Table 2. They suggest to us that there is a major source of psychological energy available to organizations. There lies, often untapped, in the belly of organizations that human desire to be fulfilled, and work can make a significant difference in how fully realized people feel. The best organizational leaders have been able to bring forth this human longing. They have been able to do this by communicating the meaning and significance of the organization's work so that the individual understands his or her own important role in creating it. When leaders clearly communicate a shared vision of an organization, they ennoble those who work on its behalf. They elevate the human spirit.

Leadership that focuses on communicating the meaning of the organization, or of a business unit within it, is what James

Table 2. Sources of Life Satisfaction: United States.

	Total	*Supervisory*	*Middle*	*Executive*
Home life	40.1%	36.8%	46.1%	37.8%
Outside interest	9.8	17.4	11.3	7.9
Career	50.1	45.8	42.6	54.3

Source: Schmidt, W. H., and Posner, B. Z. *Managerial Values in Perspective.* New York: American Management Association, 1983, p. 23.

MacGregor Burns refers to as transformational leadership. "Such leadership occurs when one or more persons engage with others in such a way that leaders and followers raise one another to higher levels of motivation and morality. Their purposes, which might have started out as separate but related, as in the case of transactional leadership, become fused. . . . But transforming leadership ultimately becomes moral in that it raises the level of human conduct and ethical aspiration of both the leader and the led, and thus it has a transforming effect on both."[14]

The most admired leaders speak unhesitatingly and proudly of our mutual ethical aspirations. They know that we want to live up to the highest moral standards. So the first requirement of enlisting others is that leaders find and focus on the very best that the culture shares in common, on what the culture—group, organizational, or national—means to its members. This communion of purpose, this commemoration of our dreams, helps to bind us together. It reminds us of what it means to be a part of this collective effort. It joins us together in the human family.

Giving Life to a Vision

The second requirement of enlisting others is to bring the common vision to life. You must animate it. You must make manifest the purpose so that others can see it, hear it, taste it, touch it, feel it. In making the intangible vision tangible, you have a kindling effect on people. You ignite human flames of passion.

Language. To give life to visions, leaders use a variety of modes of expression. Leaders make full use of all the available media to communicate to others their shared identity. Language is among the most powerful methods for expressing a vision. Successful leaders use metaphors and figures of speech; they give examples, tell stories, and relate anecdotes; they draw word pictures; and they offer quotations and recite slogans.

Review again the words of Martin Luther King. Notice his use of word images: "red hills of Georgia," "the prodigious hilltops of New Hampshire," the "heightening Alleghenies of Pennsylvania," and "transform the jangling discords of our nation into a beautiful symphony of brotherhood." Read the specific examples: "where little black boys and black girls will be able to join hands with little white boys and white girls and walk together as sisters and brothers" and "a dream that my four little children will one day live in a nation where they will not be judged by the color of their skin but by the content of their character."[15] Notice the references to the Constitution and his quotations from anthems and spirituals. All these skillful uses of language give the listener a visceral feel for the dream. They enable us to picture the future in our mind's eye. They enable us to hear it, to sense it, to recognize it.

Enriching language with stories and references and figures of speech is something that all leaders can do. In many ways, it is a natural way of communicating. One need only recall how people told each other stories as children or how they loved to have stories told to them, or recall the days before television when people loved to imagine scenes described by the announcer on the radio.

Metaphors are plentiful in our daily conversations. We talk of computers having memory and ships plowing the sea. We talk about time as money. We talk about knowledge as power. We talk about business as a game. Military metaphors are used in corporate strategy. The sports vernacular is heard daily in business meetings. Metaphors and analogies are as common in business as are numbers. Leaders make conscious use of metaphorical expressions to give vividness and tangibility to abstract ideas.

In this book, and in all our discussions of leadership, we use the journey metaphor to express our understanding of leadership. We talk about leaders taking people on expeditions to places they have never been. We talk about leaders as pioneers and trail blazers. We talk about the vision as magnetic north. We talk about climbing to the summit. We talk about milestones and signposts. All of these metaphorical expressions are our way of communicating the active, pioneering nature of leadership.

Language is a powerful tool. We remember once listening to a bank officer rallying his managers to fight for the company. He was talking about the current deregulated environment, and he wanted to get his folks charged up to take on the competition. Here are some of the phrases he used:

- "You've got to watch out for the headhunters."
- "Keep your capital and keep it dry."
- "We will act like SWAT teams."
- "We are going to beat their brains out."
- "Get the moccasin and the tom-tom going."
- "We won't tolerate the building of little fiefdoms."
- "There will be only a few survivors."

Contrast these with some of the phrases used by Jean-Louis Gassée, senior vice-president of research and development for Apple Computer, in a presentation to Apple managers:

- "What we stand for is innovation . . . also hope, freedom, fun."
- "In our hearts, minds, guts, and muscle . . . we stand for bringing computer power to the people so they can share in the fun."
- "We don't have to wear our suits in our heads."
- "Celebrate the human mind."
- "We share our love for Apple."

These two examples demonstrate how leaders can make use of the metaphorical powers of language. In the first illustration, the bank officer clearly portrayed a hostile environment and used military metaphors to rally the troops. In the second example, Gassée created an entirely different image—one of liberation and joy. Leaders learn to master the richness of figurative speech so they can paint the word pictures that best portray the meanings of their visions.

Symbols are another form of expression that can capture the imagination. The Statue of Liberty is a symbol of America as the land of freedom of opportunity. The eagle is a symbol of strength, the olive branch a symbol of peace, and the lion a symbol of courage. The bull is a hopeful symbol of rising prices in the stock market. Wells Fargo Bank uses the stagecoach to symbolize its pioneering spirit. Mary Kay uses the bumblebee as a symbol for doing what others say cannot be done. Slogans, theme songs, poetry, quotations, and humor are other ways that leaders can express the vision and values of the organization. Executives underutilize all these forms of expression. They overutilize numbers and acronyms, believing that these are more concrete or efficient ways of communicating the company's strategy and practices. In fact, numbers and acronyms are more abstract and take more time to understand. They are not nearly as descriptive as images, metaphors, analogies, and the like.

Communication professor Roderick Hart of the University of Texas has looked into the language of leaders. In his book *Verbal Style and the Presidency,* he identifies four categories of words commonly used by politicians. There are tangible and concrete words, such as *automobile* and *highway,* which he calls "realistic." There are "optimistic" words, which express hope and possibilities. "Activity" words show motion, and "certainty" words express assuredness. Hart says that Americans want language that is "highly certain, highly optimistic, highly realistic and highly active."[16] Hart's research quantifies what successful leaders know intuitively. You must make the intangible image of the future tangible and concrete. You must offer positive and optimistic predictions that the dream will be realized. You must be resolute and confident that it will be done. And you must propel the mission forward, infusing it with motion and energy.

Positive Communication Style. We don't like leaders who are negative. They bring us down. A cartoon that appeared in the *New Yorker* some years ago pictured a room full of people at a party. On the right side of the room was a crowd of well-dressed folks clearly enjoying themselves, smiling, laughing, and talking intently. On the left of the room were five people slouched in overstuffed chairs, arms folded, with frowns and puzzled looks on their faces. In the center of this group was one man with a very sad expression. Off to the side, one woman commented to another, "Sometimes I think Roswell is too much of a moderating influence." Well, sometimes managers are too much of a moderating influence. They seem to carry a cloud of gloom over their heads. When they enter a room, people turn silent and sullen. It is as if they are saying, "Be quiet and get to work." We do not like to be around people like that. They do not make us feel good about ourselves or what we are doing.

We want leaders with enthusiasm, with a bounce in their steps, with a can-do attitude. We want to believe that we are part of an invigorating journey. We want to feel alive, even at work. We follow people with a can-do attitude, not those who give 67,000 reasons why something cannot be done.

There is energy in the leaders we most admire. They are electric, vigorous, active, full of life. We are reminded of Randi DuBois, whom we discussed in Chapter Four. As you recall, DuBois's job is to get people to stretch themselves by engaging in challenging physical tasks. Typically, her clients are nervous and often a bit scared at first. But over 30,000 people—of all ages, all sizes, both sexes, and varying physical abilities—have successfully completed her course. How does DuBois succeed in leading these people? Her secret is very simple: she is always positive that people can do it, and she never says never. She conveys to everyone she meets, both verbally and nonverbally, that they have the power within themselves to accomplish whatever they desire. The authors know this from personal experience. We have been up there forty feet above the ground leaping for an iron ring while DuBois cheered us on.

Reno Taini, who works with DuBois, spent most of his career teaching kids the rest of us would call "incorrigibles." As we said in Chapter Four, most of his work with these students is done outdoors. He takes them hiking, camping, rafting, and mountain climbing; he works alongside them as they serve the homeless and hungry in the missions or clean the city streets. Taini's ability to lead some of the most difficult younger members of our society is due in large measure to his absolute expression of positive regard. What you and I might see as weirdness Taini sees as individuality. Someone that you and I might see as a loser Taini sees as a person with potential.

Here is another example of positiveness from Maria Straatmann, technical marketing manager for Computer Technology and Imaging: "Our organization is based on mutual respect: The contributions of each person are essential to our success. We have learned that creating a business (or a product) depends on people who care about each other and about the customers we serve. This caring for one another translates into integrity in our operating style. We live up to our commitments.

"We can reach for what is just beyond our grasp because we know we can rely on the support of our workers—not only for the known and defined activities, but also for the unexpected. We share the fun, excitement, and triumph of group and individual successes. We have pride in our accomplishments. We do it together, and we're the best in the business."

Positive expectations about other people and optimism about life pay hefty dividends. Research on the phenomenon of self-fulfilling prophecies provides ample evidence that other people act in ways that are consistent with our expectations of them.[17] If we expect others to fail, they probably will. If we expect them to succeed, they probably will. Much of this has to do with how we behave toward others. Our expectations shape our own behavior, not just that of others. Optimists are also far better off than pessimists. Optimists are healthier, live longer, are more successful in their careers, and even score higher on aptitude tests.[18] Pessimists tend to neglect themselves and may even weaken their immune systems. It really does help oneself and others to look at the bright side of things. So you need not be a CEO or the nation's president to raise in others a sense of hope and efficacy. One of the primary ingredients in getting others to sign up for your cause is letting your own enthusiasm show, conveying to others that they too can be great.

Charisma. The word *charismatic* frequently comes up in discussions of leadership. When we want to explain why a particular leader has a magnetic effect on people, we often describe him or her as very charismatic. But *charisma* has become such an overused and misused term that it is almost useless as a descriptor of leaders. Bernard Bass, professor of organizational behavior at the State University of New York, has done extensive research on charisma. He comments: "In the popular media, charisma has come to mean anything ranging from chutzpah to Pied Piperism, from celebrity to superman status. It has become an overworked cliché for strong, attractive, and inspiring personality."[19]

Recently, social scientists have attempted to investigate this elusive quality in terms of observable behavior. Howard S. Friedman and his colleagues, for example, studied the communication of emotions from the perspective of nonverbal expressiveness.[20] They found that those who were perceived to be charismatic were simply more animated than others. They smiled more, spoke faster, pronounced words more clearly, and moved their heads and bodies more often. They were also more likely to touch others during greetings. What we call charisma can better be understood as human expressiveness.

It is also interesting to note that similar reactions to non-verbal behavior can be observed in the world of children. The French ethologist Hubert Montagner has been studying the gestural language of children since the 1970s. He has developed a system for classifying the way kids relate to each other nonverbally into five categories of interpersonal behavior:

- Attractive actions
- Threatening actions
- Aggressive actions
- Gestures of fear and retreat
- Actions that produce isolation[21]

Montagner's findings revealed that the children who become the leaders in their groups use attractive actions, not aggressive actions. At least in the world of the very young, real leaders—those who are naturally followed—are not the young Rambos. They are not the hitters, scratchers, pinchers, biters, and pullers. The natural leaders are those who offer toys to others, lightly touch or caress, clap hands, smile, extend a hand, lean sideways, and the like. Maybe adults can learn something about leading from our children. We can learn that it is not aggression that attracts followers; rather, it is expressions of warmth and friendship that produce attachment.

Conviction. We have come to discover that what is needed for us to become more expressive in our daily lives is not just technique, using more examples, metaphors, word pictures, quotations, slogans, and the like. Neither is it simply learning to speak with more eloquence and style. While these elements do play an important role, they are not, in themselves, enough. The greatest inhibitor to enlisting others in a common vision is lack of personal conviction. There is absolutely no way that you can, over the long term, convince others to share a dream if you are not convinced of it yourself. You must be sincere in your own belief.

Imagine recruiting people to give their all for a goal that you are not convinced should be pursued. You are unable to summon the energy to be animated. You find it difficult to be upbeat and positive. Even great communicators cannot give the same speech over and over again if they do not believe in the message. The most inspirational moments are marked by genuineness. Somehow, we all are able to spot a lack of sincerity in others. We detect it in their voices, we observe it in their eyes, we notice it in their posture. We each have a sixth sense for deceit and can usually tell the fraudulent from the real. So there is a very fundamental question that a leader must ask before attempting to enlist others: "What do I want?" The true force that attracts others is the force of the heart. Inspirational presentations are heart to heart, spirit to spirit, life to life. It is when you share what is in your soul that you can truly move others.

We remember sitting across the lunch table one afternoon from Phil Turner. He had been promoted to plant manager of the Wire and Cable Division of Raychem a year before, and we were curious about how he was doing. Near the close of our interview, we asked, "Phil, why do you do what you do?" He did not answer for a few seconds. His throat got that tightness we all get when a strong emotion wells up inside and chokes us. He paused, took a breath, and replied, "Kindness." Turner cares deeply for the people he leads. That single word, his tone of voice, and his facial expression spoke more volumes than the most eloquent sermon. For us, that was truly an inspiring moment.

Commitment Number 4: Enlist Others in a Common Vision by Appealing to Their Values, Interests, Hopes, and Dreams

Leaders breathe life into their visions. They communicate their hopes and dreams so that others clearly understand and accept them as their own. Leaders know what motivates their constituents. They show others how their values and interests will be served by the long-term vision of the future.

Leaders use a variety of modes of expression to make their abstract visions concrete. Through skillful use of metaphors, symbols, positive language, and personal energy, they generate enthusiasm and excitement for the common vision. Here are some things that you can do to enlist the support of others:

1. *Identify your constituents.* The first thing that you should do is make a list of all the individuals or groups of individuals you want to enlist in your vision of the future. Your organizational superiors and subordinates are obvious groups. But in all probability, you will also want your peers, customers, and suppliers to buy into your dream. Perhaps you also want the support of the citizens of your local community. There are bound to be elements of your vision that will be of interest to the state and the nation in which you do business. You may even have a global vision. And do not limit your list to just present constituents. As your organization grows and develops, it will want to attract new people to it. As the years pass, you will want future generations to take an active interest in what you want to accomplish. Their needs and values should also be considered. Today's students are tomorrow's employees, customers, and investors. They may be the ones who actually help you to realize what you only dream of today. The point is this: identify those who have a stake today and will have a stake tomorrow in the outcomes of what you envision.

2. *Find the common ground.* In order to attract groups with a variety of needs, you must discover what aspirations, goals, interests, needs, or dreams they have in common. They are bound to differ in what they value, but you must find what can bring them together. Your ability to enlist the people you want depends upon how effective you are at detecting the tie that binds. For example, the Marines are quite clear that they want only "a few good men." They know what kind of individual they want in their organization. All their recruitment literature stresses the attributes of their organization that are most attractive to those people. On the other hand, the vision of AT&T is "universal service." Obviously, they must appeal to an entirely different set of human values.

There are numerous ways you can find out what people want, from sophisticated market research techniques to simple surveys. Each has its usefulness. But whatever technique you use, there is no substitute for face-to-face human interaction. The very best way to get to know what other people want is to sit down and talk to them about it on their turf. If you feel that you do not really understand the folks in the factory, move your desk onto the floor for the next few weeks. If you feel that you do not know much about the store owners who buy your packaged goods, ride the route trucks once a week for a year. Get out there in the flesh and make contact. Ask them just one simple question: "What do you most want from this organization?"

Then, when you have gathered the data and have a true feel for your constituents, sit down and see what patterns and themes begin to emerge. There are bound to be several. For example, Tom Melohn, the president of North American Tool and Die, found out that his customers wanted "quality, service, price"—in that order. At first, Melohn was surprised by this. He had spent twenty-five years in the packaged goods industry, where a fraction of a cent made a major difference. So he kept on asking, and the customers kept on telling him: quality, service, and price. In that order. The focus of NATD today is, not surprisingly, first and foremost on quality. "No rejects, no rejects, no rejects. That's why we're here, gang," says Melohn.

One other hint about finding the common ground: avoid being too specific. Vision statements are not job descriptions. They are not product specifications. To have the broadest appeal, visions must be encompassing. They should transcend the day-to-day work and find expression in higher-order human needs. Visions should uplift and ennoble.

3. *Take an effective presentations course.* The higher you advance in an organization, the more presentations you have to give to an ever-widening audience. If there is one course that will benefit you more than any other, it is a course in effective presentations. If you have not taken one yet, sign up for the next available class. But you do not have to wait to advance to improve your communication skills. At Stew Leonard's Dairy, every employee is eligible to take the Dale Carnegie course. They figure that the better employees are at communicating with each other and with customers, the better the organization.

Presentation skills programs can help you learn effective techniques for getting your ideas across. They can also help you gain confidence in yourself. According to Bert Decker, founder and president of Decker Communications, a nationwide communications training and consulting firm, people are more afraid of having to give a speech than they are of dying. Overcoming the anxiety of public speaking is a very important benefit of effective presentations programs.

4. *Write a five-minute speech.* We suggest that you take the next available opportunity to write and memorize a five-minute stump speech that you can deliver anywhere to anyone. Every encounter with an existing or potential stakeholder is an opportunity to teach your vision. You ought to be able to take advantage of those opportunities at a moment's notice.

In preparing your speech, use as many forms of expression as you can to transform the intangibles of your vision into tangibles. Enrich your language with stories, metaphors, analogies, and examples. Add symbols, banners, posters, and other visual aids to your presentations—anything that will help your audience hear, taste, smell, see, and touch your vision. Abstractions such as freedom, service, respect, quality, or innovation must be made concrete if others are to recognize what you imagine. When it comes to visions, we are all from Missouri. We need to be shown what they are. Ed Nelson, a plant manager for Unisys, each year shows his employees a videotape of his annual plan for the plant. In a recent tape, he included a statement of his vision. To enable his associates at the plant to better understand his long-term view, he illustrated his discussion of teamwork using the metaphor of a clock. Nelson spoke of how each person in the plant was a crucial resource, and, as in the clock, all parts are necessary to a smooth, efficient operation. He also had the camera follow him up into the foothills near the plant. The perspective of the plant in the distance visually demonstrated that the organization is part of a larger community.

If you need some help in adding tangibility to your presentations, we suggest that you spend a little time studying advertising and the performing arts. In both the theater and advertising, the performers have to get their audiences to experience something vicariously. They are rich sources of creative ideas on how to convey abstract concepts and how to appeal to human emotions.

5. *Be positive and optimistic.* When talking about mutual aspirations, do not say *try,* say *will* and *are.* There is no room for tentativeness and qualifiers in statements of vision. Sure, there

are lots of reasons why something might not happen. Sure, there are lots of contingencies. But giving eighty-three reasons why not and thirty-three conditions that have to be met will only discourage people from joining the cause. This does not mean that you have to be excessively Pollyannaish or unrealistic. Go ahead and talk about the hardships and difficult conditions. But do not dwell on them. Reasonable people know that great achievements require hard work. Let people know that you have the utmost confidence in their abilities to succeed. Tell them that you are certain that they will prevail. Tell them that you have faith in them. Remember, leaders are possibility thinkers, not probability thinkers.

Let your enthusiasm show. Smile. Use gestures and move your body. Speak more clearly and quickly. Make eye contact. All of these signals are cues to others that you are personally excited about what you are saying. If you do not perceive yourself as an expressive person, we suggest that you begin to practice expressiveness by talking to a favorite friend about what most excites you in life, about what most turns you on. As you do this, pay attention to your verbal and nonverbal behavior—or, better yet, turn on the video camera so that you can watch yourself later. We bet that you will discover that when you talk about things that excite you, you do a lot of the things we have just described.

6. *Remain genuine.* None of these suggestions will be of any value whatsoever if you do not believe in what you are saying. If the vision is someone else's, and you do not own it, it will be very difficult for you to enlist others in it. If you have trouble imagining yourself actually living the future described in the vision, then you will certainly not be able to convince others that they ought to enlist in making it a reality. If you are not excited about the possibilities, how can you expect others to be? Most of us can smell a phony. Most of us know when someone is just acting the part. The prerequisite to enlisting others in a shared vision is genuineness. The first place to look before making that stump speech is in your heart. Leaders know, however, that even the most enthusiastic followers cannot get extraordinary things done unless they work together. In the next chapter, we will explore how leaders foster collaboration and create unity of effort among group members.

PART FOUR

Enabling Others to Act

> The few projects in my study that disintegrated
> did so because the manager failed to build a coali-
> tion of supporters and collaborators.
> ——*Rosabeth Moss Kanter,*
> The Change Masters

Leaders know that they cannot do it alone. It takes partners to get extraordinary things done in organizations.

Leaders build teams with spirit and cohesion, teams that feel like family. They actively involve others in planning and give them discretion to make their own decisions. Leaders make others feel like owners, not hired hands.

Leaders develop collaborative goals and cooperative relationships with colleagues. They are considerate of the needs and interests of others. They know that these relationships are the keys that unlock support for their projects. They make sure that when they win, everyone wins.

Mutual respect is what sustains extraordinary group efforts. Leaders create an atmosphere of trust and human dignity. They nurture self-esteem in others. They make others feel strong and capable. In the next two chapters, we will explore how leaders:

- Foster Collaboration.
- Strengthen Others.

7

Foster Collaboration:
Getting People to Work Together

The collaborative goal—promote local physician participation—established early on enabled us to work through later disagreements, and as disagreements were resolved, trust was developed.
——*Robert L. Phillips,*
President,
Health Business
Development Associates

Early in our research efforts, we asked Bill Flanagan, vice-president of manufacturing for Amdahl Corporation, to discuss his personal best. Flanagan paused; after a few moments, he said that he couldn't tell us about his personal best. When we asked him why, Flanagan replied, "Because it wasn't me. It was us."

Like so many other leaders we spoke with, Flanagan understood that followers are what make the leader, and not simply the other way around. A one-word test for differentiating between leaders and managers that came through loud and clear in our case studies was the use of *we* versus *I.*

In the more than 500 cases that we studied, we did not encounter a single example of extraordinary achievement that was accomplished without the active effort and support of many people. Time after time, people like Bill Flanagan told us "You can't do it alone. It's a team effort." In getting extraordinary things done in organizations, *everyone* is important, not just the leader. Our empirical analysis substantiated the strong relationship between managerial effectiveness and *enabling others to act*. The more frequently people felt that their managers fostered collaboration and strengthened others, the higher their assessments of their managers' upward influence, credibility, and work-group esprit de corps and the higher their own levels of job satisfaction and commitment.

Fostering collaboration is all about getting people to work together. The process of collaboration must be nurtured, strengthened, and managed. In this chapter, we will discuss how collaboration can be fostered by developing cooperative goals, seeking integrative solutions, and building trusting relationships.

Developing Cooperative Goals

"Working together in democratic fashion on a day-to-day basis," explains Patricia Carrigan, plant manager for General Motors, "proved to be the hardest thing most of us had ever done. It gets easier as trust grows and mutual respect deepens—and as all can see the payoff." In Chapter Three, we described the ways that Carrigan searched for opportunities and experimented in her efforts to accomplish extraordinary things at the Lakewood assembly plant. But, as with so many other leaders we investigated, she didn't do it alone. In fact, Carrigan can't make that point strongly enough:

Management alone can't make it happen! The Phoenix risen from the ashes at Lakewood was not shaped by management, any more than it was shaped by the union or by an aggregate of employee work groups solving problems and trying out new ideas together. Its foundation, simply put, was an evolving, mutually supported and supportive human interaction process built on shared power, shared risk, and shared accountability, each fostering the development of trust, of commitment, of willingness to put the welfare of the plant first. "If the plant wins, we all win" was the guiding principle at Lakewood. When differences arose, the first question asked was "What's best for the plant?" It was asked by the union as it was by management. . . . It's not coincidence that top billing in [the mission] statement went to providing a quality workplace with involvement of all our people.[1]

What Carrigan did was get management and the union working together. She developed strategies for linking the goals of management and those of the employees. As the company succeeded or failed, so did the employees. It is not enough that leaders believe that their employees should view their goals as cooperative. The employees must believe that the goals will make everyone better off.

Teamwork is essential for a productive organization. Collaboration is needed to develop the commitment and skills of employees, solve problems, and respond to environmental pressures. Fostering collaboration is not just a nice idea. It is the key that leaders use to unlock the energies and talents available in their organizations.

Leadership is a relationship between leaders and the people that they aspire to lead. A failure to understand that leadership is a shared responsibility has led many managers to take a heroic view of leadership. Managers as "heroes" accept singly the responsibility for their departments and believe that they should know everything that is going on and be able to solve any problem that arises. It is this view of leadership that "actually *prevents* excellence from being attained in contemporary organizations."[2] The familiar aphorism "You are only as good as your people make you" has stood the test of time. Leaders alone do not make a company work. It was the realization, many people told us, that "I wasn't going to get very far until I stopped trying to do everything myself" that crystallized their leadership.

Creating competition within the team or between team members was never described in anyone's personal best as a way that they got something extraordinary accomplished in their organization. What was talked about was what people in the group had in common, how they understood each other's needs, and how they felt united as a team. What does it take to create cooperative, or collaborative, goals?

First of all, shared visions and values bind employees together in collaborative pursuits. Group tasks, complementary roles, and shared rewards also play a role. Tasks that require people to exchange ideas and resources reinforce the notion that participants have cooperative goals. As individuals jointly work together, seeing that they need information from each other in order to be successful, they become convinced that everyone should contribute and that by cooperating they can all accomplish the task successfully.[3] For example, creating project teams, work groups, task forces, or committees to solve various organizational problems promotes the sense of collaborative goals.

In our workshops, we put five people to work on a project that requires them to build five squares of equal size. Each person is given a different set of pieces to this puzzle. Some can put a square together with their pieces; others cannot. The only way that the *group* can build five squares is by sharing resources—by breaking up some of the squares already built (incorrectly). As participants soon learn, unless they each understand and are committed to their common goal, they have little incentive to work together.

Employees realize that their goals are cooperative when day-to-day organizational norms encourage them to share information, listen to each other's ideas, exchange resources, and respond to each other's requests through positive interdependence. One manufacturing manager told us how she frequently planted seed questions among her supervisors that required them to gather input from their peers before responding. Her goal was to create a communicating environment at all levels.

Helping and giving resources are tangible signs of cooperative goals. Passing along information about how a new technology might facilitate another's job, bagging groceries when the checkers are busy, or even cleaning up tables when the waiters and waitresses are running behind are visible examples that everyone has the same goals. Distorting and/or withholding information is a clear sign of competition. Showing respect and conveying warmth to other people develop cooperative goals.[4]

Consider, for example, how Mike Carrigan, executive vice-president of Springfield Remanufacturing Center Corporation, went about getting people involved in and committed to the company's planning process. He began by working up his own budget projections. He then asked each manager and supervisor to be personally responsible for verifying the accuracy of one of his projections. Over the next few weeks, each of these people went around the plant asking employees about their needs, researching past expenditures, testing assumptions, and double-checking with suppliers and buyers. When they all got back together, Mike told the group that thenceforth it was their findings that would be accepted as the budget figures for the coming fiscal year. "What happened here," explains Carrigan, "is that now these people were in effect running their own small businesses. They had to set their own budgets, and they had to live with them. If they wanted to complain, they had to complain to themselves."[5] Cooperative goals emerge when people feel a sense of ownership and responsibility.

Cooperation Versus Competition. Leaders understand that cooperation and competition work at cross purposes to one another. Trying to do well and trying to beat others are two different things.[6] Here's how management professor Dean Tjosvold describes the differences between people working in groups with cooperative goals and those in groups with competitive goals:

In cooperation, people realize that they are successful when others succeed and are oriented toward aiding each other to perform effectively. They encourage each other because they understand the other's priorities help them to be successful. Compatible goals promote trust. People expect help and assistance from others and are confident that they can rely on others; it is, after all, in others' self-interests to help. Expecting to get and give assistance, they accurately disclose their intentions and feelings, offer ideas and resources, and request aid. They are able to work out arrangements of exchange that leave all better off. These interactions result in friendliness, cohesion, and high morale.

Competitors, by contrast, recognize that others' successes threaten and frustrate their own aspirations. They are closer to reaching their goals when others perform ineffectively and fail to reach theirs. They suspect that others will not help them, for to do so would only harm their own chances of goal attainment. Indeed, they may be tempted to try to mislead and interfere in order to better reach their own goals. They are reluctant to discuss their needs and feelings or to ask for or offer assistance. Closed to being influenced by the other for fear of being exploited, they doubt that they can influence others, except by coercion and threat. These interactions result in frustration, hostility, and low productivity, especially in joint tasks.[7]

Cooperative goals promote people's working together to ensure each other's success. It is not necessary to rely on their being altruistic; when people understand that their goals are compatible, they naturally promote their own welfare by promoting others' interests. One study comparing two groups of interviewers in an employment agency bears out how people behave differently according to whether their goals are competitive or collaborative.[8] In one group, there was fierce competition among interviewers to fill job openings. Members of this group, who were personally ambitious and very concerned about productivity, hoarded job notifications rather than posting them publicly where everyone else could see them (as they were supposed to do). Members of the second group, by contrast, told each other about vacancies—and subsequently filled significantly more jobs.

Research demonstrates that individuals and groups perform better when there are cooperative goals. A group of researchers from the University of Minnesota reviewed 122 empirical studies conducted between 1924 and 1981 that considered how cooperative, competitive, and/or individualistic goal situations affected achievement or performance.[9] The results were remarkable: 65 studies found that cooperation promoted higher achievement than competition, while only 8 found the reverse to be true. Thirty-six showed no statistically significant difference. Cooperation was also found to promote higher achievement than working independently in 108 studies, while the reverse was true in only 6 studies. "Currently there is no type of task," asserts the research team, "on which cooperative efforts are *less* effective than are competitive or individualistic efforts, and on most tasks cooperative efforts are *more* effective in promoting achievement."[10]

Other research findings offer no less dramatic data refuting the popular contention that competition promotes performance. Studies involving such diverse groups as business executives, research scientists, airline reservation agents, fifth- and sixth-graders, and college undergraduates show remarkable consistency.[11] Whether achievement is measured in terms of salary levels, academic citations, work performance, or grade point averages, there is a negative relationship between achievement and competition.

Promoting Cooperation. Leaders realize that the key to doing well lies not in competition or in overcoming others but in gaining their cooperation. Political scientist Robert Axelrod employed a computer-based tournament to prove this premise.[12] He invited scientists from around the world to submit their strategies for winning in a simulation based upon the "prisoner's dilemma." In this situation, two parties (individuals or groups) are posed with a series of situations in which they must decide whether or not to cooperate with each other, without knowing in advance what the other party will do. Choosing a noncooperative strategy maximizes the individual payoff when the other party selects a cooperative strategy. In this case, one party's gain is at the other's expense. However, should both parties, each attempting to maximize individual payoffs, choose not to cooperate, then both lose. If both parties choose to cooperate, both win. It is the uncertainty and concomitant second-guessing about the other party's strategy that creates dilemmas for all of us in deciding whether or not to pursue competitive or cooperative strategies in our dealings with others.

"Amazingly enough," says Axelrod, "the winner was the simplest of all strategies submitted: Cooperate on the first move and then do whatever the other player did on the previous move. This strategy succeeded by eliciting cooperation from others, not by defeating them." He argues that cooperation based on reciprocity is the most effective strategy for creating and sustaining collaborative relationships between two parties. This strategy is successful because it demonstrates a willingness to be cooperative and communicates an unwillingness to be taken advantage of. Reciprocating cooperation establishes trust and promotes the notion that the two parties' goals are collaborative.

Recognize and encourage ongoing interactions among employees. The most essential strategy for eliciting cooperation, according to Axelrod, is to "enlarge the shadow of the future." People (and departments) are most likely to cooperate when they know that they will deal with each other again in the future. The expectation of future interactions encourages people to cooperate with one another in the present. The shadow of the future looms largest when interactions between people are durable and frequent. Durability promotes cooperative efforts between people, because it makes interpersonal relationships long lasting. It ensures that people will not easily forget about how they have treated, and been treated by, one another in future negotiations. Frequency promotes stability by making the consequences of today's actions more salient for tomorrow's dealings. Other researchers have shown that frequent interactions between people promote more positive feelings about each other.[13]

Leaders make it a point to provide team members with opportunities to associate and intermingle. They break down barriers between people by encouraging interactions across disciplines and between departments. When given the opportunity to move to their own building, the business school faculty at the University of California, Berkeley, declined. They felt that being mixed among faculty members from other disciplines across the university kept them from being isolated and offered greater possibilities for cross-disciplinary discussions and research projects. Holding a management meeting every morning before production starts, as done at Solectron, is another way to promote collaborative goals. Supervisors tell their colleagues about what they accomplished the previous day, what each hopes to be producing that day, current bottlenecks, and any problems looming on the horizon. Scheduling regular group meetings, having a common meeting space, bunching offices together, establishing times for consultation, and sharing resources (for example, secretaries and duplicating machines) are all mechanisms that you can consciously use to encourage interactions among employees.

Emphasize long-term payoffs. Another strategy for promoting cooperation is to emphasize long-term payoffs; that is, to make certain that the long-term benefits of mutual cooperation are greater than the short-term gain of not cooperating or taking advantage of the other party. Leaders do this by aligning their teams with a vision or long-term goal. City mayors such as Tom McEnery (San Jose, California) and Henry Cisneros (San Antonio, Texas) understand that changing the shape of their communities entails pulling together disparate local leaders—from labor and trade councils to political activists to business, education, and health care officials—to envision a future community that serves the best interests of everyone involved. Short-term trade-offs are negotiated and accepted in view of the long-term payoffs. Increasing numbers of hospitals are helping to finance adjacent medical office complexes to create closer partnerships between themselves and the physicians that they serve. The long-term payoff is better (more efficient) health care.

Emphasizing the long term is another strategy for helping

people deal with any short-term setbacks that they might experience. Leaders reframe such incidents as learning experiences that will help the team to meet more difficult challenges in the future. That there are shortfalls and disappointments along the way may also be seen as testing the commitment and strengthening the resolve of team members in their quest. Leaders also arrange for the rewards of cooperative efforts to be end loaded, so that they are gained and distributed when the project is completed. One variation of this strategy has been adopted at Herman Miller, Inc., the world's second-largest office furniture manufacturer. This company instituted a "silver parachute" plan, the first of its kind in the nation.[14] In the event of a hostile takeover, the parachute would be triggered, protecting all employees' jobs, salaries, and working conditions.

Set an example of cooperation and reciprocity. The winning strategy for fostering collaboration is to cooperate first, and then practice reciprocity. This means setting the example for the behavior that you desire in others. It requires you to demonstrate your commitment and trustworthiness before asking for the same from someone else. When people fail to be truthful and don't fulfull their promises, it is virtually impossible to effectively rebuild their relationships with others; there is always a nagging feeling of doubt about their credibility. Studies show that when managers who are not trusted by their subordinates try to be open and honest, their messages are perceived by their employees as fabrications.[15] Leaders must demonstrate their willingness to trust the members of their teams *first,* before the team members can wholeheartedly put their fate into the leaders' hands. We will talk more about the nature of trust later in this chapter.

One of the impressive aspects of practicing reciprocity is that reciprocity engenders a sense of obligation that is pervasive in human culture.[16] Want somebody to do something for you? Do something for them. Reciprocity leads to predictability in relationships. Relationships and negotiations often break down when people involved can't predict or figure out what others are trying to accomplish. If you are unclear about the other person's objective, you can't determine what impact your own strategy or request will have. This unpredictability, whether between individuals or between nations, is what fosters instability and competitiveness.

Reciprocity, according to Axelrod, also minimizes the losses that one party may experience. Making it clear that you will reciprocate the other person's treatment of you limits the extent to which that person can risk taking advantage of you. As a long-term strategy, reciprocity minimizes the risk of escalation, because the other party is clear about how you will respond if taken advantage of. After all, why should someone start trouble, knowing that you will respond in kind? In fact, the other party can easily see that the best way to deal with you is to cooperate, so that he or she will be the recipient of cooperation on your part.

Even during times of armed conflict, the phenomenon of reciprocity is pervasive. British and German infantry troops during World War I, for example, realized that the enemy would be likely to reciprocate cooperation in pursuit of fresh rations. As one soldier wrote in his diary: "It would be child's play to shell the road behind the enemy's trenches, crowded as it must be with ration wagons and water carts, into a bloodstained wilderness . . . but on the whole there is silence. After all, if you prevent your enemy from drawing his rations, his remedy is simple: he will prevent you from drawing yours."[17]

Seeking Integrative Solutions

Leaders who foster collaboration search for integrative solutions. In finding integrative solutions, you need to change people's thinking from an either/or (or zero-sum) mentality to a positive perspective on working together. Get people to be clear about their needs and interests, so that second-guessing and negotiation games are minimized. Make it clear that being willing to reciprocate will encourage both parties to recognize that the greatest gain will come from cooperating with one other.

The 1978 Camp David talks were an example of integrative thinking. When Egypt and Israel sat down to negotiate at Camp David, Maryland, in October of that year, it appeared that they had an intractable conflict before them. Egypt demanded the immediate return of the entire Sinai Peninsula; Israel, which had occupied the Sinai since the 1967 Middle East war, refused to return an inch of this land. Proposals for an agreement, including a compromise in which each nation would retain half of the Sinai, proved completely unacceptable to both sides. As long as the dispute was defined in terms of what percentage of the land each side would control—either/or thinking—no agreement could be reached. The stalemate was broken when an integrative solution was proposed: since what Israel was really concerned about was the security that the land offered as a buffer zone, and Egypt was primarily concerned with sovereignty over the land (and regaining prestige), they agreed that Israel would return the Sinai to Egypt in exchange for assurances of a demilitarized zone and Israeli air bases in the Sinai.

With integrative thinking, leaders frame differences and problems so that participants focus on "what is to be gained" rather than "what is to be lost." To hear Bob Phillips, president of Health Business Development Associates, tell it, there is no other way to create new ventures: "When I try to set up joint ventures, for example, a medical imaging center involving the hospital, physicians, and private investors, the only way to make it work is to demonstrate to each party what they have to gain. And how what they have to gain can *only* happen if they work together." Phillips's strategy is backed up by researchers who have shown that people respond differently to problems framed in terms of losses from the way they do to problems framed as gains.[18] These researchers found that people were more willing to make concessions when negotiators focused on the profits to be achieved than when negotiations were framed in terms of possible costs. What is most interesting about these studies is that the objective situations did not vary; the only difference was the perspective that people brought to them.

The framing effect, according to management professor Max Bazerman, "suggests that a [negotiator] should try to present information in a way that leads the opposition to see what they have to gain from a risk-free settlement." He goes on to suggest that when leaders are trying to get others to compromise, they should "strive to frame suggestions in ways that show what both sides will gain from a settlement."[19]

Rosabeth Moss Kanter has proposed five strategies, or "helpful hints," as she calls them, for leaders to utilize in promoting integrative solutions:[20]

1. *Seek many inputs.* By their very nature, integrative solutions
    begin with diverse opinions. Active listening is the source of
    considerable inspiration, as you find out about other people's
    new and creative ideas that you hadn't originally imagined
    yourself. Another advantage of seeking many inputs is that it
    makes certain that people feel consulted about decisions that
    affect them. Being consulted is no guarantee that the decision
    will be accepted, but not being consulted is almost certain to
    result in high levels of resistance. Through seeking many
    inputs, leaders also help to get people's "cards out on the
    table," where it is possible to provide a more open forum for
    competing viewpoints to be aired and kicked around. Know-
    ing how other people feel about issues enables the leader to
    incorporate aspects of different people's viewpoints into a
    project and demonstrate to others how their ideas have been
    heard and included.
2. *Meet one-on-one.* Meeting one-on-one with people lets them
    know that you personally value and care about their input. It
    also frees them from speaking to an audience and forces them
    to direct their remarks to the issues at hand. When opposition
    or criticism is expected, face-to-face communications will
    improve the likelihood of developing commonality and under-
    standing between competing perspectives. Surprise at anoth-
    er's arguments or concerns also decreases when you consult
    on a one-on-one basis. Empirical studies point out, as well,
    that as the complexity of the issues increases, greater face-to-
    face communications are required to integrate differences.[21]
3. *Keep your management posted.* The fact of the matter is that
    every boss has a boss. Only if people in upper management
    understand what you are up to can they support your actions
    to their own superiors, to whom they are responsible for the
    performance of their subordinates. Management scholar Peter
    Drucker observes that few people realize how important it is to
    protect upper management against surprises. Organizational
    surprises (even pleasant ones) generally lead to some kind of
    humiliation in the sense that the boss should know what's
    going on in the organization. Keeping your management
    posted increases their own security sufficiently so that they can
    provide any needed hierarchical blessings for your efforts. Inno-

vative middle-level managers in Kanter's studies were those who made certain that the people above them in the organization were provided with the materials and coaching necessary to effectively support the project and sell it to those higher up in the company and/or to outside constituencies.

4. *Seek specific rather than broad support.* It is easier to enlist people's support and backing for a concrete idea than for a general endorsement of anything you might want to do, points out Kanter. This reduces the level of risk taking for others in supporting your specific proposal. While broad-based support seems enticing, it is actually easier to revoke than specific support. Its very broadness creates ambiguity and provides ready excuses for torpedoing a range of specific proposals. Managers often become seduced by broad-based support, which sends them charging up the mountain only to find that the boss really had a different mountain in mind. Leaders have a knack for testing their ideas and refining vague notions before they approach high-level people for support.

5. *Generate alternative currencies.* Forging integrative solutions and making sure that people really support the project require that leaders be able to satisfy the concerns and needs of various constituents. Identifying what others want or need becomes crucial. Leaders generate alternative currencies in much the same way as insurance agents offer policies to their clients. In a discussion of insurance, the costs can be expressed on an annual, semiannual, quarterly, or monthly basis, and different amounts of interest can be applied according to the payment schedule. Dividends can be used to reduce payments, increase benefits, or generate income. Each of these various permutations of schedule, interest costs, and dividend benefits creates a currency that can be matched to each prospective insurance client's needs. Creative horse trading also takes place when leaders are able to obtain something from one part of the organization that can be given to another part in exchange for their participation. Visibility and recognition of their efforts are among the most powerful currencies available to leaders. Sharing credit for the project's success with those responsible for that success not only is common sense but pays dividends on future adventures.

Building Trusting Relationships

"It was the cooperation and support of other people," says Don Peerson, "that contributed the most toward the project's success." Peerson, director of residential programs for Pacific Gas & Electric Company (PG&E), was responsible for developing procedures and implementing the utility's Zero Interest Program. This multibillion dollar program provided financing for customers' energy conservation projects (for example, insulation), thereby enabling them to reduce their energy bills. As Peerson worked his way through the California Public Utilities Commission, the commercial banking community, the insulation contractors' association, and more than eight internal functional departments and thirteen divisions at PG&E, he came to believe that developing support, involving others, and delegating were so central to the project's success that he advised: "If you don't trust someone, get them off the project team."

Bill Sheehan, vice-president of personnel for Dana Corporation, told us about how his company turned itself around by getting employees to work together. The key element in this process: "We have no corporate procedures at Dana. We burned the 21 inches thick of policy manuals. We eliminated reports and signoffs. We installed trust."[22]

Trust, as people such as Peerson and Sheehan can attest to, is the central issue in human relationships both within and outside the organization.[23] Trust is an essential element of organizational effectiveness as well.[24] You demonstrate your trust in others through your actions—how much you check and control their work, how much you delegate and allow people to participate. Individuals who are unable to trust other people often fail to become leaders. They can't bear to be dependent on the words and work of others and consequently end up doing all the work themselves. Conversely, people who trust others too much may also fail, because they can lose touch and a sense of connectedness to their team. Delegation becomes abdication.

What does it mean to trust someone else? Trust exists when we make ourselves vulnerable to others whose subsequent behavior we cannot control.[25] By trusting another person, we become dependent upon that person. This feeling was captured by Bill

McGowan, founder of MCI: "If you're going to be in a business of any size, you're going to have to develop the kind of leadership qualities that allow you to attract good people, guide them, encourage them, and ultimately trust them—and let them go and do their jobs. Oh, sure, you have to take deep breaths occasionally. But mostly you have to trust them."[26]

What happens when people do not trust each other? They will ignore, disguise, and distort facts, ideas, conclusions, and feelings that they believe will increase their vulnerability to others. Not surprisingly, the likelihood of misunderstanding and misinterpretation will increase. When you don't trust someone, you resist letting them influence you. You are suspicious and unreceptive to their proposals and goals, suggestions for reaching those goals, and their definition of criteria and methods for evaluating progress. When we encounter low-trust behavior from others, we in turn are generally hesitant to reveal information to them and reject their attempts to influence us. This feedback only reinforces the originator's low trust. Unless there are changes in behavior, the relationship stabilizes at a low level of trust. All of the behavior that follows from a lack of trust is deleterious to information exchange and to reciprocity of influence. It increases the probability that underlying problems may go undetected or be avoided, that inappropriate solutions will be difficult to identify, and that joint problem-solving efforts will deteriorate.

The Import of Trust on Behavior. What are your reactions to people you trust? To people you don't trust? Several major research efforts have identified the impact that various levels of interpersonal trust have on work-group effectiveness.[27] For example, groups of business executives were given identical factual information about a difficult manufacturing-marketing policy decision. Half of the groups were briefed to expect trusting behavior and the other half to expect untrusting behavior. For example, in the trusting condition: "You have learned from your past experiences that you can trust the other members of top management and can openly express feelings and differences with them."

After thirty minutes of discussion, each team member completed a brief questionnaire. Other executives, who had been observing the team meetings, also completed the questionnaire. The responses of team members and the observers were quite consistent. The group members who had been told that their peers and manager could be trusted reported their discussion and decisions to be significantly better than did the members of the low-trust group on *every* factor measured. The high-trust group members were more open about feelings, experienced greater clarity about the group's basic problems and goals, and searched more for alternative courses of action. They also reported greater levels of mutual influence on outcomes, satisfaction with the meeting, motivation to implement decisions, and closeness as a management team as a result of the meeting. People were also asked to respond to the following question: "As a result of this meeting, would you give little or much serious consideration to a position with another company?" More than two-thirds of the participants in the low-trust group responded that they would give serious consideration to looking for another position. People don't hang around very long in organizations where there are low levels of trust. Would you?

Participants were later told that there were differences between the outcomes and feelings reported by the various groups in the experiment. They were asked to think about what factors might have accounted for the differences. While numerous explanations were offered, not one person perceived that trust had been the overriding variable. One executive in the study reported this insight: "I never knew that a lack of trust was our problem (back at the work site) until that exercise. I knew that things weren't going well, but I never really could quite understand why we couldn't work well together. After that experience, things fell into place."[28] Trust is at the heart of fostering collaboration.

Leaders who build trusting relationships within their team feel comfortable with the group. They are willing to consider alternative viewpoints and to utilize other people's expertise and abilities. They are also willing to let others exercise influence over their decisions. Without trust, managers often take a self-protective posture. They are directive and hold tight reins over their subordinates. Likewise, subordinates of untrusting managers are likely to both withhold and distort information.[29]

Impressions of trust make a difference. In experiments where participants were told that their manager had a low level of trust, attempts by the manager to be truly open and honest were ignored and distorted by subordinates. The mental set was so strong that the manager's candor was viewed by subordinates as a clever attempt to deceive them. They were not to be fooled and generally reacted by sabotaging the manager's efforts even further. Managers who experienced rejection of their attempts to be trusting and open responded in kind. Said one manager: "If I had my way I would have fired the entire group. What a bunch of turkeys. I was trying to be honest with them but they wouldn't cooperate. Everything I suggested they shot down; and they wouldn't give me any ideas on how to solve the problem."[30]

Organizational trust and participation in decision making are also related. Trust has been shown to be the most significant predictor of individuals' satisfaction with their organization.[31] Regardless of a person's level of participation in decision making and regardless of the fit between the levels of desired and actual participation, people who experience the most trust in organizational leaders are most satisfied with their level of participation.

Trust and Trustworthiness. The evidence about trust contradicts many popular myths. For example, if you trust others, does that make you stupid or especially gullible? Clinical psychologist Julian Rotter is one of the foremost researchers of the trust phenomenon. He's been unable, for instance, to find any relationship between individuals' trust levels and their scores on scholastic aptitude tests and concludes: "High trusters are no less intelligent than anyone else."[32]

Moreover, Rotter found no evidence in any of his studies that high trusters behave in a more gullible manner than low trusters. What studies have shown is that when there are no clear-cut data available, high trusters are more willing than low trusters to give people the benefit of a doubt. This is the equivalent of "innocent until proven guilty." The high truster says, "I will trust this person until I have clear evidence that he or she cannot be trusted." The low truster says, "I will not trust this person until there is clear evidence that he or she can be trusted." Rotter observes, "It may be true that high trusters are fooled more often by crooks, but low trusters are probably fooled just as often by distrusting honest people; they thereby forfeit the benefits that trusting others might bring."[33]

High trusters are capable of recognizing the collaborative and competitive nature of their peers and acting accordingly. Low-trusting people tend to view the world around them as filled with competitors and therefore perceive others' interests as opposed to their own.[34] This makes them unwilling and unable to build a strong team. The cost of low trust? Kanter's landmark study of innovation by middle-level managers concluded that projects failed because their managers did not build strong coalitions of supporters and collaborators.[35]

Finally, psychologists have found that, compared to those who view the world with suspicion and disrespect, trusting people are more likely to be happy and psychologically adjusted. We like trusting people and seek them out as friends. We listen to people we trust and accept their influence. For instance, in one management simulation, when the chief executive officer was a friend of the financial vice-president, he or she accepted the latter's influence far more than when their relationship was merely professional—even though in all cases the "information" presented by the financial vice-president would solve the company's problem. It is for this reason that the most effective managerial situations are those where each member of the team trusts each other.[36]

One of the clearest advantages of trusting others comes from the way people respond to trusting individuals. Trusting people are regarded by others as trust*worthy*.[37] Managers who fail to demonstrate that they trust their subordinates are perceived by those subordinates as less deserving of trust. Our perception of how trustworthy others are also affects our relationships with others. For example, if you believe that an individual cannot be trusted, you feel little moral pressure to be truthful. In fact, lying, cheating, and similar behaviors are often justified in these circumstances, with comments such as "everybody else is doing it" or "I didn't want to be taken advantage of."

The leader's behavior is more critical than that of any other person in determining the level of trust that develops in a group. A classic study conducted for the Life Insurance Agency Management Association revealed that the major difference between low- and high-performing groups of insurance sales people was the degree to which they reported that they trusted their immediate supervisors.[38] In our studies, we found statistically significant correlations between people's trust in their leader and their subsequent satisfaction with and evaluations of that person's overall leadership effectiveness.

Building Trust. While substantial levels of trust may not always be required in routine work situations, trust is almost always needed when leaders are accomplishing extraordinary things in organizations. Trust makes work easier, because it forms the basis for greater *openness* between both individuals and departments. Trust in a relationship generally develops gradually over time through the course of personal interactions. Taking some kind of risk in relation to the other person and feeling that you weren't injured (emotionally or physically) in the process is what moves trust to new levels. We see this happen in our workshops with participants in the Ropes Course—those challenging activities led by Randi DuBois and Reno Taini that we described earlier. It takes trust to fall backwards off a four-foot ladder into the hands of people you just met, but after you have completed this activity with the knowledge that someone will be there to catch you if you fall, it is easier to leap off a thirty-foot platform.

To deepen a relationship requires taking initiative in trusting another person despite uncertainty about the consequences. If neither person in a relationship takes the risk of trusting, at least a little, the relationship remains stalled at a low level of caution and suspicion. In his book *On Becoming A Person,* psychologist Carl Rogers observes that trusting another's competence, judgment, helpfulness, or concern results in a greater willingness to be open with that person. Feeling trusted also makes it easier to be open.[39]

The foundation of a trusting relationship is believing that the other person has integrity. This is demonstrated by meeting commitments and keeping promises. Going first is another way that trust is fostered. Going first is a statement of commitment— after all, you have chosen to take this action, it is public and visible, and consequently it is not easy to back out of. It's somewhat like this: "Everybody wants to go to heaven, but nobody wants to die first." When situations are risky, leaders must venture out in front of their subordinates. Going first is akin to what psychologists refer to as "self-disclosure." Letting others know what you stand for, what you value, what you want, what you hope for, what you're willing (and not willing) to do is risky. You can't be certain that other people will want to enroll, will appreciate your candor, will agree with your aspirations, will buy into your plans, or will interpret your words and actions in the way you intend. But by demonstrating their willingness to take such risks, leaders encourage others to reciprocate. Until the leader takes the risk of being open, it is difficult to get others to take a similar risk—and thereby take the first steps necessary to build interpersonal trust.

Another important ingredient for building trust is sensitivity to people's needs and interests. Listening to what other people have to say and trying to appreciate and understand their particular viewpoints demonstrate respect for them and their ideas. Still another way to build trust is by being open about your own actions and intentions. You don't find it easy to trust someone who is secretive or who "plays the cards close to the vest." Scrupulously avoiding "secret" meetings and closed-door sessions is essential, because such secrecy fuels images of organizational politics and chicanery. Keeping others informed not only prevents surprises but reduces the threat to them that the unknown often entails.

Commitment Number 5: Foster Collaboration by Promoting Cooperative Goals and Building Trust

Fostering collaboration begins with creating and sustaining cooperative goals. The best incentive for someone to help you is knowing that you will reciprocate this action and help them in return. Cooperation breeds teamwork as solutions are sought that integrate people's needs. Focusing on what is to be gained enables you to reach agreements with others over what might otherwise be divisive issues. Finally, when leaders bring people together to work on projects, they are concerned not only about the task or problem itself but also about how the group members will relate to each other in order to work effectively on the problem. Without trust, relationships interfere with and distort perceptions of the problem and divert energy and creativity from finding comprehensive, realistic solutions. Leaders help to create this trusting climate by the example they set. Trusting others is the reciprocal of being trustworthy.

With collaborative goals, integrative thinking, and trusting relationships, people are ready to work with one another to make extraordinary things happen. By strengthening others and giving power away, the leader turns this readiness into action. How this happens and what actions leaders take in the process are discussed in the next chapter. Here are some things that you can do to foster collaboration and trust:

1. *Always say* we. When thinking about and talking about what you plan to accomplish and have accomplished, it is essential that you think and talk in terms of *our* goals. Your task as a leader is to help other people to reach mutual goals, not your goals. You never accomplish anything alone, so your attitude can never be "here's what I did" but rather "here's what we did." This language reinforces the belief that goals are truly collaborative, not exploitative.

Conduct an audit of your language sometime. Take a piece of paper and divide it into two columns. Write *we* at the top of one column and *I* at the top of the other. Ask someone to observe one of your speeches or meetings, and have them count the number of times you say *I* and the number of times you say *we*. On balance, there ought to be more first person plural references than first person singular. You can use this same technique when interviewing candidates for positions in which leadership is required. Do an audit of their uses of *we* versus *I*. If you find that they use *I* more than *we*, they will probably make poor leaders, and the organization will suffer from their claiming credit for themselves.

Irwin Federman, president of Monolithic Memories, was asked in an interview how he turned his company around. He was very quick to reply: "I didn't turn the company around. I presided over it. The people in this company turned it around. I was the captain of the ship, but they were doing all the rowing."[40] Federman's attitude is typical of leaders.

When you use *we* you also share the credit. It doesn't cost you a thing to acknowledge another person's contribution. A simple thank-you from the boss is generally regarded as the most important nonfinancial compensation to employees. Sharing credit is also another opportunity to remind the team that it is *our* goal and that we are in this effort together. Bob Phillips used every small success achieved to remind the joint-venture participants that they were making progress. And with each agreement, he found group members becoming more trusting and willing to explore new possibilities. Tom Melohn uses a wonderful process to reinforce the collaborative nature of NATD's work. At one of the monthly all-employee meetings, Melohn will occasionally give employees the envelopes containing the paychecks of other employees. He will say: "Frank, do you realize that Larry earned part of your paycheck? Eleanor, do you realize that Larry earned part of your paycheck?" Then he asks each employee to find the person whose name is on the envelope and give him or her the paycheck. This ceremony reinforces the idea that all members of the NATD family are working toward shared goals.

2. *Create interactions.* Just as you can't do it alone, neither can other individuals on the project. To make certain that people are not working in isolation from one another, you need to create both physical and psychological opportunities for interaction. These might include remaining in tight cramped offices, where people can't help but see each other every day. Open office landscaping with low partitions is another way to make access to others easy. Or you might limit the size of any one department or plant to a recognizable number of people. More than one leader we interviewed said the size of a single site was limited to the number of people whose names he or she could remember.

You ought to create a way for all people who must collaborate to meet at least once a month; more frequently, if possible. Periodic celebrations, office parties, Friday afternoon mixers, and exotic food-of-the-month luncheons are all healthy techniques for bringing people together. Some managers may see these as corny and a waste of time, but we can't all be in this together unless we are face to face with each other on both a personal and professional basis. Structured, regular meetings are not only occasions for people to socialize, they are also valuable opportunities to exchange information and solve problems informally. Quality circles and other problem-solving groups that you may have formed serve the function of forcing people who must work together to get their issues out in the open and work them out.

Hundreds of executives have told us that one of the main reasons they attend the executive seminars we conduct at our university is to interact with the other executives in the room. Some participants are customers, some are old colleagues, and some are potential collaborators. We know firsthand that one of the purposes our seminars serve is to make connections. The same is even more true inside organizations.

There are even unintended positive consequences of the interactions forced upon us by physical space. Barney Rosenzweig, executive producer of the Emmy Award–winning television program "Cagney and Lacey," tells the humorous story of how the restroom is located at the opposite end of the building from his office. Each time he has to make a trip to the facility he has to pass by everyone's office or station, and predictably each person stops him to discuss some issue or other. Rosenzweig says he prays there will never be a personal emergency. Rosenzweig also has a popcorn machine outside his office door. That popcorn machine is an important gathering place for members of the cast and crew, as well as for the union truck drivers. Many an important problem has been solved at that popcorn dispenser. Why not put a popcorn machine outside your office? And, by the way, if you are ever offered an office with a private washroom, turn it down.

3. *Create a climate of trust.* One of the most fundamental bases for being perceived as trustworthy is predictability. *Predictability* refers to the degree of confidence that people have in their expectations about another person's behavior or intentions.[41] When people have little confidence about how you will behave in certain circumstances, they may have hope but not trust. So, do what you say you are going to do. That may be as simple as getting to a meeting on time. It may be as difficult as not firing anyone during a downturn if you have declared you have a no-layoff policy. Doing what you say you are going to do also enhances the sense of reciprocity needed to encourage others to increase their vulnerability with you. Being trustworthy yourself promotes trusting behavior from other people.

Delegation is fundamentally a system of trust. You signal your trust in someone when you truly delegate authority to that person. Every leader ought to have an established system of delegation. If you do not, we suggest you establish one right now.

Trust also develops when people feel safe and secure. When your thoughts and ideas are shot down or ridiculed, it doesn't take long to realize that the climate is neither safe nor conducive to making yourself vulnerable (the precursor to opening ourselves up and placing our trust in another person). Defensive communication strategies are an indication that we do not feel secure in some way, at some level. You can reduce defensive climates by providing descriptive rather than evaluative comments, avoiding game playing (such as mechanically patting people on the back) in favor of spontaneity, expressing genuine feelings of caring and involvement, and being willing to actively seek out, listen to, understand, and utilize other people's perspectives in the projects and adventures you share.

We know a leader who passionately espouses the value of creating a climate of honesty and trust. Evidence of his commitment to this value came when we observed him actually rewarding an employee for saying that an income-producing and money-saving innovation was discovered "by accident." The employee could have made up some wild story about how it was all a planned experiment, but instead chose to simply admit, without hesitation, that it was an accident. The employee got public recognition and a monetary reward. Do you have ways of rewarding trustworthiness?

There is one other thing you can do to create a climate of trust: be open about your own mistakes and vulnerabilities. Leaders have a reluctance to admit mistakes for fear they will lose their power to influence. It is seen as a sign of weakness. But, experience shows that letting others know you are human is one of the best ways to enhance your credibility. People tend to distrust those who claim to be infallible. We do not suggest you reveal your every fault to your constituents, but we do strongly recommend that you admit your mistakes and let others know you are approachable.

4. *Focus on gains, not losses.* Focus on opportunities, not problems, and create winners, not losers. Collaboration is fostered when you can integrate potentially disparate perspectives by reframing differences into commonalities. Even the fact that two parties disagree about an issue can be seen as indicating agreement about the complexity of the topic. Compromise and creative

solutions are more likely to emerge when people can be persuaded to focus on what they win, rather than what they had to give up. Realistically, often the only thing that makes the sacrifices possible in the short run is the likelihood of benefits in the long run.

A variety of gainsharing and employee stock ownership programs are getting serious attention these days. In some cases, employees have even purchased companies from their owners when there was the possibility that the organization might go out of business. There is nothing like making owners of the employees to focus attention on the long-term success of an organization.

But formal programs are not the only answer. People can be made to feel like partners in the business in a number of less-structured ways. For example, people who know how their objectives fit with the organization's objectives are more likely to collaborate. Front-line workers deserve to know the organization's strategy and objectives as much as senior managers. The usual excuse for not telling all employees the corporate strategy is that the competitors might find out. Well, that is just what it is: an excuse. Besides, it is also a signal to employees that you do not trust them. If you really trusted them you would inform them of what is going on in the organization.

In outside negotiations with customers and vendors and inside negotiations with colleagues, you can also increase the number of win-win solutions by showing how your goals and others' goals are aligned. It is one of the most effective techniques for creating a sense of mutuality. Michael Doyle, cofounder of Interaction Associates, a consulting firm specializing in collaborative problem solving, uses a simple, but extremely powerful, technique to keep people focused on gains, not losses. He often begins a problem-solving session by asking the involved parties to state their areas of agreement, rather than differences. He also stops periodically and asks the parties to list the things upon which they have agreed. By doing this, Doyle is getting people to see how many agreements they have reached rather than how many disagreements they have left to resolve.

Other techniques have been developed by Roger Fisher and William Ury of the Harvard Negotiation Project.[42] Their method of "getting to yes" can be boiled down to four basic points: (1) separate the people from the problem; (2) focus on interests, not positions; (3) invent options for mutual gain; and (4) insist on objective criteria. By adhering to these principles you can negotiate differences without people feeling like they have been taken advantage of, compromised, or defeated.

Another simple technique for keeping interactions focused on gains and not losses is to delete the word *but* from your vocabulary. *But* stimulates disagreement at best and more likely the beginning of an argument. *But* stimulates an either/or mentality and is antithetical to integrative and possibility thinking. Eliminating *but* from your vocabulary will free you from focusing on constraints and force you to consider the alternatives about how to make things happen. You may find it difficult to eliminate *but* from your vocabulary, but (well, we said it might be difficult) see what happens.

5. *Involve people in planning and problem solving.* Remember how Patricia Carrigan, the General Motors plant manager, created 133 voluntary planning and problem-solving groups involving 90 percent of the unionized work force? Carrigan attributes that "partnership with people" as the key to the extraordinary achievements of the Lakewood plant. Follow Carrigan's lead and create several groups like this yourself. It ought to be the norm in business to have 90 percent of the work force involved in planning and problem solving.

Involvement takes many forms. Edward E. Lawler III has categorized participative programs into seven areas: quality circles, employee survey feedback, job enrichment, work teams, union-management quality-of-work-life programs, gainsharing, and new-design plants.[43]

Take a good look at how you are now solving your problems or doing your planning, especially those that involve the front lines. Who is currently involved in planning and problem solving? Are you trying to do it yourself? Have you delegated it to one of the managers who reports to you? Is that person trying to do it by him- or herself? Have you delegated to staff professionals, the people with the MBAs and technical degrees? How many of the people who actually deliver the service or make the product are involved in solving the problems or planning innovative new ways to do things in your organization? Have you involved customers, vendors, and other internal organizations on whom you are dependent or who are dependent on you? Your answers ought to indicate that you have involved the people closest to the work in planning or solving problems associated with it.

Involvement in planning and problem solving does work, and it is one of the most effective ways of fostering collaboration. However, there are conditions under which it works best. To foster collaboration through involvement in planning and problem solving make sure you:

- Select people with a working knowledge of the situation.
- Clearly articulate the outcomes and standards to be met.
- Provide the resources and the authority to do the job. This means make available the necessary information, connections, training tools, money, and decision-making power.
- Set up a timetable for the planning and problem solving.
- Enable information to flow upward as well as downward.
- Periodically review progress with the groups.
- Tie rewards to performance and make sure the rewards are valued by the groups doing the work.[44]

If you are not involving people in planning, problem solving, and execution of their jobs, you are underutilizing the skills and resources in your organization. You will get more productivity through involvement. However, if you are not personally experienced in high-involvement management, we suggest you get some training yourself and also that you start on a small scale. It is too difficult a leadership task to start out by involving all or most of the work force. Begin with a pilot project, learn from that experience and then broaden your efforts.

6. *Be a risk taker when it comes to trusting others.* There is no sure way to get others to trust you. We do know, however, that it begins with you. Demonstrating your trust in other people encourages them to trust you. Distrusting them will always cause them to hesitate to place their trust in you. Also, you cannot force another person to trust you. If someone is bent on misunderstanding you and refuses to perceive you as either well intentioned or competent, there may be little you can do to change

that perception. Or you may find yourself in a situation where the previous manager created a climate of fear and distrust. It would be quite natural for those people to be reluctant to trust you as a new manager. Ultimately, all you can do is demonstrate your trust in others and have faith that they will respond in kind.

We remember a conversation with a worker who had been laid off after twenty-five years with the same company. It was quite a shock, needless to say. He moved his family to another state on the promise by a new employer of significant benefits. That employer never followed through. The worker then took a job with a company whose chief executive had a reputation for being honest and trustworthy. Having been burned twice in just a couple of years, the worker was understandably reluctant to trust anyone. Then he said to us: "But my new boss did everything he said he was going to do, and more." There is no better way to earn the trust of others than by keeping your word. We become believable to others only after they have seen us do what we say we are going to do. So, when you make promises to others, be sure you can keep them.

There are other ways to show your trust in others. One is openness and self-disclosure. When you let others know things about you and when you make yourself vulnerable by telling them about your own uncertainties and doubts, they are more likely to be open with you. This mutual openness is fundamental to trust. You can also create a trusting relationship by showing people that you depend on them as much as they may depend on you, that your success depends upon them. While displays of openness and dependency may give the appearance of weakness, they are actually some of the most powerful forces in the creation of trusting relationships.

In the final analysis only you can decide whether to take the risk of trusting others and whether the risks are worth taking. In a sense, this implies that to have others trust you, you must actively take some initiative and not simply wait for others to make the first move. The opening gambit always involves risk.[45] Leaders always find the risk worth taking. Sowing seeds of trust with people creates the fields of collaboration necessary to get extraordinary things done in organizations.

8

Strengthen Others:
Sharing Power and Information

If you want one year of prosperity, grow grain.
If you want ten years of prosperity, grow trees.
If you want one hundred years of prosperity,
grow people.

——*Chinese Proverb*

"Everyone had to feel that they could make a contribution, otherwise they wouldn't come," is how Janice Halper, corporate psychologist and seminar chairperson for the Professional Women's Network in San Francisco, started out describing how she empowered the people responsible for the Network's gala "Women of Wisdom" celebration. Halper found ways to strengthen the people involved, who, like herself, were all volunteers. She had lots of meetings—they met every other week over a nine-month period. She listened a lot: "I'd ask questions, then let others talk, record their ideas, and then play them back." She facilitated interaction by creating small two-to-three-person project teams within the larger committee and then shifted members so that everyone had the chance to work with each other on an individual basis. She made others visible by having them make the committee's report to the Network's board of directors. Most rewarding for Halper was "seeing everyone take responsibility and not having to ask for it."

Empowering the citizenry to take responsibility for governing has long been the conceptual framework upon which Sunne McPeak has created political coalitions and alliances. Now in her third term on the Contra Costa County (California) Board of Supervisors, McPeak takes great pride in the large number of people and groups she's worked with on various issues who are continuing their activities in local government affairs. Having served as co-chair of the statewide Coalition to Stop the Peripheral Canal—the first successful referendum in California over the past three decades—and chair of the California Council on Partnerships (between government and business), McPeak explains that the key factor in developing and sustaining teams involving people with diverse interests (such as growers and environmentalists on the canal issue or public- and private-sector decision makers on community renewal efforts) is in providing people with the power necessary to make a difference. This entails making certain that people have the skills and knowledge needed to make good judgments, keeping people informed, developing personal relationships among the players, involving people in important decisions, and acknowledging and giving credit for people's contributions.

In our studies we found that leaders, like Halper and McPeak, made people feel strong and in so doing enabled them to take responsibility for their team's success. If people don't know what the team's score is, don't know how to tell the score, or don't know what they can do to get on the scoreboard, then they not only can't determine whether they are winning or losing the game but are unable to figure out what needs to be done to keep their team moving ahead. Leaders don't just give lip service to the common business refrain "people are our most important resource." They really believe in their human resources and utilize them to the fullest extent possible; in the process they "grow people" and use their own power to transform their followers into leaders.

Power Is an Expandable Pie

Traditional management thinking promotes the idea that power is a fixed sum: if I have more, then you have less. Naturally, people who hold this view are reluctant to share power. They hold tightly onto what little power they may perceive themselves to have. But this view is archaic, and it seriously retards getting extraordinary things done. Moreover, Rosabeth Moss Kanter has observed that "powerlessness corrupts, and absolute powerlessness corrupts absolutely."[1] People who feel powerless, be they managers or subordinates, tend to hoard whatever shreds of power they have. Powerless managers also tend to adopt petty and dictatorial management styles. Powerlessness creates organizational systems where political skills become essential and "covering" yourself and "passing the buck" become the preferred styles for handling interdepartmental differences.

When subordinates have very little power, managers are in a position to make these people do what they want. Under these circumstances, managers can attribute people's behavior, no matter how good it is, to their orders rather than to people's abilities and motivations. This phenomenon was cleverly documented in one experiment involving small work groups. Employees in some work groups were allowed to influence decisions about their work (were made powerful), while those in other work groups were not (were made powerless). The study revealed that the managers of the powerless groups routinely complained that their employees were not motivated to work hard. These managers saw their workers as unsuitable for promotion and downplayed their skills and talents; they evaluated the work output of their employees less favorably than did the managers of powerful work groups, although the actual output of both groups was roughly equivalent.[2]

The most extensive and systematic program of research on organizational power and influence is that of Arnold Tannenbaum and his colleagues at the University of Michigan's Institute for Social Research. Their research has been carried out in a variety of public and private organizations in the United States and abroad and has included hospitals, banks, unions, factories, and insurance companies. They have learned one vital lesson that all leaders should take to heart: the more people believe that they can influence and control the organization, the greater organizational effectiveness and member satisfaction will be.[3] In other words, shared power results in higher job satisfaction and performance throughout the organization.

We used Tannenbaum's methodology to investigate why some branch offices of a nationwide insurance company were more effective than others.[4] Senior home office management, familiar with the performance of the branches, identified ten of these branch offices as high performers and another ten as low performers. These designations were highly correlated with various financial variables (for example, profit, growth, expense control) and with self-ratings by people within the branch offices. While each of the branch offices was ostensibly involved in the same business, confronted with similar policies and procedures, some did better than others. Why was that? There are many factors that might account for this difference. However, after careful consideration of financial, environmental (for example, location), and managerial factors, we found that employee power—the sense of being able to influence what was going on in their own offices—was the most significant factor in explaining differences between high- and low-performing branch offices.

Figure 3 shows that power in the various branch offices was distributed across hierarchical levels in a traditional fashion: people at every level of the organization had more total power than did the people at the level below them. Figure 3 also shows that the total amount of perceived power in the high-performing branch offices was greater at every level in the hierarchy than it was in the low-performing offices. The total amount of power (computed as the total area under the curve in calculus) was greater in high-performing branches than it was in low-performing branch offices. What the leaders in the more successful branch offices understood, and acted on, was that "power is an expandable pie"—that power is not a zero-sum commodity, requiring that for others to have more, the leader must have less. The more everyone in the organization feels a sense of power and influence, the greater the ownership and investment they feel in the success of the organization.

The expandable-power-pie concept leads to greater reciprocity of influence—the leader and the follower are willing to be mutually influenced by one another. For the leader, there is the paradox expressed by Jack Telnack, chief design executive for the Ford Motor Company: "I had to give power to gain power."[5] Telnack has been involved in shortening the new car design-production process at Ford by two years and saving over $1 billion. These results give testimony to the fact that when the leader shares power with other people, those people in turn feel more strongly attached to the leader and more committed to effectively carrying out their duties and responsibilities: they feel that a failure to carry out tasks lets themselves down, as well as the boss.

**Figure 3. Distribution of Power
in Effective and Ineffective Branches.**

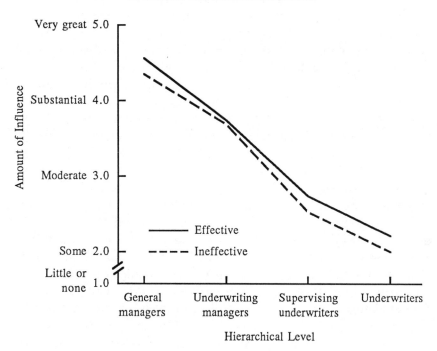

Source: Butterfield, D. A., and Posner, B. Z. "Task-Relevant Control in Organizations." *Personnel Psychology,* 1979, *32,* 773.

When you strengthen others, your level of influence with them is increased. When you go out of your way on behalf of others, you build up credit with them—credit that may be drawn upon when extraordinary efforts are required. Leaders create a sense of covenant when they help others to grow and develop. When the leader is viewed as helpful, other people will more likely be committed to the leader and the organization's goals.

By strengthening others, you place yourself on the subordinate's side. Consequently, when you make requests and demands of others, they are likely to perceive you as saying, "we are going to do this" rather than "you are going to do this." Furthermore, when you know what other people want and are sensitive to their needs, you can make assignments that effectively match people's talents with job demands. Under these circumstances, others are less likely to challenge your requests and are more likely to go along with and accept them.[6] A synergistic and cyclical process is created as you extend power and responsibility to others, and those people respond successfully. This increases their competencies so that you can extend even further amounts of power and responsibility. This in turn has the effect of allowing you to expend more energy in other areas, which enhances your sphere of influence and brings additional resources back to your unit to be distributed among the group members.

Strengthening others by enabling them to share in influencing the decisions about their daily life also has the effect of enhancing their abilities to perform as well as their sense of personal well-being. This result was well documented in a Connecticut state-run nursing home where social psychologists studied the impact of giving people power. Residents were given the responsibility for making seemingly trivial environmental choices, such as when to see a movie or how to arrange their room. Not only did general health and psychological well-being improve, but death rates were 50 percent lower than for a comparison group who was informed that it was management's responsibility to keep them well.[7] The energy that can be unleashed as a result of giving people power is awesome. How is it that leaders manage and create power and then use power to strengthen others?

Making People Feel Strong

When Steve Tritto took over as general manager of the Serial Printer Division of Dataproducts, a significant management crisis existed. There were a lot of talented people in disarray. They had no vision, and they had no camaraderie. The company had suffered five years of losses; in the preceding year, the loss had been $1.5 million. Turnover was 33 percent annually. Within one year, the division turned their losses into a $3.6 million profit. This marked the first time that the division had ever recorded a profit or exceeded corporate performance goals. Turnover was under 10 percent. These results are testimony to the attention that Tritto paid to strengthening everyone's abilities to contribute to the success of the organization. What Tritto did was to introduce a goal and ask everyone to buy into it. Then, he stressed the importance of *team* effort where before there had been divisiveness. Finally, he used the personal best theme to encourage everyone to excel.

Tritto's methods were straightforward and effective. For example, he made effective use of meetings. Every two weeks, he had "fireside chats" of an hour and a half with 25 people selected alphabetically, crossing over department and rank. Once he had met with all 310 people in the division, he started over again. "People talked. The agenda was open. Folks had a chance to influence decisions about everything from where we were as a company to the inadequacy of the lighting over the benches," Tritto recalled. Quarterly reviews were held in the company's cafeteria to give people an appreciation of how the company was doing, to give them the sense that they were part of a team, to build confidence, and to make them feel that they were in command of what was going on in their organization. Then there were the semiannual meetings. These events were more dramatic. Photographs of all the employees lined the walls of a local auditorium so that people could see pictures of themselves as they walked in. Music played in the background. The performance of the division was graphically displayed with a light and sound show. Achievement awards were given to employees who had made extraordinary contributions.

Steve Tritto understood that it was necessary to strengthen others before he could turn the division around. This ability to make people feel strong, claims Russ Barnett, managing director of MetroBrick in Western Australia, is the single most important contribution of leaders. And empowering others requires working side by side with them. Barnett echoes this observation: "Most leaders fail or succeed on their ability to know and understand the people they work with. You get the results of your efforts through other people, so you have to be very sensitive to each person and to their particular needs." Researchers from the Center for Creative Leadership substantiate Barnett's observation. "Insensitivity to others" was cited in their studies as the primary reason why successful executives tumbled off the track to the executive suite.[8] These researchers noted that the ability to understand other people's perspective was the most glaring difference between the arrivers and those executives who got derailed along the path. Other "fatal flaws" included aloofness and arrogance, betrayal of trust, and overmanaging (or failing to delegate and build a team).

Studies of executives who have been fired from their jobs portray them as loners—people who prefer to work independently of others, who are highly critical of their staffs, and who are unwilling to share control over projects and problem solutions. Fired executives viewed team participation and discussion as a waste of time and had poor interpersonal skills: they were ill at ease with others, frequently making insensitive and undiplomatic remarks, and looked on other people with a great deal of mistrust.[9]

Managers who focus on themselves and are insensitive to others fail. They fail because there is a limit to what they can do by themselves. Leaders succeed when they realize that the limits to what can be accomplished are minimal if people feel strong and capable. In fact, what leaders do, as paradoxical as it may seem, is make followers into leaders. They do this by using their own power in service of others rather than in service of self.

Power in Service of Others

People in leadership positions have a healthy share of power motivation. After all, leaders must get other people to want to do something, to influence what others say and do. Over the past two decades, social psychologists have documented that the motivation for power (that is, the need to have an impact on others) is highly desirable for people with managerial responsibilities.[10] Power needs provide the assertiveness and self-confidence necessary to organize and direct group activities effectively.

Stimulating a group of people to achieve a goal is vastly different from individually achieving a goal yourself. Power motivation, or concern for having an impact on others, requires an outlook and actions considerably different from those needed for making an individual contribution. This explains why so often the best salespeople, most brilliant design engineers, or most outstanding clinical physicians fail to succeed as managers of their groups. These high achievers prefer doing things their own way and working independently. They fail to delegate or to be influenced by others. Their subordinates fail to develop a strong sense of responsibility or commitment.

People with strong power needs are concerned with gaining the respect of others. They are willing to make unpopular decisions when those decisions are necessary for effective group performance. Such people are comfortable in setting standards and in letting people know where they stand. However, having an impact on others does not mean that you have to weaken them and make them feel small while you exercise your influence. In fact, there are two different ways that people experience and express their power needs.[11] One is with the negative face of power—a "personalized power concern," or power in service of self. The positive face of power, on the other hand, is a "socialized power concern," or power in service of others.

People with a personalized power concern have little inhibition or self-control, and they exercise power impulsively. Researchers describe them as rude to other people and suggest that they drink too much, try to exploit others sexually, and collect symbols of personal prestige, such as fancy cars or big offices. While the charisma and force of some such managers can sometimes inspire loyalty and team spirit, the subordinates' loyalties in such cases are to the individual manager rather than to the organization. When the manager departs, there is likely to be disorder and a breakdown in team spirit. Additionally, the subordinates are so conditioned to obey orders that they are immobilized when they have to act independently. In sharp contrast to the personalized power manager is the person with a socialized power concern, who exercises power for the benefit of others. Such a person is more emotionally mature, is more hesitant about using power in a manipulative manner, is less egotistical and defensive, accumulates fewer material possessions, has a longer-range view, and is more willing to take advice from others. The strong need for power is expressed by exercising influence to build up the organization and make it successful. This person is more willing to sacrifice self-interests for the benefit of the organization. Because of this orientation toward building organizational commitment, this kind of person is more likely to use a participative, coaching style of managerial behavior. Social psychologist David McClelland summarizes these two faces of power and their implications for enabling others to act:

The negative or personal face of power is characterized by the dominance-submission mode: If I win, you lose. . . . It leads to simple and direct means of feeling powerful (such as being aggressive). It does not often lead to effective social leadership for the reason that such a person tends to treat other people as pawns. People who feel they are pawns tend to be passive and useless to the leader who gets his satisfaction from dominating them. Slaves are the most inefficient form of labor ever devised by man.

If a leader wants to have far-reaching influence, he must make his followers feel powerful and able to accomplish things on their own. . . . Even the most dictatorial leader does not succeed if he has not instilled in at least some of his followers a sense of power and the strength to pursue the goals he has set.[12]

The personal best experience of Ken Kenitzer provides a good case study of using power in service of others. Kenitzer was brought into Compression Labs, Inc., as vice-president of operations. His challenge was to revamp the manufacturing organization and production systems. In reflecting on that experience, Kenitzer described the following as the key leadership practices he employed:

1. Involving peers and subordinates in planning.
2. Getting the team to enroll in the project completely.
3. Delegating responsibility to others with full trust and confidence it would be done.
4. Developing team attitude and spirit.
5. Letting people know he had confidence in them, even to the point that they could do more than they themselves believe they could.
6. Finding ways to reward accomplishment.

When asked how he would most like to be remembered as a leader, Kenitzer's reply was: "As a *team leader*—one who can get team members enthusiastically involved and committed." Kenitzer was quite successful in these efforts because he used his power to enable others to act. He believed so strongly in his team's competency that his belief was contagious. With his support, the team members felt that there was no reason to accept road-blocks—there was no way that they could fail. Kenitzer's motto, "A team that works is a working team," could be rephrased as "A team with power is a powerful team."

To better understand how to use power in service of others, let us examine where power comes from. We will also examine ways to increase the amount of power that you have.

Sources of Power

Within an organization, we generally think of power as control over valued resources.[13] Everyone has resources—personal and situational—but the key to unleashing the potential of these resources lies in creating value for them in the minds of others. Leaders are seen by others as powerful. It is, paradoxically, followers who make leaders powerful. They do this by placing value on the resources controlled by the leader. Two implications flow out of this view of power as the creation of value for resources that you control. The amount of power that individuals or units (departments) possess is derived from (1) the ability to perform important tasks and (2) the degree of discretion and visibility associated with the job.

Critical Tasks. Power flows to those who have resources that others need. The more that people want or need what you have, the more influence you will have with them. Those people who are most central to solving the organization's crucial problems and ensuring the company's long-term viability have the most power. For example, if a company is going through a merger or acquisition, then power will flow to the financial and legal specialists. If the central concern of a company is improving quality, then power will flow to the operations and manufacturing systems people. Engineering will be most dominant in technology-driven companies.

Changes in the social and political environment affect the relative importance of a leader's tasks or abilities. Faced with increasing worldwide competition, people with manufacturing experience are becoming more highly prized and rising to senior executive ranks. Just a few years ago, it was people with legal experience who were breaking into the executive ranks because of their ability to handle increasing governmental interference and litigious public interest groups. So a leader's power can ebb and flow with changing conditions.

Consequently, leaders must keep in step with the times. Our case studies of personal bests are all examples of people confronting critical organizational issues, be they improving quality, reducing manufacturing start-up times, changing customer perceptions, inventing turnkey systems, or mobilizing legislative initiatives. This requires that leaders must be attuned to the particular set of tasks and abilities needed by the organization and seek to develop or acquire the appropriate necessary skills.

Power flows to people whose tasks are helpful to the organization in dealing with critical problems. This is true not only when their resources are critical but when their resources are in short supply. Leaders have more organizational power precisely because they are not easy to replace. Power remains untapped potential, however, unless you are capable of effectively executing critical tasks. Kanter has found that a leader's ability to execute important tasks depends upon three factors.[14] The first is being able to supply the resources that a unit needs, whether money, materials, staff, or time. The second is having information, being "in the know." When you understand the premises on which decisions are based, you can exercise greater influence on the organizational system. Understanding what alternatives are available increases your maneuverability. Support is the third factor affecting your ability to perform effectively and garner power. Support from subordinates, peers, superiors, and outsiders ensures that important tasks are accomplished. Support enables you to take actions and exercise judgment generally outside of your formal scope of responsibility and authority. Superiors may act as sponsors to provide the needed backing. Peers with broad access to the corporate grapevine may offer timely information and warnings about shifting political forces. Subordinates may be counted on to pick up the slack, and outsiders can confer status and provide key external alliances. All these various forms of support are necessary for leaders to carry through with their important tasks.

Discretion and Visibility. The way that your job is designed and located in the organization also influences both the perception and reality of organizational power. Frustration, panic, and a sense of helplessness—all demotivating experiences—are what Lisa Mainiero's studies of people in powerless jobs revealed.[15] Some of the major ways in which various factors contribute to power and powerlessness are summarized in Table 3. Two key dimensions for enhancing power are by designing jobs that have discretion and visibility.

Table 3. Ways That Organizational Factors Contribute to Power or Powerlessness.

Factors	Generates Power When Factor Is	Generates Powerlessness When Factor Is
Rules inherent in the job	Few	Many
Predecessors in the job	Few	Many
Established routines	Few	Many
Task variety	High	Low
Rewards for reliability/predictability	Few	Many
Rewards for unusual performance/innovation	Many	Few
Flexibility around use of people	High	Low
Approvals needed for nonroutine decisions	Few	Many
Physical location	Central	Distant
Publicity about job activities	High	Low
Relation of tasks to current problem areas	Central	Peripheral
Focus of tasks	Outside Work Unit	Inside Work Unit
Interpersonal contact in the job	High	Low
Contact with senior officials	High	Low
Participation in programs, conferences, meetings	High	Low
Participation in problem-solving task forces	High	Low
Advancement prospects of subordinates	High	Low

Source: Kanter, R. M. "Power Failures in Management Circuits." *Harvard Business Review,* July–Aug. 1979, p. 67. Reprinted by permission of the *Harvard Business Review.* Copyright © 1979 by the President and Fellows of Harvard College; all rights reserved.

Discretion is the ability to take nonroutinized actions, exercise independent judgment, and make decisions that affect how you do your job without having to check with the boss. It means not being tied down to a standard set of rules, procedures, or schedules. The opportunity to be flexible, creative, and adaptive is what gives you the ability to make the fullest use of your skills and abilities. It also makes you feel more personally powerful and in control of your own life. If you hold a broadly defined job, you will have opportunities to use discretion, because you will have more choice about *how* to accomplish the objectives. With discretion, however, generally comes greater responsibility and obligation to do what is needed.

The New United Motor Manufacturing, Inc. (NUMMI), plant in Fremont, California (a joint venture between General Motors and Toyota), uses "pulling the rope" as a way to give people discretion and make them feel powerful. Workers have fifty-four seconds to do their job, whether it's installing steering wheels, attaching bumpers, or bolting down car seats. However, if workers fall behind or notice a quality problem, they can pull a cord overhead to stop the line. A GM internal audit showed that the NUMMI-produced car, the Chevrolet Nova, was among the best in the American auto industry. "I used to write up five or ten items on every car," says Richard Aguilar, a NUMMI inspector who worked for GM for nineteen years. "Now, only one out of ten cars has a problem."[16]

Power does not flow to unknown people. Unfortunately, as many new hires discover, simply doing a good job is not enough to get on the company's fast track. Presumably everyone is doing a good job—or they wouldn't have been hired or retained. The key is getting others to notice your achievements and their importance. *Visibility* is the means to enhancing power by calling attention to your accomplishments. Visibility is important also because being noticed is the precursor to developing key strategic alliances with others. If other people don't know about the central importance of your tasks and abilities, they will (1) take them for granted or (2) be uninterested in forming connections and relationships. Finally, unless your contributions gain visibility, you are unlikely to receive formal recognition from your organizational superiors. This reduces access to higher-level sponsors as well as to the increased resources that generally flow to successful people.

Giving Power Away to Strengthen Others

Your capacity to strengthen and empower others begins with the degree of power that you hold—your connection to lines of supply, information, and support. We are talking not about power for the sake of the leader (yourself) but about power for the sake of others. Only leaders who feel powerful will delegate, reward talent, and build a team composed of people powerful in their own right. Leaders can use the power that flows to them in service of others. They can give their own power away to others in the same way that they acquired it themselves. These four principles, articulated by Rosabeth Moss Kanter, strategically strengthen others:

1. Give people important work to do on critical issues.
2. Give people discretion and autonomy over their tasks and resources.
3. Give visibility to others and provide recognition for their efforts.
4. Build relationships for others, connecting them with powerful people and finding them sponsors and mentors.[17]

Assigning Important Tasks. Assigning people to work on critical issues is a way to help them to become central and relevant to the organization's concerns and thus acquire power and influence. At Sunset Publications, for example, making sure that the recipes in their cookbooks taste right is a responsibility that is taken very seriously. Everyone, from the most senior to the most junior people, signs up to be taste tester in the company's kitchens. Recipes don't go into the cookbooks until the taste tester gives his or her okay. This empowering process creates a sense of ownership by integrating responsibility and pride. More and more companies, especially those in manufacturing, have begun turning over to the hourly workers the job of calling on customers. In some instances, they even visit foreign competitors to determine firsthand how their own products stack up.

Leaders strengthen others by keeping people up to date on the latest developments affecting their business. They keep people informed about crucial issues, demonstrating and reminding their team about how their job (or unit) addresses these issues. For example, Chaparral Steel Company, a minimill operation thirty miles outside of Dallas, has tried to bring research right into the factory. "We make the people who are producing the steel responsible for keeping their process on the leading edge of technology worldwide," explains Gordon Forward, president and CEO. "If they have to travel, they travel. If they have to figure out what the next step is, they go out and find the places where people are doing interesting things. They visit other companies. They work with universities."[18] Staying relevant also means understanding what skills the organization values and offering opportunities for people to use those competencies. When necessary, leaders are prepared to build and develop or acquire the skills that they or others lack. In this way, leaders build for the future.

Providing Autonomy and Discretion. Leaders seek out projects that will increase the discretionary range of their team and provide greater decision-making authority and responsibility. Doug Schumer was managing a small research group at the Ohaus Scale Corporation when he was put in charge of a "crash development" program. The team had nine months to design and deliver a new product, with technical issues outside of his own area of expertise (applied physics). "A key to my success," explained Schumer, "was that I allowed the experts and leaders in the parallel activities to obtain their results their way and to tell me what had to be done to satisfy their requirements. There was no formal reporting, but I maintained very close personal contact with all the key players." Schumer also found it necessary to negotiate broadly defined objectives for his team's activities. By doing this, he enlarged the team's degree of freedom in taking action and maximized their opportunities for flexibility and creativity.

Leaders delegate important tasks and thus maximize the discretion that their team can exercise in their jobs. Gordon Forward explains how this has been done with the security guards at Chaparral Steel: "Normally, when you think of security guards at four o'clock in the morning, they're doing everything they can just to stay awake. Well, ours also enter data into our computer—order entry, things like that. They put the day's quality results into the computer system each night. We upgraded the job and made a very clear decision not to hire some sleepy old guy to sit and stare at the factory gate all night. Our guards are paramedics; they run the ambulance; they fill up the fire extinguishers; they do the checks in the plant; now they're even considering some accounting functions."[19]

Giving Visibility and Recognition. Leaders ensure that their team members are highly visible, that individual and team efforts are noticed and recognized. Telling people, both inside and outside the department, about what people are doing and publicizing their work are just two ways leaders use to increase visibility. Pictures of employees of the month on the wall, stories about people and their achievements in newsletters and advertisements, bouquets of flowers on the desks, references to interpersonal conversations in company speeches, and unsolicited letters of appreciation to the boss are other ways that leaders make the contributions of people on their team visible to others.

Major General John Stanford demonstrated his dedication to increasing the visibility of his people when he spoke at one of our workshops. He wore his full dress uniform that day, but over his own name tag he placed that of his aide-de-camp. We thought that there had been some mix-up and wondered how to tactfully tell him about it. But before we had the chance, Stanford told the group: "My aide-de-camp Albert A. A. Cartenuto III couldn't be here today. I hope I represented him well." Stanford wanted to give visibility to Cartenuto and to acknowledge the lieutenant's contributions. When Doug Schumer's project team reached milestones, he advertised their success and made the responsible individuals at all levels visible to the others. And Herman Miller's 1985 annual report, entitled *Say Hello to the Owners,* presents side-by-side, full-figured pictures of all 3,265 people who work in the company.

Helping to Build Strong Relationships. Building strong relationships is empowering in two ways. First, it helps people to more easily get in contact with others who can help them accomplish their task. This networking is the grease that often smooths the way through interdepartmental boundaries and territorial disputes. Second, relationships that are durable and require frequent interactions provide incentives for people to assist and support one another. At Herman Miller, this empowering process is referred to as "theory fastball." As Max De Pree, chairperson and CEO, explains: "In the process of work many of us are outstanding pitchers, able to throw the telling fastball, but it is also true that those pitchers can only be effective if there are many of us who are outstanding catchers."[20]

Russ Barnett describes exceptional "battery mates" as another outcome of building relationships: "You know, if you put a production fellow and a sales fellow together, you're going to find out rather quickly whether something has a chance of getting off the ground. And if it does, having them there at the start talking with one another means that you have a pretty good chance of making things work—and fast." Providing entry to senior executives, fostering outside contacts, and developing and promoting promising subordinates are some of the other ways that leaders build relational networks. Visibility is also enhanced when leaders keep their team members in contact with people outside of their department—for example, by placing people on task forces and committees whose members come from across the organization or by encouraging active participation in professional and community groups. Supervisor McPeak takes pride in the number of people she has worked with who have gone on to higher administrative and elected political offices. Good press is much of what contributes to people moving up in their organizations.

The following case study provides an excellent example of how a leader strengthens the team and what results in the process:

An otherwise successful chemical company found that it had a stubborn problem. About 10 percent of all its orders were sent from its loading dock with one sort of defect or another: wrong material, wrong size containers, too much or too little merchandise. A crackdown would bring only a month or two of improvement.

Finally, one enterprising executive decided on a new approach. He knew that in most companies the loading dock team is, at best, lightly regarded. He bet that if the low status of the loading dock worker was turned around, greater productivity would follow. Each member of his team, he decided, would no longer be a worker. He would be a manager. Each would be assigned an account list and would be held responsible for any orders going out to any of his customers.

Suddenly, every shipment that went out had a sponsor, *on* the dock. It wasn't just the company's shipment anymore. It was a manager's shipment. And each manager cared very much that his order went out without flaw. Within 90 days, the error rate dropped to two percent. And it has stayed there—or lower—ever since.[21]

By empowering the loading dock personnel, this chemical company executive *enabled others to act.* The loading dock area became a critical issue for the company. The employees were given discretion in their tasks and provided with visibility and recognition for their accomplishments. Their relationships with one another were enhanced, and connections were made between their efforts and those of other departments in the company.

Commitment Number 6: Strengthen People by Sharing Information and Power and Increasing Their Discretion and Visibility

Putting gasoline into your car engine is like strengthening other people—without power, the capabilities of the finest-tuned, highest-performance automobile will be useless. Leaders are motivated to use their power in service of others because empowered people perform better. When others are strengthened and enabled to accomplish extraordinary things on their own, the leader's own sphere of influence is enhanced.

Empowering others is essentially the process of turning followers into leaders themselves. The process of building and enhancing power is facilitated when people work on tasks that are critical to the organization's success, when they exercise discretion and autonomy in their efforts, when their accomplishments are visible and recognized by others, and when they are well connected to other people of influence and support. There are several strategies that you can use to build more power for yourself and create more power for others:

1. *Get to know people.* As we have learned in this chapter, sensitivity to others is a prerequisite for success in leadership. Insensitive leaders are eventually derailed. Sensitivity to others begins with the disclosure of facts and feelings about yourself and with the willingness to actively listen to what others have to say about themselves.

The most genuine way to demonstrate that you really care and are concerned about other people as human beings is to spend time with them. So schedule some time daily just to get acquainted with others. And we do not mean schedule time to have yet another business meeting; instead, make it unstructured time to joke and kid and learn more about each other as parents, or athletes, or musicians, or artists, or volunteers, and so on. It does not have to be hours at a time. Often five or ten minutes is sufficient, if done regularly. Walk the halls at least thirty minutes each day, stopping to talk with people who are not on your daily calendar. Go around the chain of command by chatting with subordinates' subordinates, a boss's boss, receptionists, customers, suppliers, and so on. Eat in the employee cafeteria, if there is one, or go out to lunch with folks from other functional areas. Leave your office door open, move your desk onto the factory floor, grab a cup of coffee in the employees' favorite gathering place. We know a CEO who even takes people on rides in his car, often for two or three hours, solely for the purpose of getting acquainted. Just take some kind of daily action that forces you to interact with people you know and want to know better and with people you do not know and need to.

Never take another person for granted. You demonstrate respect for other people by never taking them for granted, even when you know that you can count on them for support. To assume that you needn't talk with them, listen to their ideas, or consider their suggestions runs the risk of being seen by others as insensitive, aloof, and arrogant.

2. *Develop your interpersonal competence.* Becoming sensitive to the needs of others requires a great degree of interpersonal competence. Some people learn these skills early in life, others do not. If you feel your interpersonal abilities have room

for improvement, sign up for the first available training opportunity. There is strong evidence that you can dramatically improve face-to-face communication skills through effective training. Every leader ought to know how to paraphrase, summarize, express feelings, disclose personal information, admit mistakes, respond nondefensively, ask for clarification, solicit different views, and so on. Also, by participating in interpersonal skills training programs you demonstrate to others that you are sincere and serious about building a climate of trust and respect.

The team-building retreat is another useful way to improve relationships among members of your staff. Cross-functional retreats can help people from different functional areas learn what their colleagues do as well as learn how their functions are seen by others. We strongly suggest, however, that retreats always be led by competent and sensitive facilitators. The local chapter of Certified Consultants International can help you locate qualified group facilitators in your area.

Flexibility is another important demonstration of a leader's understanding of others. There is no one best style of leadership. You should be able to use all the practices and behaviors we discuss in this book, but you ought to be versatile enough to adapt a style that is appropriate to each different situation you face. Versatility also expands your capacity to function in a wide range of cultures and environments. If you get feedback that you are too one-dimensional in your approach to situations, you ought to look into a development program designed to expand your flexibility. Ask your organization's training director for guidance.

3. *Use your power in service of others.* There should never be any need for a leader to tell other people how powerful and influential he or she is. There is never a need for a leader to show off prestigious supplies. The thickness of the carpet, the size of the desk, and the price tag on the art are simply unnecessary displays of importance. Visible ways of drawing attention to one's power are puffery and demonstrate insecurity.

People prefer to work for managers who are upwardly and outwardly influential. Successful leaders know that it is necessary and important to let others know that you can and will use your power to help them get their jobs done. Ask the people who work for you what they need to do their jobs most effectively, then go get it for them. Watch how much your esteem goes up in the eyes of others.

Yes, leaders are power brokers. But they are power brokers on behalf of those they lead. Consider this analogy: you continue to give funds to your stockbroker only if that person is able to increase their value (make money for you). The more successful the stockbroker is, the more resources you are willing to entrust with him or her and the more willing you become to follow his or her investment advice. Since the stock market is unpredictable, the key to whether you stick with that stockbroker during turbulent and difficult times is whether he or she has developed a personal relationship with you—not that you are necessarily friends, but that you have become better informed about the stock market because of your broker and believe that, given the same information, you would have made the same decisions yourself. It is this type of interaction that sustains the personal relationship between broker and investor or leader and follower over time so that investors and followers aren't continually shopping around for some mythical guru or wizard.

As a power broker, however, you have to manage dependencies. When you create value for others' resources and, hence, power, they can become dependent on your skill, information, or support. But no one really likes to feel dependent on another person. Your challenge is to give your power away. If you get power and then hold and covet it, you will eventually be corrupted by it. The intriguing paradox of power is that the more you give away to others the more you get for yourself.

4. *Enlarge people's sphere of influence.* One way to give some of your power away is to increase the amount of autonomy and discretion others have. Delegate. Form quality circles and other problem-solving groups. Put the authority to make key decisions in the hands of others. Enable people to make decisions without checking with you. Use whatever means fits in your organization, but give people a button to push, a rope to pull, a movie to select, so that individuals have a strong sense of personal autonomy and control.

The increased sphere of influence also ought to be over something relevant to the pressing concerns and core technology of the business. Choosing the color of the paint may be a place to start, but you had better give people influence over more substantive issues. If quality is top priority, then find ways to expand people's influence and discretion over issues of quality control. If innovation is a priority, then increase people's influence over the development of new products, processes, or services. The same applies for all the critical issues of the business.

One caution: provide people with the training to make use of their decision-making power and discretionary tasks. Successful quality programs, for example, all have in common the fact that the group members receive training in basic statistical measurement methods, group communication skills, and problem-solving techniques. Without training and coaching, people will be reluctant to exercise their authority because they do not know how to perform the critical tasks or they fear being punished for making mistakes when they do.

And don't stop with training. Provide all the other necessary resources to perform autonomously. That means materials, money, time, people, and information. There is nothing more disempowering than to have lots of authority to do something, but nothing to do it with.

5. *Keep people informed.* Everett T. Suters was CEO of a small but rapidly growing Southwestern company. Everyone was putting in long hours and giving enormous effort but Suters began to pick up innuendos that seemed to say: "We're doing the work but you're getting most of the credit and all of the money." He was irritated by these comments because he didn't believe they were true, and so he called together the management team. He asked them to write down what the company profits were and how much money they thought he was personally making. When he gathered their papers he was amazed: everyone had guessed much too high. So, he passed out copies of the company's financial statement, went over it line by line, and indicated how much money was going to be needed to finance future growth. Everyone started asking questions and requesting more information. Suters says he could see them becoming "as interested in all facets of the company as I was." One manager told Suters some time later: "If I had to tell you in one sentence why I am motivated by my job, it is because when I know what is going on, and how I fit into the overall picture, it makes me feel important."[22]

The more that people know about what is going on in the organization, the better off you will be. Without information, you can be certain that people will not extend themselves to take responsibility; armed with information, people's creative energies can be harnessed to achieve extraordinary results. In our study of effective insurance branch offices, we found information and access to decision makers were significant predictors of why people felt they had influence in their organizations.[23] Information empowers people, strengthening their resolve and providing them the resources they need to be successful.

6. *Make connections.* It is not only what you know but also who you know that counts. Being connected to people who can open doors, offer support and backing, provide information, mentor and teach, and add to one's reputation are all ways power is increased. You can increase your own power by forming strategic relationships, and you can empower others in the same way. Take the time to introduce the staff in your organization to the people they need to know. Get them access to influential others. Take members of your staff to important meetings, business lunches, and customer organizations. Find ways to connect them to sources of information.

7. *Make heroes of other people.* The late Wilbert L. Gore, chairperson of W. L. Gore & Associates, once said that one of his skills was "making heroes of other people." If there is one phrase that best expresses the philosophy of strengthening others, that would have to be it. Leaders find ways to shine the spotlight on the achievements of others rather than on their own accomplishments. They make other people the visible heroes and heroines of their organizations. Gore once did this by issuing Sarah Clifton, a line worker, a business card that read: "Sarah Clifton, Supreme Commander." We reported earlier how Major General John Stanford did it by wearing Albert A. A. Cartenuto III's name tag.

There are hundreds of ways you can incorporate similar actions into your daily routine. Just think about how they do it at the movies. At the end of every film there is a long list of credits. Everyone who worked on the film is mentioned, from star to grip, from director to gaffer. Borrowing a page from the movies, John Couch took out a full-page newspaper advertisement naming and thanking all the people who worked on the Lisa project at Apple Computer. For the national conference of the Organization Development Network, the steering committee produced a poster that listed all the names of the more than two hundred people who helped to plan the conference. The poster was mailed to all the members of that professional association.

At North American Tool and Die the names of all the winners of Super Person of the Month are affixed to plaques that hang very visibly over the wash basin on the plant floor. At Stew Leonard's Dairy the pictures of all employees of the month for the last several years, not just the current month, line the walls of the store. At General Electric's corporate training facility at Crotonville, glass cases are filled with hundreds of plaques listing the names of people who attended classes there. Public speeches and newsletters are other available media for making people's accomplishments visible. And isn't it always empowering to receive a letter from someone who tells you how they heard other people talking about what a good job you have done?

We urge you to shine the spotlight on at least one person each day. Let others know how someone has contributed to getting extraordinary things done in your organization.

In the next section you will see how many of these same approaches to strengthening and empowering others also serve to build people's commitment to action. You will also read how, in order to build commitment, you must first demonstrate your own through word and deed.

PART FIVE

Modeling the Way

> I really believed we could do it. I was personally
> enthusiastic and helped others in any way that I
> could. The key: show them the way.
> ——*Maria Straatmann,*
> *Technical Marketing Director,*
> *Computer Technology and*
> *Imaging, Inc.*

A leader needs a philosophy, a set of high standards by which the organization is measured, a set of values about how employees, colleagues, and customers ought to be treated, a set of principles that make the organization unique and distinctive.

Leaders also need plans. They need maps to help guide people. Yet complex plans overwhelm people; they stifle action. Instead, leaders lay down milestones and put up signposts. They unravel bureaucratic knots. They create opportunities for small wins, which add up to major victories.

Words and plans are not enough. Leaders stand up for their beliefs. They practice what they preach. They show others by their own example that they live by the values that they profess. Leaders know that while their position gives them authority, their behavior earns them respect. It is consistency between words and actions that builds a leader's credibility. In this part of the book, we take a look at how leaders:

- Set the Example.
- Plan Small Wins.

9

Set the Example:
Leading by Doing

You can only lead others where you yourself are
willing to go.
———*Lachlan McLean,*
Production Superintendent,
Australian Paper
Manufacturers

When the men's swimming team at Stanford University won the
National Collegiate Athletic Association (NCAA) championship
in 1985, they had their picture taken with university president
Donald Kennedy. The team, naturally, wore swimsuits, and
Kennedy, naturally, wore a business suit. "If you win in 1986,"
Kennedy said, "I'll wear a swimsuit, and you can dress more
formally." Well, guess who won the 1986 NCAA swimming title?
And guess whose picture, in bathing trunks, appeared in the
student and alumni newspapers?

Of course, for those who know Kennedy, this wasn't altogether surprising behavior. He can be seen visiting the football
players in the locker room before the big game with archrival
Berkeley. He can be found backstage before major theatrical productions. He'll often jog mornings in the Stanford foothills along
with a contingent of student runners. "The two most important
speeches I make during the year are the speech I make welcoming
the freshmen and the one I make to the seniors at the end of the
commencement program," says Kennedy.

Kennedy understands how leaders model the way; how, by
the clarity and courage of their convictions and by their everyday

actions, they demonstrate to others how visions can be realized. As Kennedy observes: "The leader's job is to energetically mirror back to the institution how it best thinks of itself." Kennedy tries to be the mirror for what is best about Stanford University.

With students, Kennedy looks for opportunities to remind them about their public service responsibilities. While he's undoubtedly proud about the enormously active volunteer network that's grown among students—evidenced by such accomplishments as tripling the rate of Peace Corps volunteers in two years—he really sees the public service initiative as a vehicle for talking to the students about their own values and obligations. What emerges from the public service initiative is the idea of mutual obligation—which means that people care about one another. Kennedy tries to pick "teachable moments" to remind students about balancing their opportunities with their obligations. One of those moments emerged around violations of the university's honor code. Kennedy used this incident to increase campus dialogue about what it means to take responsibility. He doesn't miss an opportunity to model the way.

Modeling the way is how leaders make their visions tangible. It is the bricks and mortar, nails and lumber, carpeting and furniture, electrical outlets and placement of windows, and all of the hundreds of other details that go into realizing the architect's model of a new home. It is the countless lines of code, electrical subroutines, and the like that enable the computer software to produce the desired word processing output. It is the evidence— fingers on the glass, footprints on the floor—that tells us that leaders have done something. It is Kennedy's clarity about his values and how he behaves, which sends messages about what is and is not important in how the organization operates. Leaders provide the standard by which other people in the organization calibrate their own choices and behaviors. In order to set an example, leaders must know their values and live them.

Determining a Basic Philosophy and Set of Values

Values comprise the things that are most important to us. They are the deep-seated, pervasive standards that influence almost every aspect of our lives: our moral judgments, our responses to others, our commitments to personal and organizational goals. However, silently, values give direction to the hundreds of decisions made at all levels of the organization every day. Options that run counter to the company's value system are seldom considered. Values constitute our personal "bottom line."[1]

So, as Sam Boyd, manufacturing manager at Tandem Computers, puts it, "the very first step [for a leader] is to determine a basic philosophy of what you want." In describing the tremendous time and energies that went into designing a new plant, Mike Leonard, director of organization development for Alcoa Aluminum of Australia, explained: "The place we began with was developing a shared understanding of our basic philosophy about how we ought to be doing business. It was these values that served to guide us, not only with actual physical construction and socio-technical designs but also with the various recruitment, promotion, and compensation strategies as well." Before leaders can set an example, they need to be in touch with what it is that they are convinced needs to be done.

Making sure that people know what you and your organization stand for, and consequently where you and your organization stand, is a process that exemplary leaders and their organizations take quite seriously. At Tandem Computers, the company's fundamental management principle is expressed this way: "The controls are not a lot of reviews or meetings or reports, but rather the control is understanding the basic concept and philosophy of the company." Tandem takes pains to give its employees an understanding of the essence of the company's business and its five-year plan; every employee attends a one- to two-day seminar on the subject. Letting people see the big picture and peek at so-called strategic secrets, they claim, boosts loyalty and effort. The deeper purpose of such activities at companies such as Tandem is, of course, to point everyone in the right direction, explain what's happening on all sides of them, and empower them to work hard to get to where they need to be. What all this underscores is that people who understand their leader's beliefs and find their personal values aligned with them will be more likely to work hard to help the company achieve its goals.

Values are here-and-now beliefs about how things in the organization should be accomplished. While visions refer to the future and to the *what* the organization should be doing, values refer to the means (the *how*) by which these ends can best be achieved. While it is essential that the ship's captain have some vision of what lies beyond the horizon, it is also important that the crew understand the standards by which performance will be judged as they sail toward it.

In our workshops, we often ask participants to think about their fundamental values by imagining that they will be gone from their offices for the next six months and will not be allowed to communicate with people back home in the workplace. They can, however, leave behind a one-page memo that spells out how they think their business unit should be managed in their absence. In other words, we ask them to record their fundamental beliefs about what values and actions will result in an effective organization.

Consider both the simplicity and the power behind this four-part test that Tom Mathis, works manager for Kaiser Refractories, "left behind" for his supervisors: "Whatever you do, it must be (1) environmentally sound, (2) safe, (3) cheap, and (4) implementable quickly." The first rule of success for Mary Kaplan, marketing manager for Tektronix, is "We only exist for our customers, so give the best value possible." Her memo also included relying on each other, keeping informed, not giving up, and having fun. Or consider this clear and simple statement of values from Margaret Fox, owner-chef of Cafe Beaujolais in Mendocino, California: "What makes us different? I think it is a blend of satisfyingness, care, breakfast, choices, and magic."[2] Can't you just picture what this restaurant looks like? Feels like? And what do you think is the most important meal of the day that they serve?

Do Shared Values Make a Difference? Leaders need to understand explicitly what they stand for, because values provide a prism through which all behavior is ultimately viewed. The leader's values serve as the standards for others about what is important in the organization. There is tremendous energy when individual and organizational values are in synch with one another. When Tom Melohn at North American Tool and Die says "No Rejects! No Rejects! No Rejects!" there is little confusion at the end of the month about meeting shipping deadlines or reliability standards.

In our own research, we have carefully examined the relationship between individual and organizational values.[3] This research has involved over 2,300 managers from across the United States, representing all types of public and private organizations and all levels in the organizations from first-level supervisor to the highest executive. The findings (shown in Table 4) clearly reveal that senior managers' efforts to clarify and articulate their personal values has a significant payoff for both managers and their organizations. The studies show that shared values:

- Foster strong feelings of personal effectiveness.
- Promote high levels of company loyalty.
- Facilitate consensus about key organization goals and stakeholders.
- Encourage ethical behavior.
- Promote strong norms about working hard and caring.
- Reduce levels of job stress and tension.

In our studies for the Australian Institute of Management, we found that leaders talking about their values makes a difference to subordinates. Subordinates who reported that their senior managers articulated their values felt a significantly stronger sense of personal effectiveness than those subordinates who felt that they were wasting energy trying to figure out what they were supposed to be doing.[4] People tend to drift when they are unsure or confused about how they ought to be operating in order to reach shore. The energy that goes into coping with, and possibly fighting about, incompatible values is enormous, and it takes its toll on both personal effectiveness and organizational productivity. When people are clear about the leader's values and know what is expected of them, they handle better the often conflicting demands of work and personal affairs. And, in fact, research studies consistently demonstrate that in compatible work environments, people can manage higher levels of stress.[5]

Psychologically hardy individuals are those whose work lives are consonant with their personal values. In Silicon Valley (the computer chip manufacturing area of California), young start-up firms by nature require long hours from their employees. Project teams within these companies frequently work seventy

**Table 4. The Impact of Shared Values
on Perceptions of Personal and Organizational Vitality (Mean Scores).**

	Low	*Moderate*	*High*
Perceived career success[a]	5.48	5.66	6.01
Likelihood of fulfilling ambitions[b]	1.75	1.80	1.85
Intention to stay with firm	4.59	5.31	6.08
Willingness to work long hours	3.76	4.10	4.39
Clarity about organizational values	5.07	5.47	6.28
Clarity about superior's values	4.72	5.08	5.85
Clarity about peers' values	4.80	4.86	5.45
Clarity about subordinates' values	4.90	5.01	5.22
Organization guided by ethical standards	4.73	5.66	6.56
Organizational policies affect unethical actions	3.87	4.14	4.32
Willingness to execute unethical action if requested by superior[c]	2.06	1.77	1.53
Willingness to accept promotion in spite of doubts about ability[c]	2.60	2.47	2.34
Extent of ethical concern by my superiors	3.83	4.94	6.14
Extent of ethical concern by my colleagues	4.13	4.78	5.32
Extent of ethical concern by my subordinates	4.50	4.94	5.42
Stress in home and/or personal life created by work	4.07	3.45	3.04
Feeling that job keeps me from family and/or friends	4.11	3.72	3.34

Note: Analysis of variance procedures were used to test for differences between the shared values groups. All differences were beyond the 0.001 level of chance probability (probability of one in a thousand that the difference was random, or due to chance).

[a]Unless otherwise noted, all responses used seven-point Likert scales, with higher scales indicating agreement or more strongly felt perceptions.

[b]This statement was scored (1) No (2) Yes.

[c]Responses to this statement were on a five-point Likert scale.

Source: Posner, B. Z., Kouzes, J. M., and Schmidt, W. H., "Shared Values Make a Difference: An Empirical Test of Corporate Culture." *Human Resource Management*, 1985, *24* (3), 297.

hours per week, including weekends. Evidence of the dedication of these groups is the sweatshirt worn by members of Apple Computer's Macintosh development group during the intense period when they were creating that new product. On the front was the Macintosh insignia, and on the back was printed: "90 hours a week and loving it."

What Values Are Important? The research makes clear that shared values do make a difference to organizational and personal vitality and that values form the bedrock of an organization's corporate culture.[6] Unique values make for unique corporate cultures. However, less clear is whether there is some particular value, or set of values, that is the springboard to corporate vitality. Consider these examples of three electronics companies, each of which has a strong set of values.[7] The first company prides itself on technical innovation and has a culture that is dominated by engineering values. It informally encourages and rewards activities such as experimentation and risk taking. The second company is much flashier. Its important organizational values are associated with marketing, and the company gears itself toward providing outstanding customer service. The third company does things "by the numbers." Accounting standards dominate its key corporate values, and energies are directed toward becoming more efficient (for example, cutting costs). Each of these companies is quite different. Each clearly communicates its own values. Despite these differences in values, however, all three companies compete in the same market, and all are successful, although, not surprisingly, each has a different strategy. It is apparent, then, that successful companies may have very different values and that the specific set of values that may serve one company may hurt another.

The research of management professors David Caldwell and Charles O'Reilly demonstrates that while companies may have different sets of values, the more effective companies have three qualities in common: (1) clarity, (2) consensus, and (3) intensity about their core organizational values.[8] Let's look more closely at these three qualities.

Clarity means that people know what their company stands for. There is a set of beliefs about how they operate and do business that is talked about frequently and consistently. Leaders are much like a movie projector to their audience. Unless leaders are in focus and clear about their values, their audience is likely to lose interest, become displeased, and channel their energies and resources into some other activity. Being clear about the key values and principles that make the greatest difference identifies the leverage points that most directly contribute to personal and organizational vitality and success.

Consensus means that people understand the values and that they share and agree with them. There is a high degree of commitment to what the leader and his or her organization stands for. Every organization has a set of values and principles by which it does business, or at least "says" it does business. While clarity is important, its significance fades without consensus. For example, almost every organization would profess to value quality and customers, but there is likely to be considerable variation in how this value is actually operationalized across several different organizations. The greater the extent of internal disagreement, the lower the level of consensus about the "meaning" of the corporate values and, consequently, the lower the degree of organizational commitment. Consider what it means to "put in a fair day's work." Is this measured by the clock? By some union agreement? Or by consensus?

Consider the actions at Johnson & Johnson in the face of seven deaths from cyanide-laced Extra Strength Tylenol capsules. Quantities of the product valued at over $100 million were quickly recalled. James E. Burke, CEO, observed that it was the company's philosophy and values that played the most important part in its decision-making process during this incident: "We believe our first responsibility," begins the Johnson & Johnson Credo, "is to the doctors, nurses and patients, to mothers and all others who use our products and services." Consensus about the meaning of this responsibility facilitated prompt corporate actions.[9]

Intensity means that people feel strongly about the worthiness of their values. Value issues are not taken lightly. They reflect deeply felt emotional bonds. When values are intensely held, there are (1) a substantial degree of congruence between values and actions and (2) an almost moral dimension to the necessity of keeping the faith. For instance, our research shows that in companies with high levels of shared values, those values are frequently a major topic of conversation. In addition, formal mechanisms are in place within the organization to monitor values-actions congruence. One corporate vice-president of human resources describes his department's fundamental role as "Keeper of the Faith." To this end, he periodically surveys a sample of employees to determine their feelings about the published values of the company. The Organizational Behavior (OB) Teaching Society, a professional association of business school faculty, selects one of its members to serve as their "OB-1." In this capacity, the person is charged with looking broadly across the organization's activities to determine that the organizational values are intact and helping to design events that rekindle and remind the membership of the organization's mission and values.

The "Credo Challenge" at Johnson & Johnson is another example of periodically taking the organization's pulse in regard to the clarity, consensus, and intensity surrounding its values. Every few years, the company calls together a group of managers from around the world and challenges them to "get rid of, change, or rededicate themselves to" the credo. Organized religions of the world provide an ideal example of these three qualities as necessary and sufficient conditions for people to have faith. In a business organization, this faith, or what IBM's Tom Watson, Jr., called "a set of beliefs . . . which help people find a common cause,"[10] is developed around similar processes. Furthermore, studies of public-sector organizations support the importance of clarity, consensus, and intensity of values to organizational effectiveness. People within successful agencies and departments clearly understand their organization's values. Considerable agreement and intense feelings are found among employees and managers alike about the importance of their values and how they could best be implemented.[11] While some people argue that fostering shared values is worthless or impractical, because different executives can interpret such phrases as "fair," "equitable," or "best quality" exactly as they like, we believe that the process of thinking through and articulating personal values is important in itself.

Leading by Example

The challenge, as John Gardner, former cabinet secretary and founder of Common Cause, has put it, "is not to find better values but to be faithful to those we profess."[12] This is the challenge that leaders confront every day. Harvard professor Chris Argyris has referred to this challenge as the difference between "espoused values" and "values-in-use," or the difference between the values that we say and believe that we use and those that we *actually* use.[13] Employees pay attention to the values-in-use more than to espoused values. They are very critical when wide gaps exist between these values and actions. They watch to see how stated values are reinforced and how those values influence the actions of key executives.

Because values are so deep-seated, we never actually "see" values themselves. What we "see" are the ways in which people's values manifest themselves: in opinions, attitudes, preferences, desires, fears, actions, strategies, and so on. Consider this story told to us by John Schultz, a manager at Lockheed Missiles and Space Company, about his days as a high school football player:

When I played high school football, I had three coaches. The first two were exactly alike. Each said, "Men, while you are training I don't want you to smoke, drink, stay up late or fool around with girls. Got that?"

Then we would watch our coaches during the season. They would smoke, drink, stay up late and fool around with women. So what do you suppose we did? (Boys will be boys, after all!)

My third coach was the best I ever had. At the beginning of the season we had the same locker room sermon as with the other coaches. Except this coach just said, "I have only one rule. You can do anything I do. If I smoke, drink, stay up late or fool around with women, then I would expect you to do the same. But if I don't, you better not!"

That was the most difficult season I ever played football. The guy was a regular saint.

Values are intangibles. In marketing intangibles, organizations know that they must make them tangible to the customer. The only way leaders can make values tangible and real to followers is through their behaviors and actions. Employees look to their leaders as role models of how they should behave. And when in doubt, they believe actions over words, without fail. Every action that the leader takes, or doesn't take, is information about the leader's values and seriousness about those values. People around a leader are always alert to what he or she is doing. Although they attach importance to what leaders say, they will be truly impressed only by what leaders do. Consequently, leaders set an example by how they behave. Their behavior, in turn, sends signals and messages about which behaviors are appropriate and acceptable and which are not.

If leaders ask followers to observe certain standards, then leaders need to live by the same rules. That is exactly what we were told many times by exemplary leaders. "You can only lead by example," says Geno Tolari, vice-president of Informatics General Corporation. Or, as Reno Taini remarked about a particularly difficult and stressful expedition in Peru: "I was suddenly thrust in charge during one several-week-long crisis period. We survived by really pulling together as a team. One of the best things I did for morale was to rotate through every job myself."

More than ten years after a critical incident with her boss, Bruce Nordstrom, Betsy Sanders, general manager and vice-president of Nordstrom, still clearly recalled how he demonstrated to her the seriousness with which the Nordstrom organization cared about the customer.[14] She had been with the company for two or three years and was a department manager. "I was in my department busily working one day when all five of the executive officers of the company started trooping through the department. And then, to my dismay, I saw Bruce Nordstrom get the most terrible frown on his face, shake his head in disgust, and walk over toward me. He came over and he said: 'Betsy, I just overheard a conversation that really has me upset. See those two ladies over there? They were just saying how disappointed they were. Would you go find out what we did to upset them and make it right?' "

Sanders told the women that Nordstrom had overheard them and had asked her to find out what was wrong. "They were delighted to know that he cared," she said. "Well, as it turned out, the two women had fallen in love with the dresses in the Gallery—the expensive dress department—but felt they couldn't afford the prices." Sanders just happened to manage the moderate-priced dress department, and she was able to help them. The result was two more happy Nordstrom customers. Says Sanders, "I was real impressed with Bruce Nordstrom. But more so when he came out hours later out of a negotiating meeting that had certainly taken all of his time and attention and came back to check with me to find out what those customers had wanted and what I did about it." For Sanders, this event left an indelible mark. For Bruce Nordstrom, it was being clear about his values that made leading by example a natural part of his style.

Leadership is not a spectator sport. Leaders don't sit in the stands and watch. Neither are leaders in the game substituting for the players. Leaders coach. They show others how to behave, both on and off the field. They demonstrate what is important by how they spend their time, by the priorities on their agenda, by the questions they ask, by the people they see, the places they go, and the behaviors and results that they recognize and reward. Every step a leader takes and every move he or she makes is watched. Leadership is a dramatic art. Leaders are always on stage. Indeed, as social psychologist Edgar Schein has pointed out: "Leaders do not have a choice about whether to communicate. They have a choice only about how much to manage what they communicate."[15] Jack Telnack, head of Ford Motor Company's Design Center, wanted to communicate the importance of cooperation between the car and truck divisions, between which there had been friction. After winning two consecutive Car of the Year awards, the truck division was feeling that they weren't getting sufficient attention from the Design Center. To show the truck division members that he wanted to improve relations, he started driving a Bronco truck to the office. This gesture of goodwill toward the truck division demonstrated his personal commitment to collaboration. Leading by example is visible management. Employees can see what is expected and required of them by observing what their boss does. Visibility is another technique for making intangible values tangible and concrete. According to an internal report in one international franchise operation, the visibility of the manager is the crucial variable in the individual store's performance. Profits, as well as quality of customer service, were directly related to the time spent on the floor by the franchise owner. MBWA (management by wandering about) is a standard operating procedure in many companies because it ensures that managers are visible to their employees. Visibility enhances accessibility and promotes your *"walking* what you talk"—not just saying the words or going through the motions.

Moments of Truth

In our studies, we found that leaders consciously focused people's energies and efforts through intentional modeling until such actions became standard operating procedures, part of the leader's daily stream of activities and thus subconscious. Because they were "routine," they tended to become part of the accepted "way we do things around here." On the other hand, because they were *so* routine, some managers had been unaware of how powerfully these actions affect organizational life. Management consultant and author Tom Peters called these routines "mundane tools" in order to highlight the notion that leadership is inextricably bound up with the everyday occurrences that fill an executive's daily life rather than some grand techniques of structural and strategic organizational change.[16] The most powerful mechanisms for modeling the way are represented by the leader's routines.

Jan Carlzon, president of Scandinavian Airlines System (SAS), colorfully describes routines as "Moments of Truth."[17] In his business, he claims that there are 50 million (the annual number of passenger-employee interactions) moments of truth— opportunities to demonstrate a personal commitment to providing outstanding customer service. For leaders, every interaction with an employee, vendor, customer, or other constituent becomes a *moment of truth*. That interaction says more about the leader's real values than all the corporate credos in the world.

The message about what really counts in the organization is delivered, demonstrated, pointed out, and emphasized by the leader's moments of truth and how well these moments are orchestrated. Leaders, and would-be leaders, must consciously structure moments of truth to communicate and reinforce their intangible values. The most typical moments of truth center around:

- How leaders spend their time.
- The questions leaders ask.
- Leaders' reactions to critical incidents.
- What leaders reward.[18]

It is through these processes that leaders make intangible values tangible. Central beliefs are articulated and reinforced through moments of truth, providing opportunities to model how these values should be operationalized.

How Does a Leader Spend Time? Time is the truest test of what the leader really thinks is important. The conversations surrounding the leader's calendar provide clues for all employees about what's going on. While you may hear the leader say that quality is important, how much time does he or she spend in the plant addressing quality issues? For example, in the Honeywell Residential Division, a major commitment was made to improving the quality of products and services by working more closely with customers and suppliers. How could such commitment to quality be demonstrated throughout the organization? In this case, the general manager and his staff attended a five-day Quality College and then all served as faculty in subsequent Quality Colleges for employees. By devoting their own valuable time to teaching others, they visibly demonstrated their personal commitment to the value of quality. This type of role modeling took time, but the behavior was more convincing than speeches.[19]

Among the busiest days in neighborhood convenience stores are Christmas and New Year's Day. Robert Gordon, president of Store 24, wants the employees in his stores to know that he cares about them, and he wants them to be able to spend time with their families. So he and other corporate office personnel work in the stores on these holidays. Gordon could easily delegate these shifts to others, but he believes that it is important to show them his concern, not just talk about it. Other "time-sensitive" actions by leaders include the use of meetings and public statements. By attending operating meetings in the field, leaders provide vital evidence of their concerns and the directions they want to pursue. Moving a meeting to a new location, reorganizing a staff unit's reporting relationships, or taking on a new activity is often a dramatic signal that something new is afoot. Norman A. Neumann, president and CEO of Signetics, sent a message to the organization about the seriousness of his interest in improving manufacturing effectiveness by bringing together some sixty-five senior operations people from around the world for a two-day Manufacturing Effectiveness Conference. This was an important signal about his priorities—especially when, because of cost-cutting measures, this meeting was held and the annual marketing and sales conference was postponed.

Public statements can also lead to a rash of activity. Cindy Johnson, director of information services at Amdahl, found noticeable differences in people's orientation to their customers when she simply started referring to the "User Services" group as the "Customer Services" organization (a change she later formalized). Another visible public statement is the meeting roster. Who attends which meetings and who presents material can signal new approaches to management and reorient substantive directions. When the management at Quad/Graphics leaves every year for their off-site strategic planning sessions, they leave the multi-million-dollar printing equipment and all product decisions in the hands of their employees. Management by "walking away," as some people refer to this, is a public statement about the extent to which employees are trusted to act responsibly.[20]

What Questions Does a Leader Ask? Questions not only highlight particular issues and concerns but also point people in the "right" direction. The questions that the leader asks send messages about whether the focus of a company, for example, is on control of operating costs, quality, or market share. Questioning routines also demonstrate the sort of memory the leader has. Are questions asked about what was "assumed" last month? Last quarter? Are questions asked that follow up previous requests and/or dispositions of particular items? For example, "Did you follow up with the Anderson people? How did the Anderson people respond to our initiatives? Have we achieved our reliability standards on the parts shipped to the Anderson people?" Questions provide feedback about which values should be attended to and how much energy should be devoted to them.

The *first* question is an especially clear indicator of direction and interest. When we examine how leaders make people aware of key concerns or shifts in organizational focus, it is readily apparent that the leaders' questioning style has a pervasive effect on the issues that organizational members worry about. Gayle Hamilton, an area manager for the Pacific Gas & Electric Company, describes how she has tried to shift concerns from revenue to customer satisfaction. "I never let a day go by," she says, "without spreading the word that our customers are what we are in business for. I try to ask each account representative about what our customers are telling them about our services." She makes the first agenda item in her staff meetings "Customer Satisfaction."

How Does a Leader React to Critical Incidents? Another on-line signal about what really matters in the organization is how the leader reacts to critical incidents, notably in times of stress and challenge. While the general situation in the following two incidents is similar—what happens when a subordinate confronts a boss about an organizational rule—the two bosses' reactions send very strong but very different messages about "standing up to the boss" and "doing your job."[21]

(1) When Thomas J. Watson, Jr., was chair of IBM's board of directors, he tried to enter a security area one day wearing an orange badge rather than the required green one. The security guard knew who he was—Watson was surrounded by his usual entourage of white-shirted men—but insisted, "You can't enter. Your admittance is not recognized." (Guards were instructed to use precisely these words when challenging someone.) "Don't you know who he is?" someone hissed. Watson raised his hand for silence, and the group waited patiently while someone hurried off to get the proper badge.

(2) After deciding that everyone at the corporate offices should sign in each day, Charles Revson, former CEO of Revlon, stopped by the reception desk one morning. He picked up the sign-in sheet and started to look it over. The receptionist, new on the job, told him, "I have strict orders that no one is to remove the list. You'll have to put it back." They argued a bit until Revson finally exploded. "Do you know who I am?" "No, I don't," the receptionist admitted. "Well, when you pick up your final paycheck this afternoon, ask 'em to tell you."

As we all know, it's when "push comes to shove" that we learn—often dramatically—the difference between espoused values and values-in-use. Top management reactions to critical incidents such as the two previous examples give concrete content to abstract principles. They point out the truth or fiction of the importance of key organizational values. When Corning purchased Steuben Glass in 1933 and CEO Arthur Houghton, Jr., took a lead pipe and smashed $100,000 worth of crystal, he was sending an unambiguous message that Corning was not in that business any more![22]

What Does a Leader Reward? Rewards send another tangible message to followers about what to pay attention to. The game of "what grade did you get?" is one learned at an early age and keenly played by organizational members. The grades or rewards that people receive or, equally important, do not receive tell them and others about what really counts in the organization. The leader who places a premium on innovation and risk taking must be willing to "promote" in a variety of ways those who innovate. The leader must be attentive to how people are made to feel when they take risks and fail. Are people rewarded or punished when they fail? Is the leader's energy funneled into searching for the culprit or assessing what has been learned from the experience? The leader's actions in such situations set the tone for innovation and risk taking. Who is rewarded, who is promoted, and why are among the clearest ways in which leaders demonstrate their seriousness to a specific set of corporate principles. Leaders literally "put their money where their mouths are." Changing the management style at Honeywell, for example, required actively promoting managers with a participatory style and removing those who clung to the old, autocratic ways.[23] Putting greater customer orientation into Pacific Bell required making the account executives' position more visible, more prestigious, and more exciting.

More Subtle Means of Communicating Messages

For leaders, there is no getting around the interconnections between what they say and what they do. Their messages are delivered in a variety of tangible moments of truth. But there are other available means to reinforce the leader's intentions and seriousness about these messages. These include stories and language, architecture and physical space, and symbols, artifacts, and ceremonies. Using these means transmits a more subtle message to the leader's audience, because they are less under the leader's *direct* sphere of control and/or influence. They have the most impact when their use is consistent with the leader's everyday routines.

Stories and Language. In every organization, there are stories that are told that help people understand "how things really

work, or don't work, around here." Stories provide concrete
advice and guidelines about how things are done and about what
to expect in the organization.[24] Leaders are often good storytellers.
The stories they tell are clear reminders about central concerns
and suggest to those who hear them that a particular organizational value or philosophy is truly followed. They provide a concrete example of what might otherwise be a very general, perhaps
meaningless platitude.

It is not as easy to describe in mere words the "Hewlett-
Packard Way," or the "McDonald's Way," or the "El Camino
Hospital Way," but employees generally define their "company
way" by using well-known stories from their organization's history and folklore. These shared stories provide a way to explain
to newcomers and outsiders and to remind old-timers "who we
are" and "how we operate." Steve Dunne, manager of business
market planning for Pacific Bell, is fond of telling how as a
teenager he first got interested in the telephone business. He had
purchased an old candlestick phone at a swap meet and couldn't
make it work, so he called the telephone company repair office
and asked the repairperson who answered for assistance.
Together, and over the phone, they resolved the problem, and
Dunne learned an indelible lesson about the telephone company's meaning of customer service. From that one interaction,
he knew that he wanted to work for the phone company and
carry on that kind of caring service to others.

The power of stories in fostering beliefs is supported by
research conducted by organizational sociologists Joanne Martin
and Melanie Powers. They compared the persuasiveness of four
different methods of convincing the M.B.A. students in their
study that a particular company really practiced a policy of avoiding layoffs.[25] In one situation, Martin and Powers used only a
story to persuade people. In the second, they presented statistical
data that showed that the company had significantly less invol-
untary turnover than its competitors. In the third, they used the
statistics and the story; and in the fourth, they used a straightforward policy statement made by an executive of the company.
The students in the groups that were given the story believed the
claim about the policy more than any of the other groups. Other
research studies also demonstrate that information is more

quickly and accurately remembered when it is first presented in the form of an example or story.[26]

Leaders are also quite attentive to the "language" used in their organizations. Indeed, this attention focuses on the types of metaphors and analogies used to describe organizational problems and opportunities (that is, critical incidents). Whether the leader likens his or her organization to the tortoise or to the hare has implications about marketing strategies or the importance of new product development. The natural tensions generated by mergers are definitely affected by references to white knights, golden parachutes, greenmail, shark repellants, and war chests. As Tom Peters says, you would not be surprised at receiving poor service from an airline flight attendant whom you overhear remarking just before the passengers board: "Here come the animals!"

Part of the magic of Disney World can be attributed to the deliberate use of language and metaphor. For example, there are no employees at Disneyland, because everyone is a performer. That's why the "personnel department" is called "Central Casting." And in this family-oriented environment, everyone is on a first-name basis, with name badges referring to people as Hosts and Hostesses. And, of course, there are no customers at Disneyland, only Guests (always capitalized) who have come for a visit to the Magic Kingdom.

Architecture and Physical Space. Messages about architecture and physical space are often quite subtle but nonetheless powerful. They reflect the leader's messages only if consciously managed (otherwise, they reflect the assumptions and preferences of architects, facilities planners, local community standards, and the like). Factors such as the size, layout, and decor of offices and buildings convey information about what is important in an organization, the way things are accomplished, and the specific ends sought.

The significance of architecture, broadly conceived, is that it produces people's first impressions of the organization, which, in turn, often form the background for their interpretation of other corporate symbols. Many high-technology firms seem to compete for new employees upon the basis of the newness not just of their technological equipment but of their facilities. An older facility may send new employees unintended messages about how up to date the action is on the inside. Conversely, an older physical plant may transmit messages about stability or, on the negative side, obsolescence.

In one interesting set of studies, executives were asked to describe their reactions to photographs of the reception areas of the local offices of "Big Eight" accounting firms. The physical settings conveyed consistent and different messages to the executives about the warmth and comfort of relationships and about expectations regarding organizational control. What is intriguing is that these two dimensions are the ones most frequently used to describe *psychological* climate. Physical symbols about comfort and control may be important building blocks, says researcher Suzyn Ornstein, upon which people form impressions about people and organizations and which "may be particularly salient in influencing people's impressions about life in organizational settings."[27]

Leaders who have a clear philosophy and style often choose to embody that style in visible manifestations of their organization. Hewlett-Packard, for example, with its strong emphasis on communications and cooperative relationships, has chosen an open-office layout with partitions just high enough to permit a sense of privacy only when one is sitting down. Kitchens and eating facilities are provided in every work area to facilitate luncheon get-togethers, and most conference rooms have round or oval tables to symbolize the unimportance of formal status and to facilitate communication. At Sequent Computer Systems, there are no walls between departments. Everyone, not just managers, is expected to walk around the building to find out what is going on. Marketing people are expected to show their faces in engineering, engineers in manufacturing. When Scott Gibson was vice-president of operations and finance, his desk was on the manufacturing floor. Honeywell recently invested in a Corporate Conference Center (for training and development and company-wide meetings) that serves as a concrete message about the company's commitment to developing its people.

Symbols, Artifacts, and Ceremonies. We have found that leaders pay heed to the informal channels by which organizational messages are conveyed. Foremost among these are the symbols, artifacts, and ceremonies of workday life. Leaders make great efforts to link their routines and organizational issues to the history and tradition of the company. Part of the great power of Martin Luther King's "I Have a Dream" speech, we noted earlier, is owing to the ways in which he linked his message with familiar, time-honored traditions and concepts: the U.S. Constitution, freedom of opportunity, and the vulnerability of children. Things as "insignificant" as the use of first names (or the introduction of a more formal dress code) were used by one plant manager to successfully create more positive feelings about the company. Giving truck drivers the "keys to the Peterbilts" was another way employees at Quad/Graphics were given a tactile reminder that every employee was responsible for the organization's success.[28]

Artifacts are objects that stand for something else. Posters, pictures on walls, objects on desks, and buttons or pins on lapels are much more than decorative items. Each of these serves as a *visible* reminder about some key organizational value. At Mary Kay Cosmetics, the bumblebee pin serves to remind salespeople, mostly housewives, that they can successfully combine a family and a career. Bumblebees are not supposed to be able to fly, but they do; and so do women at Mary Kay. Just as your name on a parking space confers status, so Renn Zaphiropoulos's announcement, when he took over as general manager of Xerox's Office Products Division, that the names on the parking curbs would henceforth be ignored demonstrated a commitment to egalitarianism and team spirit. Phil Turner's use of the hot-air balloon at Raychem to symbolize how his department uplifted people's spirits is another example of how leaders consciously manipulate and employ symbols to send messages.

At Sequent Computers, company president Casey Powell at one critical point handed out buttons. Most of the company would wear green "How Can I Help?" buttons, but people on the critical path would get red "Priority" buttons. People with green buttons were to do anything to remove obstacles for those with the red buttons. Powell wore a green button. Handing out the buttons took fifteen minutes. Their cost was $73.50. But those hardware engineers with the red buttons got the not-so-subtle message. "I think it was a way to make sure we understood how important what we were doing was," explained one engineer.[29]

Leaders are also attentive to the use of ceremonies, both official and spontaneous, to reinforce their values (we'll say more about this in Chapter Twelve). These often mark the entry of followers into the group, as when employees at Quad/Graphics are issued company uniforms, or when employees hold dialogues with chairperson Robert Swiggett about Kollmorgen's culture.

Commitment Number 7: Set the Example for Others by Behaving in Ways That Are Consistent with Your Stated Values

Setting an example begins with the leader being clear about the "rules of the road" and then adhering to them along the journey. Clarity, consensus, and intensity are three essential factors for aligning values of leaders with those of their followers. The importance of shared values is that they channel and focus people's energies and commitments.

Through moments of truth, leaders show others how to behave. How leaders spend their time, what questions they ask, how they react to critical incidents, and what they reward make crystal clear what is really expected of people in the organization. Also important, but more subtle, are stories and language, architecture and physical space, and symbols, artifacts, and ceremonies as indications of what leaders really care about. However, leaders must consciously manage this process of modeling the way. Planning plays an important role, especially when combined with the power inherent in producing small wins with people. Both traditional and innovative strategies are involved in "planning small wins," as we discuss in the next chapter.

Here are several strategies that you can use to set an example for others:

1. *Write a tribute to yourself.* The evidence is very clear: shared values make a significant difference in how people feel and perform. But before you can get others to accept a set of values, you must be clear about exactly what values you would like them to share. You must have clear in your own mind the beliefs on which you base the success of your business. The first step in setting an example, then, is to clarify for yourself the values for which you stand.

The business values you espouse at work have their roots in your own personal beliefs about what is right and wrong. One of the best ways we know to begin the process of clarifying your values is to think first about your ideals—your conception of things as they should be or as you wish them to be. And the most important place to start is with your ideal image of yourself—how you would most like to be seen by others. So, try this exercise:

Imagine that tonight you will be honored as the "leader of the year." Hundreds of people will gather to pay tribute to your contributions to your organization and community. There will be several speeches praising your performance and your character. Now, what three to five words or phrases would you most like to hear others say about you? "She was always . . . ." "He was always . . . ." How would you like to be remembered tonight? What descriptions would make you feel the proudest? If you could influence what people say about you when you are not around, what would you want them to say?

Take the time to write down these descriptive adjectives and phrases. They may be lofty and ideal, but that is exactly the point. We all have personal standards of excellence. The greater our personal clarity, belief in, and passion for these ideals the greater the probability we will act consistently with them.

2. *Write your leadership credo.* The next step in clarifying your values is to translate those personal ideals into a set of guiding principles for your organization. Here is an exercise we find extremely useful in assisting people in translating their values and beliefs into a credo that is appropriate for their business:

Take out a piece of paper on which to write a memo. Address the memo to your team members and others to whom you wish to communicate your business beliefs. Now imagine you have been sent on an assignment to a remote post for nine months and will be unable to communicate in any manner with your team while you are gone. However, in nine months you will return and resume your present responsibilities. While you cannot communicate with people during your assignment, you are permitted to leave behind on one page your guidelines—your business beliefs, philosophy, values, credo—on how people should conduct business in your absence. These guiding principles will be given to everyone who works in the organization you lead.

Actually take the time now or in the near future to do this. Do not treat this as simply an exercise. Treat it as real. Do it, then take it to your team members, colleagues, boss, and friends and ask them to react to it. Ask them if they understand it. Ask them if they could adhere to the values you have recorded. Once you have edited your statement, send the memo. Several leaders with whom we have worked have done just that. Others have framed it and hung it on their walls.

3. *Write a tribute to your organization.* It is not just what people say about you that is important, but also what they say about the organizational unit you lead. "His organization always . . . ." "Her organization always . . . ." Another technique leaders find useful is to write a testimonial to their business units. This is similar to the personal tribute, except it is written about a unit rather than about one person.

Ask your team to do this. Ask them to write down the three to five words or phrases they would most like to have others use to describe the unit of which they are a part. Have every member of your team read these descriptions aloud and then compare notes. How similar to or different from your description are their descriptions? How similar to or different from each other are they? Is there a consistent focus? How much consensus is there within the team about the relative importance of the various standards? How consistent are they with the larger organization's values and standards? Where there are differences, resolve them. Where there are inconsistencies, set priorities. Propose hypothetical situations and determine whether there are congruent points of view.

4. *Publish your credo.* Take all the data you have generated on personal and organizational values and develop a one-page written credo for your unit. Post it prominently: in offices, branches, plants, and facilities. Publish it in the annual report. Make a videotape about it for people in other sites. Talk about the credo in your speeches. Put it on the back of business cards. Create symbols that will remind people of your organization's core values. We know many leaders who have done each of these things, and more, to make sure that employees, customers, vendors, and other stakeholders know the fundamental beliefs on which the organization is based.

5. *Audit your actions.* Words are one thing, action is another. When it comes to setting an example, people are much more inclined to believe your behavior over your words. What is critical, then, is that others see you practicing what you preach. The consistency between word and deed determines your trustworthiness.

One place to begin is by doing an audit of your actions in comparison to your values. You need to scrutinize your current routines: the things you do every day, the questions you always ask, the ways you react under pressure, and the people you recognize and reward. Are these routines, or habitual patterns of behavior, consistent with what you say is most important to you and your organization? The consistent message for the past decade from noted management consultant Tom Peters has been "attention is all there is. You are as good as, or as bad as, your calendar."[30]

Take a piece of paper and draw a vertical line down the middle. On one side list the values you preach. Now take out your calendar, meeting agenda, interoffice memoranda, and correspondence for the last two weeks. Using the information from these sources, in the other column on the page write down the actions you take that demonstrate your personal commitment to your stated values. What do you conclude from an examination of your daily behavior? Are there any glaring discrepancies between what you preach and what you practice? Any obvious priorities, based on the time you devote to the different values? Are these the priorities you want to set?

You might also want to get some independent feedback on how others now see you acting on your espoused values. One effective technique used by organization development consultants is "shadowing." Typically a leader will ask a qualified consultant to follow him or her around for a week or two taking detailed notes on every action, reading every memo, observing every meeting. The shadow consultant then offers feedback to the leader on his or her behavior. This process can be extremely valuable in assessing what your behavior communicates about your values and priorities.

6. *Establish routines and systems.* Earlier in this book we indicated that sometimes routines can stifle change, and we urged you to break some rules. At the same time we said that routines are

necessary to establish discipline. Discipline means the adherence
to a set of principles or teachings. If the credo represents the
lessons you wish others to follow, then the discipline is the systems
and structures you establish to maintain adherence to those lessons. The issue is not whether there is discipline or no discipline,
but rather the extent to which the systems and structures reinforce
the values you want people to uphold. We suggest you audit your
routines and systems to determine how consistent they are with
the espoused values. Throw out those that are inconsistent and
retain those that are. In place of those that you discard, establish
new ones that are more reinforcing of the appropriate actions.

For example, take a look at your performance appraisal
system. Does it measure how well people perform against the
standards of excellence set by the organization's values?[31] If not,
add clear performance measures to your appraisal that evaluate
how well people are doing on quality, customer service, innovation, respect of others, contribution to profitability, fun, or whatever else might be of critical value to your organization.

Start spending 30 to 40 percent of your time on your most
important strategic priority. Book up your calendar for the next
four months with activities that demonstrate your interest in and
concern about this priority. Find someone or some department
that is doing what you wish everyone else were doing, or that is at
least moving in the right direction. Hold them up as models and
make them heroes. Let everyone get a clear idea about what you
are looking for and how rewarding you can make it for them.

7. *Be dramatic.* Sometimes it will be necessary for you to
consciously stage dramatic events to make a point about what
you consider to be the fundamental values of your organization.
This is particularly important at times of change and transition.
We know one CEO who actually did a belly dance at the company's annual strategic retreat to demonstrate to senior executives
that he was personally very serious about the need for them and
the rest of the organization to get out of their conservatism and
become more creative. We know another executive team that went
mountain climbing to teach themselves about taking more risks
with one another. Driving a Bronco to work was a less flamboy-
ant, but still dramatic, way for Jack Telnack, Ford's chief design
officer, to show the truck division people that he was sincerely

interested in them. When he took over Dana Corporation, Rene McPherson took a match to the company's twenty-one inches of policy manuals, setting them ablaze and signaling his trust and respect for Dana's employees. When Maryland Governor, William Schaefer, was Baltimore's mayor, he demonstrated his willingness to deal with public complaints by making himself personally available; for example, he rode along with the city's garbage trucks in the mornings and installed a hot line for citizens to report potholes in the roads.

These actions were not drama for drama's sake. Instead they were intentional acts designed to draw attention to critical values and priorities. Leadership is a performing art; sometimes you have to be a bit of a ham and go out of your way to get the point across.

8. *Be a storyteller.* You would find it too exhausting and time consuming to be center stage each and every day. However, you can never really be completely off stage: the magic of the theater of leadership is that the story can be retold over and over again. Charles Nirenberg, chairman of Dairy Mart, Inc., told us about how one day he was visiting stores with the director of operations. He noticed a woman at the gas pump having trouble and went over and helped her out. A perfect illustration of leading by example. But Nirenberg went on to explain how this story has become legend and retold throughout the 1,200 Dairy Mart convenient store operations, as both a sales pitch and a motivating force at management meetings.

Sister Dona Taylor, chief administrator of Providence Hospital, uses the parking lot incident to illustrate her own (and the hospital's) value of equality: "Parking spaces are always in short supply, and the only reserved spaces are for our hospital vans. One morning, I pulled into the parking structure just about the same time as one of our clerical support staff was pulling into one of these reserved places. I stopped to tell her that these places were reserved, and she apologized for taking my space. I laughed and told her that I didn't have a reserved space, nor did anyone else in the hospital. We were all equal. This incident made the rounds that day throughout the hospital." Sister Dona still relates it when she wants to make a point with the staff about how they are all part of the same effort.

9. *Find teachable moments.* While every leader faces many moments of truth, you need to be on the lookout for teachable moments—those points in time when people's consciousness can be elevated. Often, these moments occur in the peaks and valleys of your experiences. At the summit, you need to remind others, for example, of what they have accomplished and why the journey was worth the effort or to provide perspective on how this achievement was a step in the right direction and proves the worthwhileness of their trials and tribulations. In times of despair, you need to make the struggle noble and reframe any setbacks as learning experiences. Don Kennedy used the honor code violations as an opportunity to focus attention on what it means to take responsibility. The success of a civic fund-raising campaign became the vehicle for learning how the power and energies of diverse interests and perspectives can be harnessed and integrated. When you are clear about your values, you will find it easier to identify these times, events, and activities of potentially momentous impact.

10. *Be emotional.* You have to care. And the way you best demonstrate that you care about something is to spend time doing it, asking questions about it, always focusing attention on it, and providing rewards for those who help achieve it. You can't be dispassionate. People around you have to know how you are feeling in order to gauge the intensity of your values and commitments. This is quite difficult to do as a public person, but you have to lead the way. When others are afraid, you have to acknowledge their fear but rechannel their energy into positive aspirations. Many leaders told us that "putting on a happy face each morning" was one of their most difficult, exhausting, and crucial performance requirements. But just as with an actor, because you practice your craft for the audience's benefit, not just your own, the show must go on. Several ways to survive the demands of being a leader, such as staying in love with what you are doing and having friends, are discussed in Part Six.

10

Plan Small Wins:
Building Commitment to Action

Planning fosters success. We broke the project up
into manageable chunks.
—*Allen Berglund,*
Software Development Manager,
Rolm Mil-Spec Computers

On July 15, 1982, Donald H. Bennett, the Seattle businessperson
we discussed in Chapter Five, realized one of his lifelong dreams
of standing on the summit of Mount Rainier. Bennett climbed to
the top of Mount Rainier on one leg, becoming the first amputee
to scale that 14,410-foot mountain. In fact, he had to make that
climb twice. The year before, a howling windstorm had nearly
blown Bennett and his climbing team off the mountain. They
had to give up 410 feet from the summit. But Bennett was not
discouraged. For another full year, he worked out vigorously. On
the second attempt, after five days of rigorous climbing, Bennett
made it to the top.

We asked Bennett how he did it. He explained: "One hop
at a time. I imagined myself on top of that mountain one thousand times a day in my mind. But when I started to climb it, I
just said to myself, 'Anybody can hop from here to there. And I
would.' And when the going got roughest, and I was really
exhausted, that's when I would look down at the path ahead and
say to myself, 'You just have to take one more step, and anybody
can do that.' And I would."

Bennett's simple advice underscores what social psychologists have observed about what is required to tackle "big" problems.[1] Problems that are conceived of too broadly overwhelm people, because they defeat our capacity to even think about what might be done, let alone begin doing something about them. Leaders face a similar challenge in trying to achieve extraordinary accomplishments. In addition, getting people to change old habit patterns and substitute new ones is a difficult process. Sometimes with the best of intentions to do otherwise, people revert back to old and familiar patterns.

Getting commitment to new behaviors, like solving big problems, is often overwhelming. So how do leaders do it? How do they get people to *want to* change the way they are currently headed, to break out of existing behavioral patterns, to tackle big problems, to attempt extraordinary performance? One hop at a time! The most effective change processes are incremental—they break down big problems into small, doable steps and get a person to say *yes* numerous times, not just once. Bennett's example illustrates the psychology of change adopted by successful leaders and adventurers. They look at progress as incremental—one hop at a time. Leaders help others to see how progress can be planned by breaking things down into measurable goals or milestones.

The scientific community has always understood that major advances in medicine, for example, are likely to be the results of hundreds of researchers conducting studies all over the world, involving experiments generally focused on pieces of the problem. Major breakthroughs are the results of countless contributions that begin to add up to a solution. It is probably accurate to claim that the sum total of all the "little" improvements in technology, regardless of industry, have contributed to a greater increase in productivity than all the great inventors and their inventions.[2]

The traditional management label for the "one hop at a time" strategy is *planning*. Unfortunately, the term *planning* fails to convey the feelings and emotions that people experience when they reach milestones. A more descriptive term is *small wins*. The small win process also helps leaders in building commitment to a course of action, in much the same way as professional fund raisers begin by asking for any size of contribution from new donors. They know that it is easier to go back for more in the future (and they do) from those who have made an initial contribution than to return to someone who has already said no.

As we said in Chapter Three, the cases of extraordinary accomplishments that we collected were all about challenging the process and going beyond the status quo. Fundamental to the leaders' success was changing the way people were currently doing their work and providing mechanisms—systems and structures—so that people remained committed to the new course of action. At the heart of this change process were two themes: small wins and incremental commitment.

Change as a Process of Small Wins

When Dan Davey arrived as the new manager for one of the Northern California offices of Pacific Gas & Electric Company, he found very poor morale, minimal efficiency, and serious interdepartmental conflicts. He was the seventh manager for this group within a two-year period. People weren't particularly glad to see him arrive and wondered how soon he, too, would be gone from the scene. What to do was not immediately obvious. He decided to start with a small win. He invited all the department supervisors and their spouses to his house for dinner. This was the first time in more than five years that this group of people had got together socially outside of work. It seemed that there had been an unwritten rule that managers were not supposed to fraternize with their subordinates or peers. "This just didn't make any sense to me," explained Davey, "if I really expected people to be helping one another out."

He followed this up with weekly breakfasts. "At first, these breakfasts were just that—breakfast; but within a few weeks, people began to voluntarily start bringing up and talking about work-related issues. Within a few months, people came to breakfast prepared to tell the other departments about problems they were having. Soon thereafter, people started offering help and suggesting ways that they could assist other departments. I convinced these people that we could achieve excellence only through a team effort!" They made such progress that after only six months Davey celebrated their accomplishments with a "night on the town" at his own expense.

Like other leaders who achieve extraordinary results, Davey utilized the small wins process. He started with actions that were within his control, that were tangible, that were doable, and that would get the ball rolling. His first steps were driven less by logical decision trees, grand strategy, or noble rhetoric than by action—action that could be built upon, that signaled intent as well as competence—just as did Debi Coleman, who, as manager of the Macintosh factory for Apple Computer, began improving productivity by refurbishing the bathrooms, waxing the floors, and painting the walls.

The success of behavior change programs such as Alcoholics Anonymous, Weight Watchers, Smoke Enders, and the like is due in large part to their incremental change philosophies. None insists that participants become totally abstinent for the rest of their lives. Although this is the goal of the Alcoholics Anonymous program, alcoholics are told to stay sober one day at a time, or one hour at a time if temptation is severe. The seeming impossibility of lifetime abstinence is scaled down to the more workable task of not taking a drink for twenty-four hours. This drastically reduces the size of a win necessary to maintain sobriety.

The idea of small wins is also compatible with studies of technological innovation. An extensive study involving five Du Pont Chemicals plants documented that minor technical changes (for example, introduction of forklift trucks)—rather than major changes (for example, introduction of new chemical processing technologies)—accounted for over two-thirds of the reductions in production costs over a thirty-year period.[3] The minor technical changes were small improvements, made by people familiar with current operations. Less time, skill, effort, and expense were required to produce them. Much of the improvements were really part of the process of learning by doing.

A small win, points out organizational sociologist Karl Weick, is "a concrete, complete, implemented outcome of moderate importance."[4] Small wins form the basis for a consistent pattern of winning that attracts people who want to be allied with a successful venture. Small wins deter opposition for a simple reason: it's hard to argue against success, and thus small wins decrease resistance to subsequent proposals. In planning a small win leaders identify the place to get started. They make the project seem doable within existing skill and resource levels. This minimizes the cost of trying and reduces the risks of failing. What is exciting about this process is that once a small win has been accomplished, natural forces are set in motion that favor stepping out toward another small win.

Small wins build people's confidence levels and reinforce their natural desire to feel successful. Since additional resources generally tend to flow to winners, this means that slightly larger wins can be attempted next. A series of small wins therefore provides a foundation of stable building blocks. Each win preserves gains and makes it harder to return to pre-existing conditions. Like miniature experiments or pilot studies, small wins also provide information that facilitates learning and adaptation.

When leaders deliberately cultivate a strategy of small wins, they make it easier for people to want to go along with their requests. People can see that the leader is only asking them to do something that they are quite capable of doing. They feel some assurance that they can be successful at the task. On the other hand, it is difficult to gain people's cooperation when either they are unsure of their ability to meet the demands placed upon them or the perceived costs of failure seem high. Consider the energy that is released when the leader can reduce the size of the demand (for example, to have breakfasts together once a week or stop drinking for twenty-four hours).

These processes are well demonstrated by the experience of LuAnn Sullivan, branch office manager for Wells Fargo Bank. While core deposits in her Capitola office had not grown for several years, under her leadership, they doubled in two years. What Sullivan did was to break her overall goal down into smaller parts so that each person could have his or her own individual monthly and weekly goals. From her subordinates' viewpoint, Sullivan made the goal of doubling core deposits seem doable. Mary Delaney, customer service representative, said that when Sullivan first told her of the goal, she thought that they would never be able to accomplish it. However, Delaney explains, "once I saw that I could achieve my weekly goals, the big goal didn't seem so crazy and it was easy to get motivated."[5] Small wins are also examples to others of what to do. When Sam Neaman helped to turn around McCrory's stores in the 1960s, he began the process with one store, in Indianapolis. His success with that store became a concrete example of what others could do. "Make me an Indianapolis" became a model for others to follow.[6]

Managing the Small Wins Process

From our studies, we discovered that successful leaders actively utilize the small win process. They break problems into manageable chunks. They tend to pursue a strategy of hitting singles rather than relying solely on the home run. They work hard at finding ways to make it *easy* to succeed. They notice and celebrate movement in the right directions. All of this is what they refer to at the 3M Company as "big wins from small beginnings." Here we discuss four ideas that leaders follow in planning projects based on the principles of small wins.

Experiment Continuously. The magic in small wins is the experimentation process, or setting up little tests that continually help you learn something. Leaders experiment in little ways all the time. They set up pilot studies, demonstration projects, laboratory tests, field experiments, market trials, and the like. Nobel prize winner William Shockley observed that in the scientific process, "you can always find something in which, in a few hours of effort, you will have made some little steps."[7] Or, as baseball great Pete Rose found out, if you get up to bat often enough, you will make more hits than anybody else has made. The idea is that in order to make forward progress, you need to have lots of ideas. This is the "one hop at a time" kind of progress.

"What have you changed?" is one of the first questions IBM's chair John Akers asks as he visits with company officials throughout the organization. And he expects to hear about several experiments, because he knows that maintaining a competitive edge in technology, or whatever function for that matter, requires improving on the status quo. The experimenting process is institutionalized at the 3M Company, where scientists and engineers are required to spend 15 percent of their time working on projects outside their normal areas of responsibility. Dan McMullin, vice-president of Mini Mart, Inc., wanted to increase average sales per transaction in the stores. His team experimented with various merchandising and display programs, identified products for "plus selling," and organized recognition and awards contests. McMullin himself spent over five weeks behind sales counters, waiting on customers in different stores, suggesting they "try out hot and tasty nachos." The results of this campaign varied in the different local stores, but it all added up to an overall 4 percent increase in average sales per transaction.

Divide Tasks into Small Chunks. Leaders understand how critical it is to break problems down into small pieces so that they are more easily comprehended. In planning, we break tasks into doable steps with milestones.[8] Because they are easier to understand, it subsequently becomes easier to integrate the separate pieces later in the process. Small chunks, like Sumo wrestlers, are not easy to topple over and, hence, tend to preserve gains and footholds made along the way. In the early days at Sequent Computer Systems when they were building their first product, whenever a goal was reached, a nickel was ceremoniously dropped into a special jar. This ritual grew out of a story often told to employees by company founder and president Casey Powell. It was a simple story about a little boy who wanted a bicycle more than anything else in the world—not just any old two-wheeler but a very flashy bike that cost $100. Being "a real process person," as Powell described him, this boy set himself measurable goals in the form of milestones to make sure that at the end of the year he would have enough money to buy his bicycle. He figured that, giving himself two weeks off for vacation, he needed to save $2 a week, or 40 cents a day, or 5 cents an hour, to earn the money in a year. The nickel dropped into the jar symbolized for Powell and Sequent employees the steady, step-by-step progress toward the launch of the new product.

André Delbecq, dean of the Leavey School of Business and Administration at Santa Clara University, was faced with the task of staying in touch with the faculty. He broke the group into three- to four-person groups across disciplines and scheduled informal luncheons with them every other week. This gave him the chance to hear what they were up to and concerned about. It was also his opportunity to tell them about issues facing the school and share feedback he was receiving about the school from the business community and alumni. Information exchanged at these luncheons generally filtered back to other members of the faculty.

Reduce Items to Their Essentials. The average executive has nine minutes at a time to spend on any one item of business before being interrupted. The pace of managerial work is fast and relentless.[9] The beauty of a small win is that it is compact, simple, upbeat, and often noncontroversial. Small wins catch the attention of people with short time perspectives who have only nine minutes to hear your idea or read your proposal. Because of their brief interactions, leaders are forced to consider their dreams within managerial boundaries. But these boundaries can be systematically expanded "one hop at a time," through the conscious use of achievable milestones.

A variation of the small win rule at Apple Computer, Procter & Gamble, and other companies is the one-page memo. New employees often spend countless hours writing and rewriting their reports until they are able to cull them down into one page—a page that is virtually certain to be read. Superior customer service emerged as a cornerstone strategy for Mac's Convenience Stores (Canada) from strategic planning sessions on corporate growth. While many ideas were generated, the most critical action was establishing a director of customer service who would report directly to the president. In this single action, noted Mac's president, Derek Ridout, "I put the organization on notice that we were serious about our commitment to superior customer service." Without this essential leverage point, most of the other actions (for example, introduction of a toll-free number for customers, complete reorganization of the new employee training program to focus on customer service, and introduction of a corporate recognition award program) would have been impossible or at least less effective.

Don't Push People into Change. Leaders wisely don't try to push people to change but rather try to move with the natural diffusion process. As in baseball, leaders focus on getting people up to bat, grinding out hits, moving people into scoring positions, and then bringing them home. Dan Beam, when he was vice-president of retail store operations for Joseph Magnin, explained how top management resisted his efforts to design a company-wide management development retreat. "Fine," he said, "I'll design it first just for my own managers." After the president got a chance to see his design, it was decided that this would be great for all of the company's management team.

The natural drive for autonomy in most people is what the leader is trying to tap. If you and I are sitting at a table predicting the probability of pulling my number out of a hat, I will predict that I have a much better chance of winning if I know that it's *my* hand that will do the picking rather than yours (even though the odds are the same). The turnaround of one department store began when the regional manager told the local store manager that he had to do something to improve the store's performance but didn't specify what should be done. People in the store got together and talked about their situation. They visited their competitor's stores. They began coming up with lots of ideas for ways to improve the store's design, appearance, merchandising, and the like. Many of the changes were small—a fresh coat of paint, clean restrooms, more interesting display setups—but each change was a small win making people feel increasingly capable. Small wins are just what people need to get themselves all fired up and going.

This is only one part of the natural diffusion process. The other part relies on sensitivity to people's interests and desires and the ability to frame issues and problems so that they are in alignment with those interests. A humorous illustration of this point is the Blondie cartoon in which Dagwood complains to the cook that the chicken croquettes are too small, and after trying one, adds, "and they taste horrible." The cook replies: "Then you're lucky they're small."[10] Employees who don't know that they have a problem are unlikely to be receptive to your helpful suggestions. The knack is giving people feedback about their progress and being in a position to provide assistance when they say, "I wonder if I could be doing this better?" Trevor Holm discovered this when he tried to institute several new procedures at the Australia Post Office, including a new sales program. Not everyone in the organization was excited about taking the time to generate the data needed for start-up, so he began by finding out what problems other departments were experiencing and in what ways he might be able to alleviate their problems—if he got certain information from them. He reframed the situation from "help me by giving me these data" to "by giving me these data, you can help solve your problems."

Obtaining Commitment

The small win process makes people feel like winners. In turn, people who feel like winners have a heightened interest in continuing with the journey. Getting people to take action is at the heart of the commitment process. To act is to commit oneself. Leaders who lead by example serve as visible models of men and women committed to a course of action. The leader's challenge is getting and keeping other people committed. In our studies, descriptions of personal bests and extraordinary accomplishments almost always recognized the importance of building, "one hop at a time," people's commitment to the task or program. In this section, we want to explain the psychological processes underlying the commitment phenomenon.[11]

People are likely to become committed to a course of action when three conditions are present: when they experience a sense of choice about their decision, when their actions (choices) are made visible to others, and when their choices are difficult to back out of or revoke. Getting others committed is important to leaders because commitment to one behavior has implications for a variety of other behaviors. Today's actions carry you into the future. Making a choice automatically leads you to resolve any internal doubts or inconsistencies between your attitudes and behavior.

Making a choice and acting upon it make the act more difficult to change. Once people have "signed up" for the project and put many hours into its success, they are unlikely to easily give up. Giving up implies an admission that they made a mistake and that their previous efforts were worthless. Being committed is a binding process. A small win gets people committed, because it makes it easy for them to take the first step.

Give People a Sense of Choice. What does it mean to experience a sense of choice? Essentially, it means that you feel personally responsible for the decision or action. It was your own choice; you were not forced. You had alternatives, and this was the one that you selected. There were no overwhelmingly external reasons for taking this action. You had a realistic picture of what this alternative would entail when you chose it, and consequently there is no one and no factor other than yourself to "blame" for this choice, decision, or action.

Choice is the cement that binds one's actions to the person, motivating individuals to accept the implications of their acts. It is the personal acceptance of responsibility for your actions. A good example of the power of choice in creating commitment comes from an internal study done by Texas Instruments. They found that the best predictor of a project's failure or success was whether people had volunteered or had been assigned to the project.[12] Think about it: by having people choose to do something, you create a situation that makes it more difficult for them to say that they didn't want to do it. *Choosing* to do something implies both a willingness and a capability to achieve the desired results. Choice unleases the power of expectations. In choosing, people are indicating their belief that they can do what is required. People who expect to succeed are considerably more likely to be successful than those who don't expect to do well.

The Soul of a New Machine, Tracy Kidder's Pulitzer Prize-winning account of the design of a new computer by a special project group at Data General, describes the process that Tom West used to get people committed to the project.[13] Almost every member of the project team passed through the initiation rite called "signing up." By signing up for the project, a person agreed to do whatever was necessary for the project to succeed. This could mean forsaking family, friends, hobbies, and all vestiges of a nonwork life until the project was completed—when, of course, a new round of getting people signed up would be started for the next project.

What is important in the "choice" process is making certain that people feel that they really have an alternative. A forced decision between working on a particular project and looking for a new job in another company would probably fail the test of choice. Accentuating the intrinsic rewards of the tasks rather than an external rationale will also create higher levels of commitment. Employees who are working hard primarily for the big bucks are unlikely to be able to sustain the energy and effort over the long haul. It's too easy for them to say, "Well, I never really liked the work or believed we could make it work successfully. I was just doing it for the money."

Finally, leaders make certain that they provide a realistic picture of the journey before asking people to sign up. The New York investment banking house of Morgan Stanley encourages job candidates to discuss the demands of the job with their spouses, because new recruits sometimes work 100 hours a week. The firm's managing directors and their spouses will take promising candidates, along with their significant others, out to dinner to bring home to them what they will face. They want to make certain that a candidate whose family will not be comfortable with these job demands will not consider taking a position with Morgan Stanley.[14]

Make Choices Visible to Others. Commitment is also more likely if choices are made visible. Taking public actions is tangible, undeniable evidence of people's belief in the purposefulness of their behavior. In addition, by making our choices and actions public, we become subject to other people's review and observation. For example, testimonials in church or in a behavior change program such as Weight Watchers make an individual's level of commitment quite visible to others. Visibility makes it nearly impossible for people to deny their choice or to claim that they forgot about it. The use of uniforms and dress codes, even codes that suggest that one can wear whatever one wants, can be seen as making visible the individual's association with the organization.

Signetics was able to achieve its goal of warranting zero defects through the efforts of all of its people. Each of the more than 9,000 employees demonstrated his or her commitment by signing unit pledges to the quality program. These signed posters were mounted on the walls throughout the corporation. They visibly reminded everyone, from the corporate management on down, that Signetics was seriously committed to quality. Visibility is also highly significant in that each member of the group serves as a role model for others. Leaders set the stage and by enabling others to act make it possible for members of the team to visibly demonstrate their own levels of commitment. Indeed, when everyone around you is contributing, and you can see this for yourself, not doing your part is difficult to excuse, even to yourself. Motivation to deliver on commitments is facilitated when individuals' performance is public.

A good example of the "going public" process is found at Solectron. Every morning before the assembly line starts, there is a management meeting, which begins with each production supervisor standing up and announcing output and reliability levels from the previous day. A different person each morning tabulates the oral reports and summarizes the company's results. Before the meeting is over, each production supervisor will once again stand up before the group and announce his or her estimated production run for that day. Leaders foster visibility by publicizing the activities of their group members, both individual and collective. They use ceremonies and symbols to promote identification. These extend from regular Friday beer busts at Tandem Computers to graduation ceremonies at Scandinavian Design's "University," from Versatec's "I Care" desk plaques to Intel's commemorative "I Survived the 125" mugs. The "125% Solution" was Intel's response to a prolonged industry slump. Employees were asked to work an extra two hours a day without pay to speed product development and enhance their units' effectiveness. When Intel ended the 125% Solution, celebrations were held for the employees, with refreshments, music, and special fifteen-ounce mugs (25 percent more than the usual mug).

Leaders encourage people to talk about the organization and their project with others; in particular, with people outside of work. This is one of the reasons why Mary Kay Cosmetics gives its most outstanding salespeople pink Cadillacs. Pink Cadillacs are "trophies on wheels." "I want everyone in town," says company founder Mary Kay Ash, "to know that this person has been successful." In this process, the salespeople's attachment to the organization is made so visible that they cannot escape being identified with their organization.

Create Choices That Are Hard to Revoke. For people to become committed to a choice, it is not enough that it merely be public; it must be a choice that cannot be easily changed. Choices that are hard to change increase your investment in the decision; such choices are not trivial. The nontriviality of a choice is often indicated by the behavior of the party offering it. For instance, consider why both large companies such as Procter & Gamble, Morgan Guaranty Trust, and IBM and such smaller organizations as Avantek, Megatrend, and ShareData make it so difficult for people to join their organizations. Professor Richard Pascale describes how companies such as these subject candidates for employment to a selection process "so rigorous that it often seems designed to discourage individuals rather than encourage them to take the job."[15] They grill their applicants, telling them the bad side as well as the good, and make sure they're not overselling the position. At Procter & Gamble and Hewlett-Packard, the process is likely to include as many as six different days of interviews, as well as a day in the field with key sales or field engineering personnel. While the process weeds out many applicants, the ratio of acceptances to job offers is fairly high. After all, think about the process at this point from the applicant's position: "I must really want this job if I am willing to spend so much energy trying to get hired. If they offer me a job after all this, I'll be sure to accept it."

The irreversibility of your behavior fosters commitment because in taking an action that cannot be retrieved you are required to find and accept salient arguments that support and justify it. This process creates a strong *internalized* rationale that deepens personal responsibility and belief in the correctness of your actions. You convince yourself that the course of action you took was the proper one, which minimizes any misgivings about alternatives not selected. Leaders understand the intensity of this process so that when they find it necessary to change a previous course of action, perhaps set by a predecessor, they provide people with *external* justifications for the predicament in which they find themselves. Typically, external rationales—for instance, this is something anyone would have done, the circumstances demanded it—make people feel that they are *not* solely responsible for their behavior. This reduces not only any pain associated with the mistake but makes it easier for people to "explain away" any personal responsibility for their mistakes and readies them to commit to a new course.

Building strong social and interpersonal ties within the project team makes it more difficult for people to leave. At the same time, it reinforces group standards regarding productive work norms. However, there are times when a leader may want to reverse the commitment-building process. Leaders know how difficult it is to change old habits and patterns, so when they want to make significant changes they may have to unbind people from their choices of actions. For example, moving people around, bringing in new people, and discouraging informal social interactions will minimize people's commitment levels.

Additional Methods for Strengthening Commitment. It is interesting that while getting people committed is one of the leader's most significant strategies, the topic is seldom mentioned in most principles of management textbooks. Psychologists, however, have long studied this binding process. Many of their prescriptions for strengthening commitment—and for getting others to *want* to do something—are consistent with the leadership practices that we have been describing.[16] For example, the strategies used to empower people are quite similar to those used to strengthen commitment. People feel strong when they take part in setting goals and their jobs offer discretion and self-determination. At the same time, having discretion and the right to freely choose your own actions increases personal commitment to these tasks.

Making people's actions visible by publicizing and recognizing their work strengthens others in two ways. First, it opens doors to potential new relationships because people are more aware of one another's contributions. Success is an attractive magnet for pulling people together and increasing their attachment to the project. Second, publicity calls attention to the significance of people's actions, creating both internal and external expectations that an action is worthy of their own and others' time and energy. County supervisor Sunne McPeak points out that building stable political coalitions is often based on making certain that participants' involvement is publicized. "Good press," she notes, "is an essential political currency." While publicizing other people's actions heightens their sense of personal power, it builds commitment because it makes it more difficult for people to disassociate themselves from the actions and activities that they were recognized for. It is simply more compelling to find reasons to support our previous course of action than to admit that we were duped or foolish.

McPeak also knows that giving people significant work to do increases their attachment to the project. Letting them make decisions in their areas of responsibility, she points out, builds ownership so that individuals take a personal interest in the outcome of their investment. Not only does giving people meaningful work strengthen them by building their competencies but commitment is enhanced when people feel that their jobs are intrinsically rewarding and are part of a means to some greater end. Thus, those jobs become hard to leave. Meaningful work is more likely to strengthen people's commitment to their jobs and to the company than work that has no significance or challenge. In the former case, you do the work because you want to, not because someone else is telling you to. Also, both commitment and the sense of power are enhanced when people don't feel closely supervised or monitored by the leader.

It is also clear that leading by example, which we discussed in the last chapter, is a perfect illustration of the process of commitment. Leaders make choices and, especially from the follower's perspective, are believed to have considerable latitude in what they say and do. Leaders always have an audience. Their behavior is quite public and conspicuously visible to others. The leader's actions tend to be binding because they are irrevocable: leaders take a position and stake their reputation on the prescribed course of action.

Commitment Number 8: Plan Small Wins That Promote Consistent Progress and Build Commitment

The ancient philosophers remarked that "the journey of a thousand miles begins with the first step." It is leaders who get us started. They convince us that the impossible is possible. They show us the way. Planning small wins moves us off dead center. Small wins breed success and compel us down the path. Experiments, pilot projects, and skunkworks (innovative off-line programs) all facilitate the process of getting started. Breaking problems into manageable chunks keeps people's capacities from being overwhelmed. Remembering that executives have only nine minutes, on average, before being interrupted encourages leaders to be focused in their aspirations and actions. Moving with the tide and spreading the good news make the journey both less traumatic and more fun.

Planning small wins is all about getting people to change and to remain on the new path. Commitment—staying the course—is facilitated when you feel that you have a choice to make, other people know about your choice, and you can't easily deny or back out of your actions.

Modeling the way requires being clear about your personal values. It demands being a role model and demonstrating to others what is expected of them. Modeling the way means planning the journey so that many opportunities for collecting small wins are provided. And modeling the way produces the ingredients needed for getting, and keeping, people committed. Here are six strategies that you can employ to facilitate the small wins process:

1. *Make a plan.* We have devoted the majority of this book to discussing the behavioral side of getting others to want to achieve exceptional results. That has been intentional, since most of what people told us involved the human dimension. But it would be misleading to say that people will commit themselves to a course of action that is unconscious and unarticulated. High performance projects are carefully planned. No mountain climber would ever think of just setting out to scale a summit without selecting a route, choosing a competent team, assembling proper food and equipment, and so on. Every personal best we examined was characterized by attention to the details of planning and preparation.

There are a few things to keep in mind when planning. First, your planning should be driven by your values and vision, not by technique. There are many useful planning tools, but none should determine what you want to do. Second, involve in the planning process as many as you can of the people who will have to implement the plan. Remember, both empowerment and commitment are increased through choice, and involvement in planning increases people's discretion over what they do. Third, break the project into manageable chunks. Specifying needed events and milestones is one of the greatest benefits of planning. Fourth, use the planning process as a means of getting people to mentally walk through the entire journey. This act of visualizing the events, milestones, tasks, and goals enables people to both anticipate the future and imagine their success.

2. *Make a model.* One very effective way to get started on the road to success is to select one site or program with which to experiment. Use it as a model of what you would like to do in other programs or locations. Your model should probably not be in your highest profile operation, which may be too visible and subject to too much outside interference. As we noted earlier, Sam Neaman did this with the Indianapolis McCrory's store. He started by asking people to look at their competition and then come back to the store and determine what they could do to improve. They experimented with every aspect of the store, starting with changing the floor layout, widening the aisles, and painting the walls. There were regular meetings, and they celebrated reaching every milestone. As a result of their efforts, employees created a model store that everyone else wanted to see. General William Creech also began turning around the performance of the Tactical Air Command on a trial basis, in a few installations, by creating smaller units with more involvement between the operational squadron and its companion maintenance group.[17]

Do not, however, require that every project or facility do it in exactly the same way as the model. One of the things that increases people's commitment is a sense that what they are doing has its own distinctive image and is unique. If people are forced to copy the model, they will not develop a feeling of ownership for it. Instead, use the model as a visual aid in teaching people about the principles of achieving excellence, and then challenge them to improve on it and adapt it to their environments.

3. *Take one hop at a time.* Once you have set your sights, move forward in incremental steps. Do not attempt to accomplish too much at once, especially in the beginning. Provide orientation and training at the start of every new project, even if the members of the team are experienced. The group may never have worked together as a unit and the project is likely to be unique. Every new project has a shakedown period.

The key to getting started is *do*ability. Identify something that people feel that they can do with existing skills and resources; this, of course, makes it easier for people to say yes. Make sure you include a few early successes in your plan. There is nothing more discouraging than being confronted initially with tasks that you don't know how to do and at which you know you will fail. It's like learning to ski. You start on the beginner's slope, then work your way up to the advanced.

Keep people focused on the meaning and significance of the vision, but also remind them to take it one day at a time, or one hour at a time if necessary. Implement things in small, planned chunks. It is a lot more efficient to count one hundred cards by stacking them in ten piles of ten than it is to count them in one stack of one hundred. Why? Because you will inevitably be interrupted, lose your place, and have to start all over again. Try it sometime. There are countless little daily steps that can be taken to signify progress. If your task is to improve the productivity of your plant, painting the walls and refurbishing the bathrooms, such as Debi Coleman at Apple Computer did, are little things that move in that direction. Phil Turner had the machines that spool wire in Raychem's Wire and Cable plant torn down, repaired, and reassembled one by one instead of trying to do them all at once. It is a lot more productive to make a little progress daily, than it is to attempt to do the whole task all at once, as any college student who pulls an all-nighter before final exams knows too well.

The same is true for other work activities such as writing reports and memoranda. The one-page memo and the executive summary are ways you encourage people to read what you have written. Meetings are other events that we can break into smaller pieces. You can have people stand instead of sit, or you can break the large group into sub-groups, as Jan Halper did, to work on different agenda items.

Be certain to make progress very visible. Some manufacturing plants now use electronic signs controlled by a computer to visibly display hourly or daily progress. If you do not have access to high-tech hardware, a cardboard sign will do. The point is to let people know how they are doing in a timely manner. We cannot imagine any sports team that would wait until the end of the game for some official to tell them the score. Also, schedule regular opportunities for people to meet to discuss progress and problems. Davey's weekly breakfasts at PG&E is an example of this.

4. *Reduce the cost of saying yes.* If you want people to take risks and experiment, you have to be prepared for mistakes to be made. It is easier for people to say yes when you can minimize the costs of their potential mistakes. For example, in teaching would-be pilots to fly an airplane, a colleague of ours lets them make mistakes, but he doesn't let them crash. Most people are risk aversive, so it is more important to reduce the negative consequences of a new action or behavior than to enhance the positive consequences or payoffs. Reducing the costs of failure makes it easier to take the first step and facilitates the experimenting and learning processes in an organization.

In getting people to make commitments to actions, it is also wise to get them to say yes a number of times, not just once. That is the effect of multiple interviews on job candidates. Each time they agree to return for another interview, they are saying yes to the company. Find ways to get people to publicly state their agreements more than once.

5. *Use the natural diffusion process.* There are two ways to bring about change: you can force it or you can let it happen naturally. The former is faster, but it increases resistance and can be extremely expensive. The latter is slower, but it tends to receive greater acceptance. Wherever possible, you should make use of the natural dynamics of change. That does not mean you must sit idly by while people slowly learn to accept new ideas. Rather you should understand how change works and put that knowledge to productive use.

For example, it is widely known, by sales people as well as change agents, that an innovation that offers the promise of solving a persistent and difficult problem and that is a clear advantage over existing solutions for a critical mass of people will have a higher degree of acceptance than one that appeals only to a select group or does not appear to address a felt need. You stand a better chance of gaining acceptance of and commitment to an innovation if you show people how they will benefit from it. Sales people call this "benefit selling." So, when you begin a change effort in your organization, clearly communicate the benefits of the change; do not assume that they are obvious to others just because they are obvious to you.

It is well understood that innovations are more easily adopted if they seem to be compatible with accepted values and norms. Rather than position changes as something new and revolutionary, it is better to show how they fit into the already accepted beliefs and expectations of the company and the individuals. Changes that are easy to understand and to implement will be accepted far more quickly than those that are not. This is what is often referred to as "user friendly" in technology. User friendly changes are more likely to succeed. So keep things simple, design them for use at the skill level of the largest number of potential users, and provide training where necessary. Champions and opinion leaders are also natural allies in the diffusion process. Successful innovations are always strongly advocated by influential people. Find highly respected individuals or groups in the organization who might agree with you and have them introduce the change with their peers.

6. *Give people choices and make choices highly visible.* You need to give people choices about what to accomplish and how to accomplish it in order to build commitment and create ownership. Making people feel like owners is important—after all, when was the last time you washed a rental car? Unless people have choices to make, they aren't really exercising responsibility. So talk it over with your team. What needs to be done? Who is going to do what? What decisions will they have to make along the way? If you've established a clear vision and have consensus and strong feelings about the right way to do things in your organization, then you've created the necessary conditions for the paradox of "guided autonomy"—people on your team have autonomy, but they understand the ball park within which decisions and reponsibilities must be carried out. Finally, by making visible the choices that people have made you create binding-in forces that increase the energy and drive directed at accomplishing and succeeding with the task. With the team assembled, let people know what choices others have made. Better yet, let others tell their peers what they have decided to do and why. Publicize the decisions in newsletters, memos, and posters. The halls of IBM's San Jose research facility are lined with posters

signifying individual's commitment to quality. Each poster includes the person's photograph and personal statement about what quality means to him or her. Each poster is personally, and prominently, signed.

Once people get started, your job is to keep the ball rolling. We describe a variety of techniques that leaders use to keep momentum going in the next section, "Encouraging the Heart."

PART SIX

Encouraging the Heart

Love 'em and lead 'em.
>——*Major General John H. Stanford,*
>*Commander,*
>*Military Traffic Management*
>*U.S. Army*

Getting extraordinary things done in organizations is hard work. The climb to the summit is arduous and steep. Leaders encourage others to continue the quest. They inspire others with courage and hope.

Leaders give heart by visibly recognizing people's contributions to the common vision. With a thank-you note, a smile, an award, and public praise, the leader lets others know how much they mean to the organization.

Leaders express pride in the accomplishments of their teams. They make a point of telling the rest of the organization about what the teams have achieved. They make people feel like heroes.

Hard work can also be fun work. Hoopla is important to a winning team. Everybody loves a parade. Leaders find ways to celebrate accomplishments. They take time out to toast a milestone with champagne.

And what sustains the leader? From what source comes the leader's courage? The answer is love. Leaders are in love—in love with the people who do the work, with what their organizations produce, and with their customers.

In the next two chapters, we see how leaders:

- Recognize Contributions.
- Celebrate Accomplishments.

11

Recognize Contributions: Linking Rewards with Performance

If you don't show your appreciation to your people, then they're going to stop caring, and then you are going to find yourself out of business.

——*LuAnn Sullivan,*
Branch Manager,
Wells Fargo Bank

"I was teaching math to sixth-graders. We were working with students who had been 'low performers' and felt like they were already failures in math. Their attention spans seemed to be about two minutes long! The challenge was to increase their speed and accuracy in solving math problems." So begins Cheryl Breetwor's "personal best"—her story about a time when she accomplished something extraordinary in an organization. Breetwor, who went on to direct investor relations for Rolm Corporation before starting her own company (ShareData), chose this experience as a sixth-grade teacher as one of her personal bests. Why?

"Because it's all about how you make work fun and rewarding. We wanted to show these kids they could win. If you can do that, you can get the best out of anybody," explains Breetwor. "And, what's more, I knew we could do it!" Every day, Breetwor handed out awards—awards primarily for "speed, skill, and accuracy" but also for persistence. Breetwor used these opportunities to recognize the small wins and milestones reached by the kids on their path toward mastering mathematical fundamentals.

In our personal best case studies, it was not unusual for
people to report working sixty-, seventy-, even eighty-hour work
weeks. Along the way, some people may be tempted to give up.
To persist for months at such a pace, people need encouragement.
Literally, they need the heart to continue with the journey. One
important way that leaders give heart to others is by recognizing
individual contributions. When participants in our workshops
and seminars summarize the five or six key leadership practices
that make a difference in getting extraordinary things accomplished in organizations, recognizing people's contributions is
on every list.

But there is much more at stake here than simply recognizing individuals for their contributions. Consider the other elements in Breetwor's personal best story: (1) her high expectations
for the students and her self-confidence that she could help them
achieve those expectations; (2) her ability to directly link the
students' performance and the rewards that they earned; (3) her
creative use of rewards—besides grades—such as stickers, gold
stars, fun pages, and the like; and (4) her positive and hopeful
outlook. Putting into practice these four factors provides leaders
leverage so that by recognizing contributions, they can stimulate
and motivate the internal drives within individuals.

High Expectations: Enabling Others to Achieve Their Best

Successful leaders have high expectations, both of themselves and of their followers. These expectations are powerful,
because they are the frames into which people fit reality. In this
way, you see what you expect to see, rather than what may be
actually occurring. Social psychologists have referred to this as
the Pygmalion effect, based on a Greek myth about Pygmalion, a
sculptor who carved a statue of a beautiful woman, fell in love
with the statue, and brought it to life by the strength of his perceptions. Leaders play Pygmalion-like roles in developing people.

One of the clearest and most often mentioned responses by
subordinates at all levels to the question "What is the difference
between leaders and managers?" is that leaders bring out the best
in us. They get us to achieve even more than we originally
believed possible ourselves. Their belief creates a self-fulfilling

prophecy—we do as we are expected to do. Psychologists have found that rats whose handlers are told that they are "maze bright" run mazes more quickly than do rats introduced to their handlers as slow; students presented to their teachers as intellectual bloomers do better on achievement tests than do their counterparts who lack such a positive introduction; and job trainees pointed out to their supervisors as having special potential have higher actual job performance than do trainees not so identified.[1]

Leaders treat people in a way that leads to extraordinary achievements. The leader's expectations have their strongest and most powerful influence in times of uncertainty and turbulence. When accepted ways of doing things are not working well enough, then a leader's strong expectations about the destination, the processes to follow, and the capabilities of the team to complete the journey serve to make dreams come true.

It is also true that leaders have a high degree of self-confidence. To be sure, some people mentioned that they were nervous or anxious on the eve of their personal bests, but each was also ready for the plunge. Each was excited by and willing to accept the challenges they faced, either by circumstance or by choice. Without exception or hesitation, these people expressed confidence that they could work well with others and assemble a team to address whatever problems might lie ahead. The high expectations that leaders have of others are based in large part on their expectations of themselves. This is why leaders model the way. What gives their expectations for others credibility is their own records of achievement, dedication, and daily demonstrations of what and how things need to be done.

What's more, leaders tend not to give up on people, because doing so means giving up on themselves, their judgment, and their ability to get the best out of other people. Cheryl Breetwor was convinced that she was a good enough teacher to improve that group of sixth-graders' math skills. She never gave up on them. She never gave up on herself.

Often you are not aware that your behavior toward people is based upon your expectations about them. Systematic studies indicate that people communicate their expectations primarily by the character of the socioemotional support and encouragement that they provide people. Treating people in a friendly, pleasant, and positive fashion and being attentive to their needs produce increased performance because of the favorable effect on employee motivation. When you have high expectations of others, you also tend to give them more *input*—that is, more suggestions, helpful hints, and responsive answers to their questions—and more *feedback* about the results of their efforts. Both of these factors enhance the employee's learning such that competencies and mastery are achieved rather than mistakes repeated or ineffective habits ingrained. Finally, the standards of performance (or *output* levels) that you set communicate what your expectations of them are and, in turn, affect their own levels of aspiration. Pygmalion in the workplace is a reciprocal process whereby leaders' expectations affect the expectations of their constituents about how hard to try and how far to reach.

Linking Performance and Rewards

The outcomes of our present actions play a major role in determining our future actions. People repeat behavior that is rewarded, avoid behavior that is punished, and drop or forget behavior that produces neither result.[2] If extra hard work and long hours on a project go unnoticed and unrewarded, people will probably soon find ways to minimize their efforts. That's why manufacturing support manager Russ Douglass used what he called *"spot strokes:* instant payoffs like 'have this lunch on me' or 'take the afternoon off.' Sometimes we'd put on a party in the parking lot on a half-hour notice."

One of the oldest, most important, and strongest prescriptions for influencing employee motivation is to tie job-related outcomes (such as rewards and recognition) to job effort and/or performance.[3] If a concern for quality is desired, then rewards should be given to those who consistently meet quality standards, and low-quality performers should not be rewarded until they conform to this norm. Janet Scacciotti, of the Old Stone Bank, wanted to increase employees' attention to customer service. She instituted a "Smile Program": when a customer or supervisor is impressed by an employee's attitude or behavior, they give that employee a "smile" check as recognition of the importance of providing good customer service. Putting the photographs of such employees in the bank's in-house newsletter serves to reinforce and call attention to desired behaviors.

Another example of a specific performance-reward linkage comes from Jack Welch, CEO of General Electric. When Welch was an up-and-coming group executive, he had a special telephone installed in his office with a private number that was made available to all the purchasing agents in his group. If the agents ever got a price concession from a vendor, they could phone Welch on his special telephone. Whether he was making a million-dollar deal or chatting with his secretary, Welch would interrupt what he was doing, take the call, and say, "That's wonderful news; you just knocked a nickel per ton off the price of steel." Then straightaway, he'd sit down and scribble out a congratulatory note to the agent.[4]

There are three key criteria for an integrated performance-reward system: make certain that people know what is expected of them, provide feedback about performance, and reward only those who meet the standards. While in practice it is not always easy to meet these objectives, their significance should not be underestimated.[5] We have found that successful leaders work more skillfully and diligently than others to see that the system does work.

Reward systems work best when performance can be measured accurately and objectively. When objective standards are difficult to set and performance measures are subjective, the acceptance of performance appraisals depends upon the extent to which employees trust those who make the evaluation decisions. That is one extremely important reason why the relationship between leaders and their followers must be founded upon mutual respect and trust. Another important characteristic of effective reward systems is that employees should be able to influence the work being measured. Officials at one airline offered incentives to pilots for on-time arrivals, but actual performance improved only slightly. What management failed to realize was that arriving on time is determined more by weather and traffic conditions than by any particular action taken by the pilots. Because of the importance of reward systems being based on attainable performance standards, the people affected should participate in establishing those standards.

Clear goals, feedback about results versus efforts, and rewards tied to performance achievement have been shown in a wide variety of organizational settings to improve the job performance of such diverse work groups as clerks in a small grocery store, mountain beaver trappers, engineers, telephone service crews, truck drivers, and salespeople.[6]

One production section in a B.F. Goodrich plant in Ohio was not performing well. After identifying some problems, the production manager introduced a performance-reward linked system. The program provided cost, scheduling, and goal-accomplishment information directly to the first-level supervisors once a week. Daily meetings were also held to discuss how each group in the plant was doing. Illustrative charts were developed that showed achievement as compared to objectives. Over a five-year period, production in this plant increased over 300 percent, while production costs decreased steadily.[7]

Another example of how specific performance-reward linkages affect behavior comes from the Big Boy Restaurant System (Marriott Corporation). Traditionally, store managers were evaluated only on profits and on other somewhat subjective factors. These factors, however, were not the ones that customers used in deciding whether to patronize the stores. In an effort to be more customer oriented and to focus the attention of store managers on the customer, the performance-reward criteria were changed. Now, in addition to sales and profit, all store managers are assessed on customer satisfaction measures, such as store cleanliness, employee friendliness, and promptness of service.

Social psychologists and leaders alike have found that rewards usually work better than punishment. Punishment may be necessary for continuous poor performance. Unfortunately, what punishment usually teaches people is how to avoid being punished—not the same as doing things right. The challenge is to "catch people doing something right" and then to let them know it.[8] One Southern California hospital has institutionalized this challenge through the use of "Catch Me" buttons for employees. Every time a manager or fellow employee catches—notices—someone else doing something right, he or she tells that person about it and in return gets that person's button. The buttons are redeemed at the end of the month for further prizes and awards.

Using a Variety of Rewards

There are many types of rewards that you can use to recognize the effort and contributions of your team members. Indeed, the creative use of rewards often distinguishes leaders from managers. Leaders tend not to be dependent upon the organization's formal reward system, which offers only a limited range of options. After all, promotions and raises are very limited and scarce resources and cannot be applied frequently. On the other hand, verbal or written praise, "spot strokes," buttons, and other informal and more personal rewards are almost unlimited resources. Relying upon an organization's formal reward system typically requires considerable effort as well. In one study, we found that the time lapse between performance and promotion, for example, is seldom less than six months. Most organizations' performance appraisal systems allow for raises and any other merit awards to be handed out only once per year.[9]

Instead of relying only on formal rewards, leaders make tremendous use of *intrinsic* rewards—rewards that are built into the work itself, including such factors as a sense of accomplishment, a chance to be creative, and the challenge of the work—immediate outcomes of an individual's effort.[10] For Cheryl Breetwor at ShareData, an intrinsic reward is giving people the satisfaction and pleasure of being able to list on the wall each new customer installation along with their own names. But intrinsic rewards are also, as the Apple University staff at Apple Computer pointed out, as subtle as "a helping hand" and "listening without interrupting." Other more personal currencies include lunch with the boss, a night out on the company, tickets for the ball game or theater, and the afternoon off.

Some managers make the mistake of assuming that individuals respond only to money. Although salary increases or bonuses are certainly appreciated, individual needs for and appreciation of rewards extend much further. Verbal recognition of performance in front of one's peers and visible awards, such as certificates, plaques, and other tangible gifts, are powerful rewards. Spontaneous and unexpected rewards are often more meaningful than the expected formal rewards. The motivational impact of Christmas bonuses, for example, is limited, because they are expected, and the only unknown is what their amount will be. Many employees consider these "bonuses" as part of their annual salary expectations, not as something extra for their efforts during a particular year. During one very difficult trek across an ice field in Don Bennett's hop to the top of Mount Rainier, his daughter stayed by his side four hours and with each new hop told him, "You can do it, Dad. You're the best dad in the world. You can do it, Dad." This spontaneous act of verbal encouragement kept Bennett going, strengthening his commitment to make it to the top. Bennett told us that there was no way he would quit hopping to the top with his daughter yelling words of love and encouragement in his ear.

Praise and coaching are significant forms of recognition. For example, few managers make enough use of one very powerful but terribly inexpensive two-word reward of thank you. Personal congratulations rank at the top of the most powerful non-financial motivators identified by employees.[11] There are few, if any, more basic needs than to be noticed, recognized, and appreciated for our efforts. And that's true from the maintenance staff right on up to the executive suite. There's little wonder, then, that a greater volume of thank-yous is reported in highly innovative companies than in low-innovation firms.[12] Extraordinary achievements do not come easily and seldom bloom in barren and unappreciative settings.

Larry Frost, as senior vice-president of Wells Fargo Bank, put a bell in the middle of the office. Every time someone made a loan, he or she got to ring it. The individual who made the sale was instantly recognized, and others were challenged to make a sale so that they, too, could ring the bell. At Mervyn's Department Stores, executives send note cards with "I heard something good about you" printed at the top to other officers, clerks, buyers, trainers, and other line employees. Where are they likely to end up after being received? You find them on bulletin boards, office desks, filing cabinets, drinking fountains, and stockroom walls. Many are mounted and framed. Sharon Kneeland, when she was manager of employee development at Eaton Corporation, handed out brightly colored, often humorous stickers whenever she could to employees who had shown "extra effort" on some assignment. At the end of the month, she held "sticker redemption nights" where employees could exchange the stickers for food and beverages.

Such actions provide a healthy opportunity for recognition. They make visible the efforts of people that help the group meet its goals. For example, the "Super Person of the Month" award at North American Tool and Die Company is given to the person who contributes most to the company's achieving its goal of "No Rejects." A plaque and a check for $50 accompany the award, which is given at a public ceremony.

Certainly, you can't buy people's commitment—to get them to care, to stay late, or come in early—with ringing bells, thank you notes, stickers, or plaques. Social scientist Daniel Yankelovich points out that overall organizational effectiveness and efficiency depend on employees' personal dedication and sense of responsibility. You get these intangibles, he says, "only when people are motivated to work hard, to give of themselves."[13] The public recognition that Tom Melohn gives the NATD employees is one way he is able to show that he cares and to heighten the employees' sense of caring. With this kind of motivation, leaders are able to help others get extraordinary things accomplished.

Consider the case of Albert "Smitty" Smith, room service captain for Marriott's Marquis in Atlanta. National Football League (NFL) teams playing in Atlanta had been staying with the Marriott for several years when one of its local competitors substantially reduced its rates and some teams began staying at that hotel instead. Smith was deeply disappointed. He loved football, and he wanted the NFL teams back at Marriott. So, whenever a team was staying at the competing hotel, Smith would take the day off and contact all of the coaches and team management to let them know that he was available to meet all of their special needs, which he understood after working with them for so many years. Each of the teams was so impressed by Smith's one-person marketing effort that they all returned to the Atlanta Marriott the following year. At Marriott's International Marketing Meeting, Smith was featured as the guest speaker on salesmanship and received a special leadership trophy from J. Willard Marriott, Jr. Following his remarks, the group gave Smith the first standing ovation to be received at any marketing meeting.[14]

You have to be constantly on the lookout for ways to spread the psychological benefits of making people feel like winners, because winners contribute in important ways to the success of their projects. Often you are like a mirror for the team—reflecting back to others what a job well done looks like and making certain not only that the members of the team know that they have done well but that others in the organization are aware of the group's effort and contributions. Of course, in this way, you also build the team's reputation and strengthen the members of the group.

Consider the impact of the "fabulous bragging sessions" held once per quarter at the corporate headquarters of Milliken and Company in Spartanburg, South Carolina. While attendance is voluntary, as many as 200 people participate in each Corporate Sharing Rally, as the sessions are called. Dozens of teams of workers from all areas of the company give crisp, five-minute reports in rapid-fire succession about improving product quality, describing their programs and quantifying their impact. Everyone who attends receives an award signed by the president and framed on the spot. And everyone who attends is likely to go back to one of the company's sixty plants with a host of ideas—not demands that have been forced on them by top management but suggestions from their peers about how all of them can be doing their jobs better and making their company more competitive and successful.[15] The "fabulous bragging sessions" are a wonderful example of providing recognition and celebrating people's accomplishments.

What happens when you provide both intrinsic and extrinsic rewards? Unfortunately, while the idea of an additive effect is intuitively appealing, it does not always occur. There is some evidence that intrinsic and extrinsic rewards are negatively related and may actually work against one another. For example, in a situation that is already intrinsically rewarding, the addition of extrinsic rewards may actually reduce the effectiveness of the intrinsic rewards.[16] This is what causes an amateur musician to avoid acquiring professional status or a starving artist to resist selling his or her paintings. On the other hand, some studies show that while achievement-oriented people do find success rewarding in and of itself, money and fame are also important rewards, serving as symbols of that success.[17] One executive referred to this as the "fun being in playing the game down on the field, while the results are posted on the scoreboard." What we found among leaders was not so much an either/or mentality as a both/and type of thinking. Leaders are remarkably skillful in using these two types of rewards in additive ways. Their success is due, no doubt, to their application of two important principles: first, leaders make certain that rewards are given in close proximity to the behavior they are trying to encourage. Second, leaders make the rewards contingent upon performance.[18]

Russ Douglass's spot strokes mentioned earlier are an excellent example of this. So is the Paul Revere insurance companies' Program for Ensuring that Everybody's Thanked (PEET). Each Monday morning, members of the executive committee get "PEET sheets" listing three quality team leaders and highlighting what their teams have been doing. Also noted are who visited the team last and when. The executive committee makes it a top priority to visit each of these teams during the week. There are also bronze, silver, and gold awards given to recognize each team member's contribution to "Paul Revere Quality."[19] The Limited Stores have a full-time manager of nonmonetary compensation, Lynn Buckmaster-Irwin. She produces the company's monthly magazine *Applause Applause!* Every issue features people who have earned (for example, a promotion) or won (for example, a sales contest) something—sometimes twenty to fifty people, sometimes over two hundred people—whose names and pictures are displayed.

Providing Courage

Through recognizing individual achievement, leaders give courage to their followers. This courage enables people to maintain composure during anxiety-producing situations and to endure hardships. Courage to continue the quest and hope in a positive future were central elements of Don Quixote's legacy: "to dream the impossible dream."

Research points to the role that "encouraging the heart" has upon motivation and physical stamina. One study involved soldiers undergoing a forced march.[20] They had just finished several weeks of intensive training and were competing for places in special units. Motivation was extremely high among the recruits;

failure to maintain the pace during the forced march meant losing the chance to join the special units. The soldiers were divided into four groups, which were unable to communicate with one another. All the men marched twenty kilometers (about twelve-and-a-half miles) over the same terrain on the same day. The first group was told how far they were expected to go and were kept informed of their progress along the way. The second group was told only that "this is the long march you hear about." These soldiers never received any information about the total distance they were expected to travel. Along the way, they were given no information about how far they had marched. The third group was told to march fifteen kilometers, but when they had gone fourteen kilometers, they were told that they had to go six kilometers farther. The fourth group was told that they had to march twenty-five kilometers, but when they reached the fourteen-kilometer mark, they were told that they had only six more kilometers to go.

The groups were assessed as to which had the best performance and which endured the most stress. The results indicated that the soldiers who knew exactly how far they had to go and where they were during the march were much better off than the soldiers who didn't get this information. The next-best group was the soldiers who thought that they were marching only fifteen kilometers. Third best was the group told to march a longer distance, then given the good news at the fourteen-kilometer mark. Those who performed worst were the soldiers who received no information about the goal (total distance) or the distance that they had already traveled (feedback). Blood tests taken during the march and again twenty-four hours later showed similar patterns. Blood levels of cortisol and prolactin (chemical substances whose levels rise as stress increases) were, as expected, highest for the group that knew the least about the march and lowest for those soldiers who knew exactly where they were and how much farther they were expected to go.

Even with highly motivated, achievement-oriented people, the type of leadership provided makes a definite difference in performance, in the levels of stress experienced, and in long-term healthiness. Leaders, as we have said before, need to provide people with a positive sense of direction. In the case of the marching soldiers, having a clear goal, even if it changed, produced superior results. People also produce best when they are given feedback about how they are progressing. Without feedback, though production (marching) may continue, it will be less efficient, and a significant toll will be taken in the form of increased levels of stress. Recognition signals successful accomplishment, reinforcing both employees' "I can do it" attitudes and the leader's expectations: "I knew you could do it." By giving people hope, you enable them to persevere and persist in moments of hardship and times of uncertainty and turbulence. Indeed, it is persistence that the CEOs of America's 100 fastest-growing small companies report as the vital factor underlying their organizations' success.[21] Often, says one company president, success is just a day-by-day grinding-out process. With hope, you make the impossible a possibility and then motivate people in their drive to transform the possible into reality.

Commitment Number 9: Recognize Individual Contributions to the Success of Every Project

Leaders have high expectations both of themselves and of their constituents. They create self-fulfilling prophecies about how ordinary people can persist and by doing so achieve extraordinary results. They provide people with clear directions, substantial encouragement, personal attention, and feedback. Along the way, feedback creates small wins that stimulate, rekindle, and focus people's energies and drive. When the journey is complete, feedback helps to ensure that learning takes place so that people acquire the competence that comes with experience.

Leaders make people winners, and winning people like to up the ante, raise the standards, and conquer the next mountain. They want to enlarge market share, lower costs, increase production, reduce reject rates, experiment with technologies and processes, and explore uncharted territories. Leaders recognize and reward what individuals do to contribute toward vision and values, goals, other people, and so on. And leaders express their appreciation far beyond the limits of the organization's formal performance appraisal systems. Leaders enjoy being spontaneous and creative in saying thank you—from sending personal notes, ringing the bell, and using stickers and buttons to just listening without interrupting. Leaders also cheerlead when it comes to the *group's* accomplishments. The next chapter adds to our discussion of individual recognition by focusing on how leaders encourage people to work together as a team. Here are seven strategies that you can use to recognize accomplishments:

1. *Develop tough measurable performance standards.* Earlier in this book we reported that strong-culture companies were characterized by high performance standards. Before you can design an adequate reward system you must clarify and communicate your standards. Those standards ought to be extraordinarily high, yet achievable. At North American Tool and Die (NATD), the standard is 99.9 percent acceptance of parts by all customers on all parts. It is intentionally 99.9 percent and not 100 percent. NATD has proven that 99.9 is achievable, while 100 percent is not as likely, even though they often achieve it.

Your performance standards must be linked directly to what is important to the success of your business. Make sure that your performance standards include what is important to the customer as well as what is important to management and stockholders. Not all organizations or business units will have the same priorities regarding standards. Accuracy, for example, has a higher value in the accounting department than in the research and development department, where innovation is at the top of the list. However, the company as a whole might set a high standard for everyone on "respect for the dignity and worth of the individual," for example. So develop performance standards that are relevant to each business unit as well as to the company as a whole.

2. *Install a formal systematic process for rewarding performance.* Once you have developed your standards, determine ways to measure them daily, and regularly reward people for their achievements. The annual performance appraisal is an adequate summary report for an entire year's performance, but employees should not have to wait twelve months to know how they are doing on every performance standard. Every reward system ought to meet these criteria: each employee must know (1) what the performance standards are, (2) how the standards will be measured, (3) how they are going to get feedback, and (4) what the relationship between their efforts and the available rewards is.

There are numerous ways to measure performance, from satisfaction surveys to electronic counters, from units sold to words typed per minute. The most powerful measurements are those that offer timely feedback and can be monitored by the employees themselves. No one could imagine designing a measurement system for driving in which only the police could determine how fast you were going. Instead, each automobile is equipped with a speedometer. Why, then, do we design feedback systems in business where only inspectors and managers (the police) have the tools to monitor performance?

3. *Be creative about rewards.* You need to use the organization's formal reward system to recognize people's achievements; however, that's not enough. People respond to all kinds of rewards other than promotions and raises. One shop foreman presented employees with new chairs after they achieved their production objectives. But a bigger reward, and even more pleasurable to the employees, was being called into the foreman's office, presented with the new chair, and being wheeled in the chair back to the work station by the foreman amidst the cheers of coworkers. One of our university colleagues takes his highest-performing students each term out for lunch and bowling to show his appreciation. In this chapter, we've already given examples of other creative rewards, such as "super person of the month" awards, photographs with the president, verbal encouragement, spot strokes, pictures in annual reports and company newsletters, and the life. Place your emphasis on noticing and recognizing small wins. Movements in the right direction warrant your personal seal of appreciation and encouragement to continue the effort.

4. *Let others help design the nonmonetary compensation system.* People become most excited about activities and events that they have had a hand in designing. When you involve others, you also are more likely to design a system in which rewards are closely linked to performance norms. Because it's *their* system, people will more strongly feel that they can influence it directly through their efforts. In an illustrative case, a hospital's CEO told the food service staff what a great job they were doing and how proud he was of their creativity and conscientiousness in showing that hospital food could be really imag-

inative and tasty. Though they were pleased with this feedback, what they really wanted was a chance to demonstrate just how good they were, that working in a hospital didn't mean that they were second-class restaurateurs and chefs. After some discussion, they initiated a Sunday buffet operation in the hospital cafeteria, complete with ice sculptures and a string quartet and open to the public. The crew's pride in their food preparation as they walked the line talking with customers (many of whom were on the hospital staff) created an atmosphere of sheer delight, increased their motivation, and was reflected in more efficient operations overall.

Of course, you should be cautious about making everything that people accomplish a reason for celebrating. For one thing, you don't want to replace people's intrinsic motivation (internal pleasure and satisfaction in the accomplishment itself) with external motivators or justifications ("I did it only for the reward"). You can also trivialize recognition to the point that it is taken for granted and so becomes meaningless or less a benefit than a right. In that case, the only payoff related to an extra bonus (such as one given at Christmas) comes when you don't deliver the expected reward, and that "payoff" is usually negative. However, in our studies, *over*doing recognition and celebrations was not a problem; more typically, the concern was about how to increase encouragement and recognition.

5. *Make recognition public.* Tell people that they have done well as soon as you find out about it. And let other people know about the accomplishment. When recognition is public, not only is a person's self-esteem bolstered, but his or her behavior serves as a model to others of what's right and how doing the right things will be noticed and rewarded. Recognition also helps to empower recipients by increasing their visibility. Public recognition builds commitment in that it makes people's actions visible to their peers and difficult to deny or revoke. At Stew Leonard's Dairy in Norwalk, Connecticut, mounting photographs of the employees recognizes their completion of the Dale Carnegie program and honors their commitment to enhancing their professional skills for the store's (as well as their own) benefit. Military organizations make tremendous use of medals and insignias—they are almost always handed out ceremoniously.

6. *Go out and find people who are doing things right.*
Rewards are most effective when they are highly specific and in
close proximity to the appropriate behavior. Selecting someone
as the employee of the month but never telling that person why
is not an effective use of recognition. You ought to say: "Sue was
selected as the employee of the month because she called five
different locations to locate an item the customer requested but
we did not have in stock. And because the store could not deliver
it until the next week, she went out of her way to personally pick
up the item on her way home from work so the customer could
have it in time for an important event. That is the kind of
behavior that makes us so highly valued by our customers.
Thank you, Sue. We award you this $50 check in appreciation of
your contribution to our organization."

Now in order to be able to provide such timely and specific
feedback you have to go out and find it. One of the most important results of being out and about as a leader is that you can
personally observe people doing things right and then reward
them on the spot or at the next public meeting. It is also advis-
able to have a system for collecting information from employees
and customers about people who are observed doing things right.
Weekly breakfast meetings are perfect opportunities to ask for
such incidents. Add to your agenda the question, "Who have
you seen do something special this week that has really helped
our business?"

7. *Coach.* Coaches don't wait until the season is over to let
their players know how they are doing; the same should be true
in your business. Coaching involves the on-the-job, day-by-day
spending of time with your people, talking with them about
your game strategies, and providing them feedback about their
efforts and performance. And when the game is over, you get
together with the players and analyze the results of your efforts.
Where did we do well? Where do we need to improve our efforts?
What will we have to do differently, better, or more of the next
time? And then it's practice and getting ready for the next game.
Even the grand masters in chess can recall each move in the
match and analyze the lessons to be learned for the next tournament play. The best teams in athletics and business always
emphasize the fundamentals of their game. In business, this

means being clear about your vision and values, which is what recognition and celebration should always be linked back to. We take up this issue in the next chapter.

12

Celebrate Accomplishments:
Valuing the Victories

When you give someone a check, don't mail it, have a celebration.

——*Renn Zaphiropoulos,*
President,
Versatec

We began the previous chapter with Cheryl Breetwor's personal best example of turning around the attitudes and math skills of her sixth-graders. Some days, the only rewards she handed out were for persistence. But these were the most significant achievements, for without persistence, there would be no other performance awards. Students received persistence awards because their classmates came to care about them. Peer encouragement to reach the goal was crucial, and so the kids helped each other out. What the kids remembered most about receiving an award was the applause from their classmates.

Russell Singleton, a project leader at KLA Instruments, recalled that he spent most of his time during his personal best wandering around, making sure that the different pieces of the project were moving along and that people "knew I cared about their part." He held meetings with the project team at the start of each work day, generally before the rest of the office and operating staff arrived. "We broke bread (sometimes doughnuts, or fruit) together each day," Singleton explained. "Everyone gave a status report of their progress and problems. Everyone had a personal goal for each day. The goals were short range and very visible. Everybody knew what everyone else was doing . . . and when we achieved good results, we would gather together and demo the result to the whole team. And cheer."

Cheerleading—not cheer managing—is a large part of the leader's function. After all, leaders can't get extraordinary things done in organizations alone—they need the help of their teams. The best quarterbacks in the National Football League are usually the first ones down the field to congratulate the receivers who carry their passes into the end zone. "Encouraging the heart" is not only the process of recognizing individual achievements; it also includes celebrating the efforts of the entire group. The persistence award is not left on the students' desks when they arrive in the morning; it is given out in a class celebration. The technical breakthroughs at KLA were demonstrated not to the boss's satisfaction but to the entire team's delight. What often distinguishes one department or unit from others in a large organization, researchers document, is the wide variety and frequency of celebratory and expressive events.[1]

Cheerleading and celebrating are the processes of honoring people and sharing with them in the sweet taste of success. When leaders cheerlead, they base their celebrations on three central principles: (1) focusing on key values, (2) making recognition publicly visible, and (3) being personally involved.

Cheering About Key Values

Determining what you want to celebrate is the starting point for cheerleaders. People lose interest and really never get into the game if a rally cry goes up every time the team simply gets the ball. The hoopla and celebration are not for the sake of fun only but for the sake of calling attention to and reinforcing key organizational values. If the main departmental objective is to obtain new contracts, then celebrate when they're signed. If a company values employee loyalty, then celebrate with years-of-service dinners and recognition pins. And if developing new products is a goal, then hand out awards with every patent granted. The point here is that everything about a celebration must be matched to its purposes.[2] Without expressive events to recognize an achievement, important organizational values have little impact upon people's behavior. Celebrations are to the culture of an organization "what the movie is to the script or the concert is to the score—they provide expression of values that are difficult to express in any other way."[3]

Old Stone Bank of North Carolina in High Point, is extremely proud of the job its tellers and savings counselors do. In order to recognize and show their appreciation, top management established Project ROSE—Recognition of Superior Effort.[4] Charles Huff, Jr., CEO and president, kicks off the program by presenting every one of Old Stone's customer contact personnel with a red rose. Each quarter, three winners are selected; at a group meeting, they are presented with a rose corsage, a cash prize, and a framed certificate. Quarterly winners are entitled to compete for the year's grand prize award. One winner wrote, "I appreciate the fact that management has created a program to recognize our efforts. I feel this program gives each of us the incentive to do our best, knowing that our efforts are recognized by management."

To further the ROSE program theme in other areas, new employees are presented with a bud vase of fresh flowers on their first day of work. In instances of customer complaints, the customer receives a personal letter and a dozen red roses from the president. As one formerly irate store owner responded, "What a wonderful surprise to receive the roses from you. We certainly do appreciate them and the fact that you care about our business. Everyone has problems, but it's how you handle them that counts." A letter from another disgruntled customer also included thanks for the fresh flowers. She went on to write, "I appreciate you taking the time, trouble and expense but most of all I appreciate your obvious concern. Your explanation of the situation was most helpful in improving my understanding and therefore quieting my feelings. I did not expect such overwhelming attention. My concern was as much for your employees as for myself. However, judging by the great consideration you have shown me, I am quite sure you are showing the same to them."

In any celebration, the need for consistency with key values is an essential part of maintaining a leader's credibility. What you say and what is being celebrated should be one and the same; otherwise, the celebration will come off as inconsistent, insincere, and phony. Authenticity is what makes most conscious celebrations work.[5] The celebration must be an honest expression of your commitment to certain key values and to the hard work and dedication of those people who have lived the values.

While we were doing a seminar for Advanced Decision Systems, everyone was in a dither from the very start of the day, anticipating the announcement of a major government contract. It was difficult at times to keep everyone's attention, because at each break several participants would gleefully run around shouting, "Has anyone heard?" "Is the party on?" The enthusiasm was infectious, and even we got caught up in it. At two o'clock, the director of human resources asked that we take a break at three so that everyone could hear the announcement together in the conference room. At ten minutes before three, we joined sixty to seventy people packed into the conference room and the hallways on both sides. The general manager began speaking in a quiet and somber voice about all the hard work, time, and sweat that had gone into drafting the proposal. He told a funny story about a person who thought that she had lost some critical papers that she had left in her car when it was towed away because she had stayed so long at the office; another story told about the speeding ticket that he had received on the way to work because he was daydreaming about the proposal. He thanked several people personally for their efforts. And he spoke about the challenges and opportunities that receiving this contract would bring and how everyone in the company would have to "make more sacrifices doing more of the work they loved doing." Then he gave a wink, a sheepish grin, reached into his ancient leather satchel—and popped the cork, spraying champagne on everyone nearby, screaming, "We got it! We got it! We got it!" We finished the seminar in the warm afterglow of this celebration, with people talking about how they loved working for this leader and this company. He was demanding and caring, challenging and supportive, intense and playful.

Public Ceremonies

In an earlier chapter, we talked about how the *public* nature of events makes your actions more visible to others and, therefore, has a stronger binding-in effect. Celebrations and cheer-leading are public events. They reinforce corporate commitment to key values and demonstrate visibly to others that the organization is serious about the importance of adhering to these values. Fifteen or more times a year, some new and promising project at the 3M Company reaches the level of $1 million in profitable sales. You might think that this does not get much attention in a $7 billion company, but it does. Lights flash, bells ring, and video cameras are called out to recognize the entrepreneurial team that is responsible for this achievement.[6]

Public ceremonies and rituals are the ingredients that crystallize personal commitment. They help to bond people together and let them know that they are not alone. There's nothing worse than celebrating alone, whether it is a birthday, an anniversary, or New Year's. Generally lighthearted, celebrations tend to reduce conflicts and minimize differences. Celebrations are also organized in order to inform and thereby empower those who attend. There is a family feeling about celebrations. While fun, they also provide a meaningful reminder about which key values are celebrated in the organization.

When Gayle Hamilton, local area manager for Pacific Gas & Electric Company, first started her assignment in Pajaro Valley, California, she noticed some animosity between the staffs of the office and the field service center, which were located at opposite sides of the town. She took two actions. The first was to institute a "ride along" and "sit along" program. People from the two groups made half-day visits to each other's areas, working side by side with their hosts, answering customer service calls on the telephone or driving to construction sites for utility installation discussions. She also organized a dinner dance and involved people from both groups in the planning process. The dance was a grand success. It brought people together and promoted common interests. Before she could initiate the plan for the next dinner dance, employees from the two groups beat her to the punch. They thought it was such a good idea that they had institutionalized it.

Some of the most significant and memorable public celebrations are those that occur spontaneously. From the pat-on-the-back and let-me-take-you-out-to-lunch variety to the "party in 30 minutes in the parking lot," relatively unplanned celebrations create a favorable impression on the recipients. They create a real sense of importance because of their timeliness, when the thrill of victory is still a thrill. Because there are no rehearsals, the feeling of celebration is on a more personal level. Messages such as "we're in this together" and "I really care about you" are most sincerely communicated in small group settings and on less planned occasions.

Personal Involvement

Think about your impressions of your own boss. When we ask people to talk about their bosses, they relate personal details that significantly affect their overall impressions of them and their relationship. Leadership is a relationship predicated on personal involvement.

When we organized a conference for the National Association of Convenience Stores, we asked the chief executives to prepare for it by writing descriptions of true-life critical customer service incidents, detailing how they, by their own examples, had demonstrated excellence in customer service. One company president wrote, "When a store celebrated its 'Grand Opening' I was there greeting customers and carrying groceries. By personally participating, I was showing the customers that we are happy to be in and a part of their community. It also shows everyone with the company the importance I give to customer service. I did not realize the importance that people in the company placed in my being there. I used your letter as a tool to interview several people in the company and learned that my absence at the past several 'Grand Openings' was noted. I was missed! I have learned not to miss any more."

Leaders play a very special role in the art of celebration because they are enormously visible to others in the organization and serve as role models. Because organizations, like any living system, go through a multitude of changes, leaders have many opportunities to provide celebration and, in so doing, to focus attention on key organizational values and to interpret key organizational events. Certainly, not all celebrations have to be parties. However, they are intended to be joyous. Mass, for example, is a solemn ceremony that celebrates the sacrament. The orientation of new M.B.A. students at Santa Clara University begins with a half-day series of outdoor activities intended to reinforce the need for students to work together and to take an interest in one another's welfare. The Fourth of July, Labor Day, and Memorial Day are examples of national celebrations in which we are reminded of struggles, sacrifices, legacies, and continuing responsibilities. Every organization has its equivalent "national" holidays or events. Cathy DeForest, an expert on this subject, provides these examples of reasons for organizational celebrations:

- *Stages of organizational change:* expansions, reorganizations, closings, mergers, the end of an old technology and the introduction of a new one, moves to new locations.
- *Success:* financial success, promotions, awards, expansions to new markets.
- *Loss:* of old procedures, financial opportunities, contracts, a job, status; death of a colleague; an experiment that failed.
- *People:* teamwork, team successes, founders, winners of sales contests, employee awards, individual birthdays, marriages, reunions.
- *Events:* a company's anniversary, opening day, holidays, articulation of an organization's vision.
- *The unknown:* paradox, ambiguity in the marketplace.[7]

The importance of celebrations and the leader's role in them often comes as a surprise to some people. "I was unprepared for the scrutiny, of being placed under a microscope, by the people around me," explains Leigh Beldon, president of Verilink. "But I soon learned that I was on stage. And while I'm not always comfortable with the role required, I look for natural opportunities to celebrate with others our accomplishments and hard efforts." Leaders are always on the lookout for people who are doing the right things in the right way so that they can celebrate the victories.

James Treybig, president and CEO, attends nearly every one of Tandem Computers' Friday afternoon celebrations. By doing so, he signals to others not only that it is okay to celebrate but that it is a desired part of corporate life. Even when it comes to celebrating, leaders model the way. And when times get tough, they don't stop celebrating. So look for small wins. Try celebrations for "The Martyr of the Week" or "The Best Try."[8] One sure sign that you're building a spirit of celebration in your organization is that others begin leading the way, as when Gayle Hamilton received an invitation to what has become the *employees'* party, or when Jack Kilmartin, former chairperson of Mervyn's *received* an "I heard something good about you" card from one of his store managers.

While special celebrations such as kick-off meetings, annual award dinners, jubilees, and rallies serve an important purpose, they are insufficient unless the day-to-day behavior of top managers reflects concern about key values. Renn Zaphiropoulos, CEO at Versatec, personally cooks dinner at his home for top-performing employees. There is no regular schedule for these celebrations; they are all determined by something special—for example, he recently prepared a special dinner for the European group because they had an exceptional year. During the meal, they talk about where the organization is going and what everyone will need to do if they are to be successful. This personal touch has enormous importance, especially in a high-tech world. On these personal occasions, leaders also find further opportunities to let others know what they value, what they consider important, and to share stories about corporate heroes and heroines.

Bob Greene, a syndicated columnist for the Chicago *Tribune,* describes talking with a group of people about a particular boss. Some of them liked the boss, and some of them didn't. But they all vouched for one thing about him: he never said thank you. As Greene pondered this behavior, he concluded that perhaps for some bosses the reluctance to say thank you was a device used to maintain a symbolic distance between themselves and the troops.[9] Saying thank you establishes a personal and very human connection between people. And that's exactly what you, as a leader, need to do. Once a human connection has been established, it's much easier to create a commonness, to share visions, values, and experiences, and to establish deeper empathy with other people. Personal involvement, created through public and mutual celebration, brings about the sort of togetherness and commitment that the old preacher showed each morning when he prayed, "Lord, ain't nothing going to happen to me today that You and I can't handle."

Creating Social Support Networks

Russ Douglass found that the surprises and unexpected "ya dunn goods" that he provided served a number of purposes besides positive reinforcement. "Many times they were pressure relief valves," he explained, "ways of loosening things up and letting people know we were all in this together." Researchers investigating the workplace have long recognized that supportive relationships at work are critically important to maintaining personal and organizational vitality.[10] In the process of celebrating accomplishments, leaders create social support networks. People who share the same goals are likely to come to care about one another on more than just a professional level. Celebrating achievements together reinforces the common stake that people have in reaching the destination. Making people feel included is a major function of celebrations. That we are not just part of the team but part of something significant and larger than the moment creates a compelling motivation to achieve and succeed. Being included and close to others increases our sense of belonging and esprit de corps. The purpose of the Friday afternoon beer busts at Tandem is not just celebration, insiders explain, it is also exchanging information, team building, and collectively letting off steam.

Many managers have a difficult time with personal relationships. Traditional managerial wisdom has asserted, "Don't get too close to your people, or they will take advantage of you." But it works both ways. Extraordinary accomplishments are not achieved without everyone—leader and follower alike—getting personally involved with the task and with the people. Some leaders liken the emotional attachment to being in a chorus. Others say it's like a feeling of being family. Matt Sanders, who has successfully helped several new start-up companies, says that "the people you hire have to be your partners." Our personal best cases were filled with the importance of building genuine personal relationships between the members of the team and the leader.

The conference and catering department at UCLA was preparing for its summer season—its busiest time—when it became aware that other departments on campus (such as physical plant, central receiving, and scheduling and facilities) were upset that they would have to put out a great deal of effort to help conference and catering be successful, but would receive very little in the way of rewards themselves. Mary Pat Hanker, director of Conference Services, realized that the department's success was dependent on the helpfulness of these other units and she decided to figure out a way to gain their support, commitment, and involvement. She realized that the intervention had to be pleasant, playful, and humorous in order for people to want to participate—and feel good about participating wholeheartedly—rather than feel threatened and hence reluctant to comply.

So they staged a celebration. They held a barbeque for the people they were calling upon for help. Unlike most office parties, however, the people responsible for generating the heavy summer business traffic—the managers—were the ones who cooked and served the food. This symbolic reversal of roles did indeed foster a spirit of cooperation. At the summer's end there was another celebration. This time, conference and catering passed out T-shirts bearing a humorous version of their logo, which showed three surrealistic conferring stick figures that were bedraggled, bandaged, and on crutches as though they'd been through a war. Beneath the caricature was the phrase, "I survived the '86 UCLA conference season." These were distributed to the people who had been particularly helpful to the success of the summer season.

Hanker separated these celebrations from everyday work roles and work relationships. People across departments had the opportunity to interact with one another outside of the more formal and structured work context. Peter Tommerup, an ethnographer studying these events, explained how these celebrations gave people permission to interact with one another in a friendly and intimate manner, increasing their feelings of camaraderie, cooperation, and appreciation of the reasons behind the hectic summer season. This social support network enhanced collaborative efforts and facilitated amiable interpersonal relationships throughout a stressful and highly productive period.[11]

Investigations from a wide variety of disciplines consistently demonstrate that social support—the quality of interpersonal relationships—serves to enhance not only productivity but also psychological well-being and physical health. The California

Department of Mental Health states strongly that *Friends Can Be Good Medicine.*[12] They report that social support not only enhances wellness but also buffers against disease, particularly during times of high stress. This latter finding was true irrespective of an individual's age, gender, or ethnic group. Even after adjusting for such factors as smoking and histories of major illnesses, people with few close contacts were dying two to three times faster than those who regularly had friends to turn to.[13]

Animal studies also support the notion that company prevents misery. Squirrel monkeys become more agitated when confronted with a boa constrictor when alone than when several monkeys confront the snake together. Mice that are injected with cancer cells and then isolated develop tumors more rapidly than those who remain with their mates. The morbidity rates of widows are three to thirteen times as high as those of married women for every known major cause of death. The warm family support given to artificial heart recipient Barney Clark was considered by his doctor to have been crucial to his remarkable endurance after receiving the heart. Even studies of former Vietnam prisoners of war have revealed that communication with fellow captives, sometimes involving complex tapping codes, was a vital factor in their survival.[14] Celebrations create positive interaction among people, providing concrete evidence that people generally care about each other. Knowing that you are not alone in your efforts and that you can count on others if necessary provides the courage to continue in times of turmoil and stress.

The case for social support also includes the exchange of information facilitated by both official and informal interactions.[15] When celebrations cut across functional and hierarchical boundaries, as they frequently do, people get a chance to exchange ideas and be stimulated by people outside their own specialties. The monthly "Thank Goodness It's Friday" (TGIF) get-togethers at our university mix faculty and administrators outside of their formal responsibilities and committees and give them an opportunity to get a sense of the others' agendas. While we might not make an appointment to let the academic vice-president know our concerns about some particular campus issue (for example, changing from a semester to a quarter system), we're likely to say "Let's catch Paul's attention at the TGIF and ask him about the calendar." It's at these same events that we've been asked informally about serving on a university task force or invited to nominate people for awards or given the chance to brag about our research and discuss how it might be useful to someone else in the organization (or could be expanded with further funding).

Our experience is echoed by others in their own contexts. Without corporate celebrations, we might all come to believe that the organization revolved around our work and that we were independent and not responsible to others. Social interaction and support work both ways—as you give, you get, and you become interconnected and caught up in other people's lives. It always takes a group of people working together with a common purpose in an atmosphere of trust and collaboration to get extraordinary things done.

The Secret of Success Is Love

We once asked U.S. Army Major General John H. Stanford to tell us how he would go about developing leaders, whether at Santa Clara University, in the military, or in private business. He replied, "When anyone asks me that question I tell them I have the secret to success in life. The secret to success is stay in love. Staying in love gives you the fire to really ignite other people, to see inside other people, to have a greater desire to get things done than other people. A person who is not in love doesn't really feel the kind of excitement that helps them to get ahead and lead others and to achieve. I don't know any other fire, any other thing in life that is more exhilarating and is more positive a feeling than love is."

"Staying in love" is not the answer we expected to get, at least not when we began our study of leadership bests. But after numerous interviews and case analyses, we noted that *love* was a word that many leaders used freely when talking about their own motivations to lead. The word *encouragement* has its root in the Latin word *cor*, meaning "heart." When leaders encourage others, through recognition and celebration, they inspire them with courage—with heart. When we encourage others, we give them heart. And when we give heart to others, we give love.

Vince Lombardi, the unforgettable coach of the Green Bay Packers, believed in love. In a speech before the American Management Association, he made these remarks: "Mental toughness is humility, simplicity, Spartanism. And one other, love. I don't necessarily have to like my associates, but as a person I must love them. Love is loyalty. Love is teamwork. Love respects the dignity of the individual. Heartpower is the strength of your corporation."[16] Of all the things that sustain a leader over time, love is the most lasting. It is hard to imagine leaders getting up day after day, putting in the long hours and hard work it takes to get extraordinary things done, without their hearts being in it.

Not everyone with whom we spoke talked about love. But many did. And it led us to suspect that just possibly the best-kept secret of successful leaders is love: being in love with leading, with the people who do the work, with what their organizations produce, and with those who honor the organization by using its work. Leadership is an affair of the heart, not of the head.

Commitment Number 10: Celebrate Team Accomplishments Regularly

Celebrating team accomplishments recognizes that extraordinary performance is the result of many people's efforts and reinforces bonding feelings of "we are in this together." Making hard work fun and exciting is what encouraging the heart is all about. There are several strategies that you can use to celebrate team accomplishments:

1. *Schedule celebrations.* While many celebrations are, and should be, spontaneous, you should select a few celebrations that you want people to put on their calendars. Just as New Year's, Thanksgiving, and the Fourth of July all fall at the same time and have the same meaning each year, certain organizational celebrations should do the same. Your first task is to decide which organizational values or events of historical significance to the company are of such importance that they warrant an annual ritual, ceremony, or festivity. Perhaps you want to commemorate founder's day, recognize the top 5 percent of the sales force, honor the people who created the year's important innovations, praise those who gave extra special customer service, or thank the fam-

ilies of your employees for their support; whatever you wish to celebrate, formalize it, announce it, and tell people how they become eligible to participate. At a minimum, you ought to have at least one celebration each year that involves everyone, though not necessarily at the same site, and one that draws attention to each of the key values of your organization.

In addition to these annual affairs, bring celebration into as many other critical events as you can. We suggest you review the list of reasons for celebration that Cathy DeForest developed earlier in this chapter and make a list of all the ways you can bring more ceremony, ritual, commemoration, observance, and convivial good times into your organization.

2. Be a cheerleader, your way. You can cheerlead for your group better than anyone else: this is another instance of leading by example. Some people find this difficult, because they have very limited views of what it means to cheerlead that are based upon traditional views of school cheerleaders. There is much more to this than just "Rah! Rah!" gyrations. Foremost is being clear on your personal values and what it is that you want to celebrate. Celebrations must be organized around evident performance-reward linkages, as we described in the previous chapter. For example, in the Chemicals Division of Milliken Textiles, everyone receives free doughnuts and coffee when quality milestones are achieved. A sign is prominently displayed giving the responsible group credit for achieving the milestone—and for the free doughnuts!

As with individual recognition, all kinds of rewards exist for celebrating. Use your imagination. But most importantly, be authentic. You may be comfortable giving out plaques, flowers, T-shirts, and the like, or you may not. So do it your way, but do celebrate. When leaders give gifts of the heart, it is the thought that counts the most. Can't think of anything to celebrate? Try "thank goodness it's Friday" and "we made it through another week together" (this works in both tough times and good times). Try celebrating with champagne every milestone achieved, as one design group did at Apple Computer. Think they had lots of milestones? You bet, *and* lots of milestones *achieved.* Try "coloring the ball," which is one way Ken Best at McDonnell Douglas publically celebrated achievements in one high-performing project he led. The project team tacked up their entire scheduling document on the conference room wall and when they got together each week to review their progress, each team member used his or her color-coded marking pen to fill in circles representing the completed milestone. Best found that these sessions were excellent ways to acknowledge progress and review bottlenecks, and that there was always some small win that could be noted and colored in on the chart.

If there are others in your organization who are better at celebrating than you are, give them your support and encouragement. Join in the fun. You don't have to lead it, but be a part of it, letting others around you know that it's okay to laugh, to have fun, and to enjoy each other's company. In this way you let people know that you are human, creating an important commonality that minimizes we-they (for example, leader-follower or boss-subordinate) differences. And if you want others to join in the party, then give it your personal support and your visible presence.

3. *Secure your social network.* There are two perspectives to this strategy. The first we have described as creating or building social support for the people on your team. You do this in many ways, not the least of which is by celebrating their accomplishments visibly and in group settings. Social interaction increases people's commitments to the standards of the group, and when the group is aligned with your vision and values, the results are strong peer pressure for individuals to do their fair share and consensus about required behaviors. When people are asked to accomplish the extraordinary, social support also enhances their resistance to the debilitating effects of stress.

Secondly, you need to examine your personal social support network, which may include the members of your team but probably includes others outside your immediate work group. Try this. Stop reading for a moment. Take out a piece of paper. Draw a circle in the middle about the size of a half-dollar. Write your name in it. Now begin drawing smaller circles around the big circle. These circles represent members of your support group. Think about the people with whom you have the strongest and closest bonds and begin filling in the various circles with their names. Draw the circles and jot down names quickly, just as they come to mind. Include the people who have given you strong social support all through your life, as well as those who give you support now.[17]

What does your support network look like? Where does your boss fall? Where would your subordinates put you? Examine who are your friends, close colleagues, mentors, and sponsors. Are there people whom you've gotten out of touch with and have not seen for a long time? Think about clubs, associations, even religious or political groups you belong to now or have in the past. Determine which relationships need to be strengthened or renewed and get in touch with those people now. Unfortunately, what happens all too frequently is that when you really need these people's support, because you have neglected the relationship or taken it for granted, their support becomes unavailable.

Take another few minutes and respond to the six questions below and circle one response for each item. The California Department of Mental Health calls this a measure of the strength of your social support network.[18]

1. At work, how many persons do you talk to about a job hassle?
    none (or not employed) (0)   one or two (3)
    two or three (4)   four or more (5)

2. How many neighbors do you trade favors with (loan tools or household items, share rides, babysit, and so on)?
    none (0)   one (1)   two or three (2)   four or more (3)

3. Do you have a spouse or partner?
    no (0)   several different partners (2)   one steady
    partner (6)   or married or living with someone (10)

4. How often do friends and close family members visit you at home?
    rarely (0)   about once a month (1)   several times
    a month (4)   once a week or more (8)

5. How many friends or family members do you talk to about personal matters?
    none (0)   one or two (6)   three to five (8)
    six or more (10)

6. How often do you participate in a social, community, or sports group?
rarely (0)   about once a month (1)   several times
a month (2)   or once a week or more (4)

Add the numbers in parentheses next to each item you circled. If your score is less than 15, then your social support network has low strength and probably does not provide much support, says the Mental Health Department. You need to consider making more social contacts. If your score is 15–29, your support network has moderate strength, and it is likely to provide enough support except during periods of high stress. Your support network has high strength if your score is 30 or more, and it is likely to support your well-being even during periods of high stress. Indeed, you need to maintain and sustain personal relationships, especially in times of change and crisis and when extraordinary accomplishments are desired, in order to assist you in coping with excessive stress levels that cause mental and physical illness.

4. *Stay in love.* In an earlier chapter, we asked "Are you in this job to do something, or are you in this job for something to do?" And if it is the former, what is it that you want to do? We now know that this was a much too rational question, because so much of leadership is a "fire in the belly" kind of experience. You must, to paraphrase IBM's founder, Thomas J. Watson, Sr., put your heart in the business and the business in your heart. So many extraordinary leaders have told us, "I really love what we're doing." Ask yourself, "What is it that I love to do?" Your passion for leadership will emanate from there, so find ways to put that into your business.

We typically end our leadership seminars by asking participants in small groups to encourage the heart—to recognize individual achievements and celebrate team accomplishments within the context of the seminar. We realize that encouraging the heart doesn't necessarily come at the end of the seminar, belong just at the conclusion of a project, or follow sequentially the other leadership practices we have been describing. It is not the end of the process but a continual part of the leadership journey. It is vital that leaders give courage, spread joy, and care about people, product, and process all along the way. In the next and final chapter, we describe how you can develop yourself as a leader. Before turning to this issue, this is the way Douglas M. Molitor, account executive at Regis McKenna, Inc., contributed to the celebration at the conclusion of one of our leadership workshops:

Stump Speech
On connecting leadership with modeling, enabling, vision,
climbing over walls, jumping out of trees, and the Tao

When I get back to RMI
These are the lessons
   I'll try to fly.

Challenge the process
   Push the status quo
Try new ideas
   Don't say no.

Share a vision
   First foot on the way
Enlist in a dream
   Its rewards begin today.

Provide others the tools
   Let them draw from within
Remove the path's barriers
   Shout praise over the din.

Do as I do
   Do what you may
If I listen to you
   You'll show the way.

Celebrate history
   A wake for a loss
Life is a journey
   Venture the cost.

Never leave it be said
   "If only I had . . ."
Time's too short
   Inaction is sad.

First step outward
   With friends gathered round
Envision the future
   Feet on the ground.

PART SEVEN

The Beginning of Leadership

> You never conquer the mountain. You only conquer yourself.
>
> —*Jim Whittaker,*
> *First American*
> *to Climb Mount Everest*

People frequently ask us, "Are leaders born or made?" It's a judgment call. No one knows for sure. Our experience tells us that leadership is a set of learnable competencies. We can, however, tell you this for certain: every exceptional leader we know is also a learner.

The self-confidence required to lead comes from learning about ourselves—our skills, prejudices, talents, and shortcomings. Self-confidence develops as we build on strengths and overcome weaknesses.

Formal training and education can help. Many leadership skills are successfully learned in the classroom. But training alone is insufficient. We also learn from other people and from experiences. Those who become the best leaders take advantage of the broadest possible range of opportunities. They try, fail, and learn from their mistakes. Leaders develop best when they are enthusiastic participants in change.

Ultimately, leadership development is self-development. Musicians have their instruments. Engineers have their computers. Accountants have their calculators. Leaders have themselves. They are their own instruments. In this final chapter, we learn how we can develop ourselves and become better leaders than we are today.

277

13

Become a Leader Who Cares and Makes a Difference

> The greatest rewards come only from the greatest commitment.
>
> ——*Arlene Blum,*
> *Mountain Climber and Leader,*
> *American Women's*
> *Himalayan Expedition*

In our study, we wanted to know what common practices leaders used to get extraordinary things done in organizations. Through an analysis of hundreds of personal best leadership cases and thousands of surveys of leader behaviors and characteristics, we found that there are essentially five fundamental practices and ten behaviors in exemplary leadership:

Leaders challenge the process. They *search for opportunities* to change the status quo. They look for innovative ways to improve the organization. They *experiment and take risks.* And since risk taking involves mistakes and failure, leaders accept the inevitable disappointments as learning opportunities.

Leaders inspire a shared vision. They passionately believe that they can make a difference. They *envision the future,* creating an ideal and unique image of what the organization can become. Through their strong appeal and quiet persuasion, leaders *enlist others* in the dream. They breathe life into visions and get us to see the exciting future possibilities.

Leaders enable others to act. They *foster collaboration* and build spirited teams. They actively involve others. Mutual respect is what sustains extraordinary efforts, so leaders create an atmosphere of trust and human dignity. They *strengthen others*, making each person feel capable and powerful.

Leaders model the way. They establish values about how employees, colleagues, and customers ought to be treated. They create standards of excellence and then *set an example* for others to follow. Because complex change can overwhelm and stifle action, leaders *plan small wins*. They unravel bureaucracy, put up signposts, and create opportunities for victory.

Leaders encourage the heart. Getting extraordinary things done in organizations is hard work. To keep hope and determination alive, leaders *recognize contributions* that individuals make to the climb to the top. And every winning team needs to share in the rewards of their efforts, so leaders *celebrate accomplishments*. They make everyone feel like heroes.

How do leaders learn these practices? How can you become a better leader? In this closing chapter, we offer insights from our and others' research on the development of the capacity to lead.

When Philip L. Smith, president and chief operating officer of General Foods, discusses leadership with a select group of senior managers in the company's executive development program, he asks each to "share a story about a leader or leaders who have had a profound impact upon his or her life and values." As a result of the free and open exchange, "Participants get a strong message: just as they have been influenced by leaders, so too they can have a lasting and compelling impact on the people they manage."[1]

Virtually all of us can name at least one leader whose compelling impact we have felt. Sometimes it is a well-known figure out of the past who has changed the course of history. Sometimes we choose contemporary role models who serve as examples of success. Still others are those who have helped us learn—coaches, teachers, parents, friends, bosses. But if we are to become leaders, we must believe that we, too, can be a positive force in the world.

"Now the very concept of leadership implies the proposition that individuals make a difference to history," observed historian Arthur M. Schlesinger, Jr. Yet there has never been universal acceptance of this proposition. Determinism and fatalism govern the minds of many.[2] Some management scholars claim, in fact, that their evidence suggests that leaders have little impact on organizations, that other forces—internal or external to the organization—are the determinants of success. And because this is true, some claim, the role of the leader is largely symbolic, enabling us to justify our belief in individual efficacy.[3] Our evidence suggests quite the contrary. When the leaders in our study used the five practices more frequently, they were seen by others to:

- Have a higher degree of personal credibility.
- Be more effective in meeting job-related demands.
- Be more successful in representing their units to upper management.
- Have higher-performing teams.

Additionally, those working with these leaders felt significantly more satisfied with their practices and strategies, more committed, and more influential and powerful. In other words, the more you act like a leader, the more likely it is that you will have a positive influence on others in the organization. Leaders can indeed make a difference.

Other researchers have also found that leaders can have a significant impact on their organizations. Bernard M. Bass of the State University of New York investigated the nature and effects of two types of leaders: *transactional* and *transformational*. In terms of practices, his transformational leader closely resembles the leader we describe in this book, inspiring others to excel, giving individual consideration to others, and stimulating people to think in new ways. The transactional leader, on the other hand, tends to maintain a steady-state situation and generally gets performance from others by offering rewards. (The transactional leader closely resembles the traditional definition of the manager.) In measuring the influence of both types of leaders, Bass found that while both were positively associated with effectiveness, "transformational leadership factors, particularly charisma and individualized consideration, were more highly related than transactional leadership factors to satisfaction and effectiveness."[4]

Smith, Carson, and Alexander investigated the effects of leadership on organizational performance in a longitudinal study of ministers. They concluded that outstanding ministers have a very positive effect. "Churches that superior performers led repeatedly experienced greater giving, membership growth, and property development than did other churches."[5] Leaders can make a difference. If you want to have a significant impact on people and on organizations, you would be wise to invest in learning to become the very best leader you can.

Learning to Lead

So how do you become the best leader possible? To find the answer to that question, we asked the people in our study to tell us how they learned to lead. Typical responses included:

- "I don't know. I suppose it's a combination of personality, schools, books, personal experiences in observing leaders in action, etc." (Phil Lemay, Amdahl Corporation).
- "I am not sure I have yet. 'learned to lead.' I have observed methods and skills of my bosses that I respected. I have had some experience (trial and error) since this project was initiated, and I previously had some courses relating to people skills, communications, etc. The skills to do this 'Personal Best' could only have come from a combination of my experience as a nonleader and a strong desire to take on a leadership position" (Tom Kellett, Harshaw/Filtrol Partnership).
- "By mistakes" (Tom Voehl, Lam Research Corporation).
- "I learned to lead from experience and from trying to adapt techniques used by others that I thought were successful. I also enjoy reading autobiographies of leaders I admire to try to understand how they think" (Don Danielson, KLA Instruments).
- "'Classes/books can give you concepts, bosses/mentors role models, but you learn best by doing, trial and error, reflection" (Jan Johnson, Signetics).
- "Bosses, intuition, trial and error" (Gayle Hamilton, Pacific Gas & Electric).
- "Most of my leadership traits are based on my basic value system of dealing with people, as ingrained in me in my

youth and fine tuned through experience" (Dan Wible, Unisys).
- "Being calm, confident and trusting of myself, others gravitate toward me and put me in a leadership role. I actively take opportunities for leadership. I view learning as a high priority in my life and learning about leadership is key—through role models, books, direct experience" (Dan Beam, Interaction Associates).

Our analysis of all responses suggests three major categories of opportunities for learning to lead. In order of importance, they are trial and error, people, and education.

Two other studies support our findings. The first was conducted by the Center for Creative Leadership as an outgrowth of their study on derailed executives. The center interviewed successful executives to find what career events they considered to be important to their development.[6] The second study was done by the Honeywell Corporation. At Honeywell, senior executives wanted to improve the ways they developed their managers. As a part of this project, Honeywell undertook a six-year research program to determine how managers learn to manage.[7] While neither of these studies asked exclusively about leadership, as we did, the results are so similar that we believe that important lessons can be drawn from them.

The Center for Creative Leadership clustered their results into these categories:

- Job assignments that the executives had had.
- Other people with whom they had come into contact.
- Hardships that they had endured.
- Miscellaneous, including formal training.[8]

Job assignments accounted for the highest percentage of developmental events. Thirty-eight percent of all learning opportunities were connected with tough job assignments. Learning from other people accounted for 21 percent, and hardships for 19 percent. Of the 22 percent miscellaneous, only 9 percent were related to course work.[9]

The Honeywell study resulted in similar categories:

- Job experiences and assignments.
- Relationships.
- Formal training and education.

The Honeywell ranking is identical to ours and that of the Center for Creative Leadership, although the percentages vary slightly: 50 percent for job experiences, 30 percent for relationships, and 20 percent for training.[10] Also important in the Honeywell research is the finding that managers contend that training must occur at the right time in their careers. That time is "at or near the time of a significant change in assignment."[11] This finding suggests that training would be more effective if it were more tightly coupled with job experiences. While managers find it difficult to schedule training just as they are entering a new assignment, they should ideally take part in skills development as soon as possible after assuming a new role.

What is quite evident from all three studies is that, whether you are talking about managing or leading, experience is by far the most important opportunity for learning. Other people are a close second, and formal education and training are a distant third.

Trial and Error. There is just no suitable surrogate for learning by doing. Whether it is facilitating your team's meetings, leading a special task force at work, heading your favorite charity's fundraising drive, or chairing your professional association's annual conference, the more chances you have to serve in leadership roles, the more likely it is that you will develop the skills to lead—and the more likely that you will learn those important leadership lessons that come only from the failures and successes of live action.

Just any experience, however, does not by itself support individual development. In Chapter Three of this book, we talked about how important challenge was to doing our best as leaders. Seeing change as a challenge was described as important to psychological hardiness, and challenge was also the key ingredient in people's enjoying what they do. Now it turns out that challenge is also crucial to learning and career enhancement.[12] Boring, routine jobs do not help you improve your skills and abilities. They do not help you move forward in your career. You must be stretched. You must be given opportunities to test your-self against new and difficult tasks. So experience can indeed be the best teacher, if it contains the element of personal challenge.

There are other ingredients in the recipe of job assignments that advance careers and learning. Cynthia D. McCauley, of the Center for Creative Leadership, found in her review of develop-mental experiences in managerial work that managers must be given broader and broader responsibility if they are to blossom into senior executives. It also helps to have those leadership oppor-tunities early in careers. Staff assignments at corporate headquar-ters that give a person high visibility are useful—and personally empowering. However, staff jobs that have low visibility tend not to be stepping stones to senior management. For example, Patricia Carrigan, plant manager of the General Motors Bay City plant, began her corporate career as a human resource staff member at corporate headquarters. There she mastered valuable consulting skills that serve her well as a line manager. She also discovered that she would rather be a manager in a plant than a corporate staff member. Project teams and task forces can add to a prospec-tive leader's abilities to work with diverse groups inside and out-side the company. Hardships and business crises can be especially powerful triggers for self-insight and lessons in handling loss.[13]

The first prescription, then, for becoming a better leader is to broaden your base of experience. People are more likely to follow you if they have confidence that you understand their area, the organization, and the industry. Job rotation is one way, but we suggest going beyond that. Volunteer for leadership roles in your professional associations and community groups. They are always in need of good people. And volunteer groups are great places to develop skills in getting people to want to do things. Begin to seek new assignments early in your career. Do not hesi-tate to ask for a new assignment within two or three years. If you are in the same job for longer than five years, you are out of the learning curve. Also, volunteer for the tougher assignments. Those are some of the most beneficial to your development. They are higher risk, but the payoff is greater.

Yet even the most venturesome jobs will not help you grow if you do not take the time to reflect upon what you have learned from life's trials and errors. When we do recall, in vivid detail, the people, the places, the events, the struggles, the victories—the very smell and texture of the action—we discover lasting lessons about how to more effectively lead others. We find embedded in experience the grains of truth about ourselves, others, our organizations, and life itself. Unexamined experiences do not produce the rich insights that come with reflection and analysis.

Inductive learning—where we proceed from observations based on experience to principles and applications—is a far better process for learning leadership than beginning with an a priori "truth." Learning from experience is much like watching the game films after an athletic event. These documentations show us how we executed our plan, what we did well, and where we need to improve. Athletic teams make extensive use of postgame review. Why not leaders?

The personal best case methodology is one approach to reaping the educational benefits of experience. While we used this technique to gather data on exemplary leadership practices, those we studied were able to draw lessons about their own strengths, weaknesses, assumptions, strategies, and tactics. You may wish to write a personal best for yourself. We would also recommend a "personal worst." Failures can be as instructive as successes, if we take the time to reflect upon them.

People. Other people have always been essential sources of guidance. We all remember the parent we looked to for advice and support; the special teacher who filled us with curiosity for our favorite subject; the neighbor who always let us watch, even take part in, the tinkering in the garage; the coach who believed that we had promise and inspired us to give our best; the counselor who gave us valuable feedback about our behavior and its impact; the master artisan who instructed us in the fundamentals and nuances of a craft; or the first boss who taught us the ropes to skip and the hoops to jump. McCauley found that of all the potential relationships at work, the three most important are mentors, bosses, and peers.[14] Mentors are particularly valuable as informal sponsors and coaches.[15] They help us learn how to navigate the system, they make important introductions, and they point us in the right direction. However, not every successful leader has had a mentor or believes that one is essential to getting ahead.[16]

Bosses are obviously important to our careers. They can help us to advance or they can slow our progress. They serve as extremely important sources of performance feedback and modeling. The best bosses are those who challenge us, who trust us, who are willing to spend time with us, and who are consistent in their behavior.[17] Bosses, like all other leaders, must be credible to us if we are to learn and develop as their subordinates. Chances are that most of us have had good and bad bosses in our careers. Good bosses are obviously preferred, but bad bosses are not necessarily roadblocks to development. They can, however, create unwanted stress in our lives.[18] If you ever find yourself stuck with a bad boss—whether a tyrant or a weakling—your best bet is to learn to manage him or her. It is unlikely that you will change that person. Your own best growth strategy is to treat your boss as you wish to be treated, remain positive about yourself, and deal with your boss directly in an assertive but nonconfrontational manner.[19] Bad bosses may not be pleasant to work with, but they can be great examples of what not to do. And in some companies, surviving an unbearable superior can even earn you a badge of courage.

All managers are in a network of relationships. Not only must they influence bosses and subordinates, they must also influence peers and important external groups where they lack formal authority. John Kotter of the Harvard Business School found in his study of general managers that this was one of their critical job challenges.[20] When managers develop effective lateral relationships, they are more likely to be successful in their careers. Peers are valuable sources of information; they can tell us what is happening in other parts of the organization. Trusted peers can also serve as advisers and counselors, giving us feedback on our personal style and also helping us to test out alternative ways of dealing with problems.

Finally, we do not have to have a relationship with people to learn from them. As often as people mention learning from bosses, peers, or mentors, they mention outside role models. It was interesting to find how many people look to historical figures or to well-known contemporary leaders for inspiration and learning. We are just as apt to look to great men and women of the past for guidance as we are to look to those we work with today.

While much has been written about the importance of mentors, bosses, and peers in adult development, very little has been said of the influence of historical role models. Biographies have always been a rich source of information on the great military, governmental, and business leaders of the past. The popularity of biographies of modern business executives—and of their books about management—is evidence of a keen interest in discovering the secrets of others' successes. Advancements in video technology make contemporary leaders even more accessible as exemplars of the art of leadership. To gain access to the wealth of knowledge others have about leadership, we recommend that you interview or observe leaders you admire.

Mentors are difficult to find—usually they find you—so many of us will never have the experience of being the protégé of an influential leader. However, you can still learn firsthand from those you think are masters of the craft. Ask a leader whom you look up to whether you may interview her or him. Usually, he or she will be flattered. (After all, that is how we got the material for this book.) It is tougher to get a busy executive to allow you to follow him or her through a typical day, but if you ever have the opportunity, take it. Also, the next book you buy or check out of the library ought to be a biography of a leader you admire. Then make a practice of reading one a month for the next year.

Education and Training. Formal leadership education and training represent a third way you can learn to lead. Every large company, and most medium-sized firms, have some type of internal training department. Most also send their employees to external programs for further development. A report by the Carnegie Foundation estimates that corporations spend nearly $40 billion each year for employee education.[21] While only about 30 percent of this total is spent specifically for leadership training, that amount is not trivial.[22]

However, those we surveyed said that the classroom was less important as a source of learning than either experience or other people. The Center for Creative Leadership and the Honeywell Corporation found the same result. Yet, we also find that formal training and education can be of greater importance in developing your skills as an executive and leader than you might assume. While it may be true that these activities account for somewhere between 9 percent and 20 percent of our managerial development, training is a high-leverage way of improving your chances of success. Most managers are lucky to spend two weeks per year in formal training programs. That's about 5 percent of your time. But for that 5 percent, you get two to four times the educational value from the hours you spend in training than you do from the hours you spend on "the job." We would say that is a pretty efficient and effective use of resources. Perhaps you would get even greater payoff if you spent more time consciously trying to improve yourself through organized programs.

Training and education are vastly underdeveloped and underutilized opportunities for creating a personal edge in learning to lead. At the same time, we can be encouraged by an explosion of new leadership programs on and off the college campus that may fill the chasm between need and resource availability.[23] If, as the Honeywell study recommends, training were more closely linked to changes in assignments, then it could become a more effective process in leadership development.

We recommend that you devote at least two weeks each year to formal personal development programs. Do not wait to be sent "to get fixed." Initiate the request to participate in outside training and development programs. While we learn mostly from experience and other people, we need to get away from our day-to-day work to get some perspective. Take advantage of both internal company programs and external ones. Your own organization may have the best programs, and it may have the best employees of any company in the industry, but you need the stimulation from other sources. There is also great value in the connections you can make at external executive programs.

In developing leadership abilities, concentrate on interpersonal skills and strategic thinking skills. Also, take courses in functional areas about which you know least. It is important to stay up to date in your field, but the most effective leaders are generalists. Get as much breadth as early as possible.

While part of the job of your boss and the staff of the training department is to help you develop, do not wait for them to tell you what you need to do to improve. Instead, go to them with your own list of developmental needs. If you are not clear about your strengths and weaknesses, sit down right now and begin your assessment. Ask for feedback from people you know. Ask personnel or colleagues if they can recommend any useful diagnostic questionnaires. If, for example, you would like to assess how you use the practices we describe in this book, you might consider taking our Leadership Practices Inventory (see Appendix B). Initiate your own learning agenda, and find the opportunities to build on your strengths and overcome your weaknesses.

Can Leadership Be Taught?

Every time we conduct a workshop or give a speech on leadership, someone will ask, "Can leadership be taught? Are leaders born or made?" The only honest answer to this question is, "No one knows for sure." All the other answers are either opinions or matters of definition.

The Case for Leaders Being Born. In 1954, management scholar Peter F. Drucker made the following assertion in his book *The Practice of Management:* "We have defined the purpose of an organization as 'making common men do uncommon things.' We have not talked, however, about making common men into uncommon men. We have not, in other words, talked about leadership. This was intentional. Leadership is of utmost importance. Indeed there is no substitute for it. But leadership cannot be created or promoted. It cannot be taught or learned."[24] Drucker had not changed his mind by 1985, when he wrote a new preface to the book. His position is crystal clear on this issue. "Leadership," says Drucker, "requires aptitude—and men who are good chief engineers or general managers are rare enough even without aptitude for leadership. Leadership also requires basic attitudes. And nothing is as difficult to define, nothing as difficult to change, as basic attitudes. . . ."[25]

Researchers at the University of Minnesota may have provided some empirical support for Drucker's assertion. They investigated the formation of adult personality, studying 350 pairs of identical twins, some raised apart and some raised together. The researchers put the twins through extensive psychological and physiological tests to measure the roots of key personality traits.

Comparing twins raised apart with those raised together allows researchers to compare the relative influence of heredity versus environment. If twins raised with different parents are more similar than different, then researchers attribute the characteristics to heredity. On the other hand, if the twins are more different than similar, researchers conclude that the distinctive characteristics are due to environmental influences.[26] The University of Minnesota researchers concluded that leadership is one of those traits that are most strongly determined by heredity. They came to this conclusion after analyzing the results of a personality questionnaire measuring eleven factors, including leadership, which was defined as "social potency." A person high in social potency "is masterful, a forceful leader who likes to be the center of attention." When social potency was exhibited in one twin, it tended to be exhibited in both, even when they had been raised apart. Researchers estimate that 61 percent of that trait is inherited.[27]

Tracy Gibbons, an organization development professional with Digital Equipment Corporation, took another look in her doctoral dissertation at the question of whether the potential to behave as a leader is the result of heredity and early childhood experiences or whether it is the result of skill acquisition in the adult years. Gibbons specifically investigated the development of transformational leaders—those who shape, alter, and elevate the motives and values of followers.[28] She surveyed a total of forty-seven individuals who were nominated as leaders by knowledgeable colleagues; of these forty-seven, she conducted in-depth interviews with sixteen. On the basis of these interviews, Gibbons concluded that formal education, mentoring, and other activities in adult life had less influence on the development of transformational leaders than did parental expectations and values and innate skills reinforced very early in life. She states, "Predisposition, either from inborn characteristics or early influences, plays a significant part in the development of transformational leaders. These effects set the stage early on which other events and experiences will unfold and also influence heavily the behavioral patterns and meaning making system which gets established."[29] Gibbons's findings suggest that the desire, willingness, and skill to lead result mostly from inborn abilities and early childhood experience. Gibbons also found that these predisposed leaders use structured developmental opportunities and influential people as vehicles for actualizing their natural talents and that these learning opportunities tend to be for personal development rather than skills training. Furthermore, they see all experiences as learning experiences, not just those times spent in a formal classroom or workshop. Gibbons concludes that efforts to formally train and develop transformational leaders will have limited payoff. She recommends more careful screening and selection processes in order to identify those predisposed to lead.

Similar conclusions could be drawn from a study conducted by AT&T. While the AT&T study tracked managerial progress, and did not examine leadership traits per se, it provides some useful insight into the development of leaders. Beginning in 1956, AT&T set out to establish a more scientifically sound basis for selection and development of managers. To do this, they decided to conduct the Managerial Progress Study (MPS) and followed the managerial careers of 422 recruits for thirty years.[30] As a basis for determining the predictors of a manager's progress through the ranks, AT&T conducted an intensive series of assessment center exercises at the beginning of the study, at year eight, and at year twenty. The exercises consisted of behavioral simulations, personality tests, interviews, and aptitude tests. At the end of the exercises, each participant was rated by management and psychology experts on twenty-six dimensions measured through assessment activities. These dimensions ranged from areas such as administrative skills and interpersonal skills to work motivation and dependency needs. On the basis of these ratings, in 1956 the experts predicted who would succeed—defined by the AT&T researchers as attaining higher levels of management.

Of the college-trained recruits in the study, 64 percent of those predicted to reach middle management by year eight did so. Of the noncollege new managers, 40 percent of those predicted to reach middle management did so. The researchers then asked the crucial question, "How did they get this way?" They concluded: "One fact, expected by any personnel selection expert and well confirmed in the MPS, was that, to a great extent, measurable differences in managerial abilities and motivations that would foretell success were present when the men first came to the original assessment center. . . . Most of the original 26 assessment dimensions had significant correlations with success after eight years, and most of these relationships held even after 20 years."[31]

These studies of managerial and leadership success make a strong case for the "leaders are born" proposition. It would appear from their evidence that leadership is a natural talent and that it is either innate or developed as the result of very early childhood influences. If this is so, then organizations ought to focus most of their efforts on selecting and developing the naturally talented leaders. Those who do not possess the talents would not benefit much from attempts to train them to be leaders. Before we accept this conclusion, however, we must examine the case for "leaders are made."

The Case for Leaders Being Made. We would be intellectually dishonest if we did not say that some individuals clearly have a higher probability of succeeding at leadership than others. Some people are born with it. Some people are especially fortunate to have parents who promote the development of leadership abilities in their children at a very early age. It is the same in any life activity: it is easier for some people than for others. But this does not mean that ordinary people cannot get extraordinary things done, that ordinary managers cannot become extraordinary leaders. We make this assertion for one simple, but often overlooked, reason in this argument over whether leaders are born or made: there is no perfect predictor of leadership. There is no one factor that anyone can point to in any study ever done on leadership that accounts for 100 percent of the variance—and that includes ours. There is no way that we can say for certain that "This person will become a leader, but this person will not." Researchers can only talk in terms of probabilities. As we said earlier, people do not get extraordinary things done with probability thinking. They achieve greatness through possibility thinking. And it is possible that an ordinary human being can learn to lead.

Take the Minnesota twins study, for example. The researchers say that 61 percent of the trait of social potency is inherited. That leaves 39 percent that is determined by other factors. The researchers also admit that further study will probably change this percentage. Says Thomas Bouchard, director of the study, "In general, the degree of genetic influence tends to be around 50 percent."[32] So we could conclude that about half of the tendency toward leadership is innate and half is influenced by other factors. That seems to us to be reason for optimism. That's better odds than a professional baseball player has for getting a hit in the majors.

We also take issue with how leadership was defined in the Minnesota twins study. Social potency—dominance, taking charge, wanting to be the center of attention—may be one aspect of leadership. But it is certainly not all of the leadership practices we have uncovered in our research. Leadership is a complex set of behaviors and traits, not just one. We simply cannot rely upon one measure as the determinant of our leadership potential.

Psychoanalyst and author Michael Maccoby took a different approach to studying leaders. He conducted lengthy in-depth interviews and administered the Rorschach test—a recognized psychoanalytical measure—to six recognized leaders in a variety of settings. In summarizing his analysis of these leaders, he stated that they were "alike in their ability to bring together different types of people for a common goal, to transform adversarial competition into principled problem solving leading to consensus. They differ in talents, temperament, and traits that equip them to work at different levels of business, unions, and government."[33] In other words, while some of their practices were similar, their personalities were different. Maccoby also implies that character traits as well as an individual's actions may differ from setting to setting. There is no one way to lead, nor is there one and only one leadership personality.

The AT&T study of managerial potential discussed earlier also demonstrates that there is no perfect predictor of managerial advancement. Thirty-two percent of those college-educated new managers who were predicted not to reach middle management within eight years actually did so. And 9 percent of the noncollege group predicted not to reach middle management actually did so. Thirty-six percent of the college group and 60 percent of the noncollege group predicted to advance to middle management did not. Even personnel experts using twenty-six tested dimensions cannot predict success with 100 percent accuracy.

Another intriguing bit of information emerges from the AT&T study that has even greater significance for leadership development. When the researchers analyzed the relationship between job challenge and the actual management level attained, they found that there was a "strong and statistically highly significant relationship between ratings of Job Challenge and advancement, although, once again, all the percentages are lower for the noncollege than for the college group. Those whom the assessors had not predicted to reach middle management are of considerable interest. Here 61 percent of the college graduates who had not been so predicted, but who had experienced high Job Challenge, had arrived at middle management. The corresponding figure for the comparable noncollege group was 28 percent."[34] In other words, a job high in challenge nearly *doubled* the chances of success for those predicted not to succeed. It is apparent that it is possible to structure the environment to dramatically improve a manager's chance of advancing.

Leadership ability is only one part of the AT&T Managerial Progress Study. We cannot conclude from that research alone that job challenge would significantly enhance the development of leadership skills. However, our own finding that challenge plays a critical role in doing our leadership best would support this assumption. The Center for Creative Leadership's finding that 60 percent of all executive learning opportunities were associated with tough assignments and hardships further reinforces the potency of challenge in stimulating individual growth and development.

Believing That You Can Lead. There is another danger in accepting too readily that innate personality is the principal determinant of leadership ability. That is the danger of the "self-fulfilling prophecy." It is well documented that adults in the workplace and children in school tend to perform to the level of the authority figure's expectations.[35] A boss's high expectations of his or her team are likely to produce higher levels of performance, provided that the subordinates perceive the high expectations as achievable and realistic. Similarly, a boss's low expectations of employees are likely to lead to lower performance. If we, as parents, teachers, bosses, or friends, begin with the assumption that some people have it and some people don't, then we are likely to get exactly the kind of leaders we expect.

Certainly we should not mislead people into believing that they can attain unrealistic goals. Neither should we assume that only a few will ever attain excellence in leadership or any other human endeavor. Those who are most successful at bringing out the best in others are those who set achievable but stretching goals and believe that they have the ability to develop the talents of others.[36] It is far healthier and more productive for us to start with the assumption that it is possible for everyone to lead. Maybe that leadership will be exhibited on behalf of the school, or the church, or the community, or the scouts, or the union, or the family. In our study, everyone had a leadership story to tell. Somewhere, sometime, the leader within each of us may get the call to step forward.

Harry Levinson and Stuart Rosenthal, both psychiatric experts, make this comment about the development of leaders: "Our point of view is that some leaders want to be leaders and see themselves as leaders. Others rise to the occasion. In either case they see what has to be done and do it. They provide stability and support while defining goals and providing reassurance. Sometimes they become leaders when they become angry about something, catch fire, and start to lead. . . . Managers become leaders when they learn to take a stand, to take risks, to anticipate, initiate, and innovate."[37] The same can be said for the leaders we studied. Many of them did not initiate the personal best leadership projects that they wrote and talked about, yet they rose to the occasion. Some got angry and caught fire. Others accepted an assignment and then found something within them that they had not known they had. None of us may know our true strength until challenged to bring it forth.

In discussing theories of how leaders develop, leadership scholar James MacGregor Burns observed, "I think we suffer to a great degree from the excessively Freudian emphasis on childhood and on a particular culture. While Freudian analysis is indispensable to leadership study, it is certainly not adequate. What is left out is the enormous variety of cultures, the large variation and changeability of motivations, the role of skill, and the tremendous impact of later years. I think, for example, a person's 20s have been insufficiently addressed as a time of enormous psychological influence. And the impact of life's experiences goes on into the 30s, 40s, and 50s as well."[38]

To take the determinist's view that only some of us have it and others do not is to settle for less than we can become. "Determinism," writes Arthur M. Schlesinger, Jr., "may or may not be true, but it unquestionably violates our deepest human instincts. It abolishes the idea of human freedom by discrediting the presumption of choice that underlies every word we speak and every decision we make. It abolishes the idea of human responsibility by depriving the individual of accountability for his acts. No one can live consistently by any deterministic creed."[39]

It is interesting for us to note that people have never asked us, "Can management be taught? Are managers born or made?" These questions are always raised about leadership, but never about management. It is a curious phenomenon. Why should management be viewed as a set of skills and abilities but leadership be seen as a set of innate personality characteristics? We have simply assumed that management can be taught and on the basis of that assumption established hundreds of business schools and thousands of management courses. In the process, our schools and companies have educated hundreds of thousands of managers. Certainly some of those managers are better and some are worse than others. There is also a normal distribution of high-performing chefs. But in general, schools have probably raised the calibre of managers by assuming that people can learn the attitudes, skills, and knowledge associated with good management practice. The same can be done with leadership. By viewing leadership as a nonlearnable set of character traits, a self-fulfilling prophecy has been created that dooms societies to having only a few good leaders. If you assume that leadership is learnable, you will be surprised to discover how many good leaders there really are.

We would not have written this book if we did not believe that it is possible for ordinary people to learn to get extraordinary things done. We would not have written this book if we did not believe that ordinary managers can become extraordinary leaders. Gibbons, who makes a strong case for attention to predispositional factors, also found that transformational leaders had to an extraordinary degree a focus on their own self-development. We cast our votes on the side of optimism and hope. Chances are that you also believe that leadership can be learned, or you would not be reading this book. One thing we do know for certain is that effective leaders are constantly learning. They are constantly looking for ways to improve themselves and their organizations. By reading this book and engaging in other personal development activities, you are demonstrating a predisposition to lead. So even if some other people may not be able to learn to lead, you believe that you can. And that is where it all starts—with your own belief in yourself.

Jim Whittaker, president of Whittaker/O'Malley, Inc., of Seattle and the first American to climb Mount Everest, once observed: "You never conquer the mountain. You conquer yourself. Your doubts and your fears." We would say the same for leadership. You do not conquer your organization. You do not conquer leadership. You conquer your own doubts and fears about leading.

Leadership Development as Self-Development

Wanting to lead and believing that you can lead are only the departure points on the path to leadership. Leadership is an art, a performing art. And in the art of leadership, the artist's instrument is the self. The mastery of the art of leadership comes with the mastery of the self. Ultimately, leadership development is a process of self-development.

The quest for leadership is first an inner quest to discover who you are. Through self-development comes the confidence needed to lead. Self-confidence is really awareness of and faith in your own powers. These powers become clear and strong only as you work to identify and develop them.

As you begin this quest, you must wrestle with some difficult questions: How much do I understand about what is going on in the organization and the world in which it operates? How prepared am I to handle the complex problems that now confront my organization? Where do I think the organization ought to be headed over the next ten years? What are my beliefs about how people ought to conduct the affairs of our organization? How certain am I of my own conviction as to stated vision and values? What are my strengths and weaknesses? What do I need to do to improve my abilities to move the organization forward? How solid is my relationship with my constituents? Am I the right one to be leading at this very moment? The questions continue.

Honest answers to these questions tell you that you must become more worldly-wise. The leader, being in the forefront, is usually the first to encounter the world outside the boundaries of the organization. The more you know about the world, the easier it is to approach it with assurance. Thus, you should seek to learn as much as possible about the forces that affect the organization, be they political, economic, social, moral, or artistic. Honest answers to these questions also tell you that if you are to become as effective as possible, you must strive to improve your own understanding of others and build your skills to mobilize people's energies toward higher purposes. While scholars may disagree on the origins of leadership, there is a strong consensus that leaders must be interpersonally competent. You must be able to listen, take advice, lose arguments, and follow. Unless you can develop the trust and respect of others, you cannot lead.

Struggling with these questions also reveals fundamental contradictions in leadership. Taken to extremes, any leadership practice can become destructive. Challenging the status quo to promote innovation and progressive change, taken to extremes, can create needless turmoil, confusion, and paranoia. The singular focus on one vision of the future can blind us to other possibilities as well as the realities of the present. Exploiting our powers of inspiration can cause others to surrender their will. An overreliance on collaboration and trust may indicate an avoidance of making critical decisions or cause errors in judgment. An obsession with being seen as a role model can push you into isolation for fear of losing privacy or being found out or cause you to be more concerned with style than substance. Constantly worrying about who should be recognized and when you should celebrate can turn you into a gregarious minstrel.

Far more insidious than all of these, however, is the treachery of hubris. It is fun to be a leader, gratifying to have influence, and exhilarating to have scores of people cheering your every word. It is empowering to set directions and have people fired up to march at your command. In more subtle ways than you would like to admit, you can be seduced by your own power and importance. All evil leaders have been infected with the disease of hubris. They have become bloated with an exaggerated sense of self. They have used the gifts of leadership to pursue their own sinister ends. Leadership practices are amoral. But leaders—the men and women who use the practices—are moral or immoral. There is an ethical dimension to this discussion of leadership that cannot be ignored or taken lightly, by leader or follower.

John Gardner, former Secretary of Health, Education, and Welfare and founding chairperson of Common Cause, has written that there are four moral goals of leadership:

1. Releasing human potential.
2. Balancing the needs of the individual and the community.
3. Defending the fundamental values of the community.
4. Instilling in individuals a sense of initiative and responsibility.[40]

Attending to these goals will always lift your eyes to higher purposes. As you work to become all you can be, you can start to let go of your petty self-interests. As you give back some of what you have been given, you can reconstruct your communities. As you serve the values of freedom, justice, equality, caring, and dignity, you can constantly renew the foundations of democracy. As each of us takes individual reponsibility for creating the world of our dreams, we can all participate in leading.

You can resolve the conflicts and contradictions of leadership only if you establish for yourself an ethical set of standards on which to base all your actions. You can avoid excessive pride only if you recognize that you are human and need the help of others. All of your individual complexities are held together by a fundamental set of values and beliefs. Developing yourself as a leader begins with those key convictions. It begins with your value system. Clarifying your own values and visions is a highly personal matter. No one else can do it for you. To exhibit to others harmonious leadership—where words and deeds are consonant—you must be in tune internally.

All great leaders have wrestled with their souls. For instance, Martin Luther King, Jr., while attending Crozer Seminary, read extensively in history. The more he read, the more he questioned whether Christian love could be a potent force in the world. He doubted his own capacity to be a pacifist. His faith in love was deeply shaken by Nietzsche's writings glorifying war and power and proclaiming the coming of a master race to control the masses. It was not until he was introduced to the teachings of Gandhi that King was inspired to live by the discipline of nonviolent resistance. And it was through reading Gandhi's biography that King also learned that the Indian lawyer himself had struggled to overcome his own tendencies to hatred, anger, and violence. Only after resolving his internal conflicts was King able to enthusiastically embrace the philosophy of nonviolence.[41] Such personal searching is essential in the development of leaders. You cannot elevate others to higher purposes until you have first elevated yourself. Like King, you must resolve those dissonant internal chords. Extensive knowledge of history and the outside world only increases your awareness of competing value systems, of the many principles by which individuals, organizations, and states can choose to function. You cannot lead others until you have first led yourself through a struggle with opposing values.

When you clarify the principles that will govern your life and the ends that you will seek, you give purpose to your daily decisions. A personal creed gives you a point of reference for navigating the sometimes stormy seas of organizational life. Without a set of such beliefs, your life has no rudder, and you are easily blown about by the winds of fashion. A credo to guide you prevents confusion on the journey. The internal resolution of competing beliefs also leads to personal integrity. And personal integrity is essential to believability. A leader with integrity has one self, at home and at work, with family and with colleagues. He or she has a unifying set of values that guide choices of action regardless of the situation.

This does not mean that leaders are one-dimensional people who only focus narrowly on their work. Leaders may have numerous pursuits and interests—arts and literature, science and technology, entertainment and sports, politics and law, religion and family. Nor does it mean that leaders are flawless, perfect human beings. Leaders are human and make mistakes. We are not suggesting that the ideal leader is a saint. However, we are suggesting that leaders who cannot personally adhere to a firm set of values cannot convince others of the worthiness of those values. Leaders without integrity are only putting on an act. The believability and credibility so essential for leadership are earned when your behavior is consistent with your beliefs. The first step in summoning the courage of your convictions is clarifying for yourself the beliefs that will guide your actions.

We have said that leaders take us to places we have never been before. But there are no freeways to the future, no paved highways to unknown, unexplored destinations. There is only wilderness. If you are to step out into the unknown, the place to begin is with the exploration of the inner territory.

Appendix A

The Personal Best Questionnaire

In collecting information on exemplary leadership practices for our study, we asked each leader to write a description of one "personal best leadership experience." The leadership practices model was derived from an analysis of the common patterns and themes that emerged from these personal bests. The Leadership Practices Inventory (Appendix B) was developed from the model that we derived from these cases. Following is the original personal best questionnaire as revised for use in our leadership workshops. You may want to take a couple of hours to complete a personal best case for yourself. You will find the answers helpful in assessing your own leadership skills.

Preparing to Write Your Case

1. Think about all the leadership experiences that you have had. Let them pass by in your mind, as if you were viewing a movie of your leadership career or hearing a tape recording of your personal leadership history.
2. A few of these experiences will undoubtedly look, sound, or feel like personal best experiences. Select one of these experiences.
3. Spend some time getting a clear mental picture of the extraordinary experience. See, hear, and feel it again as intensely as you can. Get as vivid an image as possible.
4. Once you have recalled and reviewed your personal best leadership experience, turn to the worksheets and answer all the questions.

Getting Started

Personal Best. A "personal best" experience is an event (or series of events) that you believe to be your *individual standard of excellence.* It is your own "record-setting performance," a time when you did your very best. It is something you use to measure yourself by, a time you look upon as your peak performance experience. A useful and simple guide to the selection of your "personal best" is "When I think about this, it makes me smile a lot."

Leadership Experience. You have been involved in many experiences in your career. For purposes of this exercise, we ask that you focus your thinking on only those in which you were *the leader.* You might use these criteria to select your leadership experience:

1. Your experience does not need to be restricted to a time when you were an appointed or selected leader. It can be either a time when you emerged as the informal leader or a time when you were the official leader or manager.

2. It can be in *any functional area,* in a service or manufacturing organization, in a public or private institution, in a staff or line position.

3. It can be the start-up of a new business, a new product or service development program, a quality or productivity improvement project, and so on.

4. The experience does not need to have occurred in your present organization; it could be a past work experience. It could also have occurred in a club, a professional organization, a school, or any other setting. Let it be any time when you felt that you performed at your very best as a leader.

Personal Best Leadership Experience Worksheet

The Situation

1. Where did this take place (name of the organization, division, and so on)?
2. When did this take place? How long did it take to complete from start to finish?
3. Who initiated this project? If you did, indicate your title and function at the time. If someone else did, what was this person's relationship to you (boss, peer, outsider, and so on)?
4. Who else was involved, either directly or indirectly, in the project? It is not necessary to name everyone. Please just indicate their functional areas and whether they were bosses, peers, subordinates, and so on.
5. What was your specific role or title in this project?
6. What were the actual results of this project, both quantitative and qualitative?
7. Indicate any awards, bonuses, or other special recognition that you and/or your group received.

Opportunities and Challenges

1. If you were the one to initiate this project, why did you want to do it? What drove or motivated you? If someone else asked you to take on this project, what made you believe that you could do it?
2. What did you do, if anything, to challenge the status quo, the existing ways of doing things? What changes did you make? What novel or innovative things did you do? What risks did you take?
3. How did you challenge others to attain high levels of performance, to excel, to do better than ever before?
4. As best as you can recall, how would you describe your feelings at the beginning of this project? How did you feel immediately after accepting or initiating this project?

Destinations

1. As you looked forward to the time when the project would be completed, what did you dream that you would accomplish? What was your ideal outcome, your vision, your fondest wish for the project?

2. If you used any slogans, metaphors, catchy phrases, logos, or symbols to describe your dream or vision, what were they?

3. How did you sell others on your project? What did you say to convince them that they ought to enlist and sign up?

4. How did you build a sense of enthusiasm and excitement for this project?

Involvement

1. How did you involve others in planning and decision making? Did you use any special methods or techniques?

2. How did you build a team out of the individuals who worked for you? Did you use any special methods?

3. How did you foster cooperation and collaboration among those whose support you needed, even if they didn't work for you? Did you use any special methods?

4. How did you develop trust and respect among those who worked on the project? Did you use any special methods?

5. How did you help your team members to feel strong and capable? Did you use any special methods?

Leader Actions

1. For this project, what were the values that you believed should guide everyone's actions? What were the standards to which everyone was accountable?

2. How did you show others, by your own example, that you were serious about these values and standards? How did you "lead by example"?

3. What structures and systems did you use to plan, organize, or control the project?

4. What dramatic or unusual actions, if any, did you take to get people to pay attention to important aspects of the project?

Encouragement

1. How did your team celebrate its accomplishments, its milestone achievements?

2. What festive events, if any, did you have?

3. How did you recognize individual contributors? Did you use any special incentive systems, recognition programs, and so on?

4. How did you get the word out to the rest of the organization about your group's accomplishments?

Summing Up

Please review your responses to the previous six sets of questions. In summary, what would you say were the five or six key leadership actions that you took that enabled this to be a personal best leadership experience?

Character of the Experience

1. What five or six words would you use to best describe the character (the feel, the spirit, the nature, the quality) of this experience?

2. Please write down a few words that describe how you felt personally as the leader of this experience.

Leadership Lessons

1. What did you learn about leadership style and practice from this "personal best leadership experience"?

2. If you were going to teach someone else about leadership on the basis of your own personal best experience, what morals and lessons about leadership would you pass along? What would you tell others to do to be an effective leader?

3. Of all the things that contributed to the success of this project—whether actions that you took or other factors—what was the most important contributor to the project's success? What action, attribute, and so on, made the most difference?

4. If you were going to contribute one quotation of your own, one personal saying, to a book about leadership, what would that quotation be?

In Conclusion

1. As a leader, how is it that you would most like to be remembered?

2. Why did you select this project to write about? When you look back on it, what made this one so special, unique, memorable?

3. How have you learned to lead? Just how have you gained the skills to lead? Please select and rank order the three ways that have contributed most to your leadership development.

Appendix B

The Leadership Practices Inventory

Some claim that never has there been a time when more and better leadership is required than today. A plethora of research studies on leadership have been conducted over the past three decades. Recent best-selling books focus on leadership and leaders. Still, the field lacks consensus about just what leadership is, how it differs from management, and whether it can be measured and developed. Over the past five years, we have asked hundreds of managers to describe a "personal best"—an experience in which they got something extraordinary accomplished in an organization. This is their personal best experience as a *leader*. This is an experience in which they feel that they led, not managed, their project to plateaus beyond traditional expectations. These were experiences in which "everything all came together." As we listened and investigated people's experiences, we discovered that everyone had a story to tell. The stories they told were seldom about traditional textbook management. We learned that there was a pattern of behavior that people used to lead and to achieve extraordinary results.

The personal best survey is twelve pages long and consists of thirty-eight open-ended questions, such as: Who initiated the project? What made you believe you could accomplish the results you sought? What special, if any, techniques or strategies did you use to get other people involved in the project? Did you do anything to mark the completion of the project, at the end or along the way? What did you learn most from this experience? What key lessons would you share with another person about

For more information about the use or purchase of the Leadership Practices Inventory, contact University Associates, 8517 Production Avenue, San Diego, California 92121, (619) 578-5900.

leadership from this experience? Completing the personal best survey generally requires about one to two hours of reflection and expression. More than 550 of these surveys have been collected. A short form (one to two pages) of the survey is available and has been completed by an additional 780 managers.

In addition to these case studies, we have conducted forty-two in-depth interviews, primarily with managers in middle- to senior-level organizational positions in a wide variety of public- and private-sector companies. These interviews have generally taken forty-five to sixty minutes but in some cases have lasted four or five hours. The various case studies (from surveys and interview notes) have been independently content analyzed by two outside raters. While the category labels have gone through several iterations, the fundamental pattern of leadership behavior that emerges when people are accomplishing extraordinary things in organizations is best described by the following five practices, each of which consists of two basic strategies:

1. Challenging the process
   a. Search for opportunities
   b. Experiment and take risks
2. Inspiring a shared vision
   a. Envision the future
   b. Enlist others
3. Enabling others to act
   a. Foster collaboration
   b. Strengthen others
4. Modeling the way
   a. Set the example
   b. Plan small wins
5. Encouraging the heart
   a. Recognize contributions
   b. Celebrate accomplishments

More than 70 percent of the behavior and strategies described in respondents' personal best case studies and interviews can be accounted for by these factors. While there may appear to be a somewhat linear or sequential flow to these practices, the actual dynamics are much more complex. In the course of personal best experiences, individuals are likely to describe an iterative, or developmental, flow to the leadership process. Their cases provided illustrative examples of the dynamic interconnectedness among the various behaviors and strategies.

The more complete description of the model and relevant conceptual materials has already been presented in the text of this book. The purpose of this appendix is to report the development and validation of a leadership measurement instrument (Leadership Practices Inventory) based upon this conceptual and empirical framework.

Instrument Development

The Leadership Practices Inventory (LPI) was designed on the basis of lengthy and repeated feedback from respondents and factor analyses of various sets of behaviorally based statements. Each statement was cast on a five-point Likert scale. A higher value represented greater use of a leadership behavior: (1) rarely or never do what is described in the statement, (2) once in a while do what is described, (3) sometimes do what is described, (4) fairly often do what is described, and (5) very frequently, if not always, do what is described in the statement. Sample statements include: "I seek out challenging opportunities that test my skills and abilities." "I let others know my beliefs on how to best run the organization I manage." "I treat others with dignity and respect."

The LPI was originally completed by 120 M.B.A. students. These students were employed full time and attending school part time at a small private West Coast university. Their average age was twenty-nine years, nearly 60 percent were males, and almost half had supervisory experience. After the subjects completed the instrument, an item-by-item discussion was conducted. The items that were reported to be difficult, ambiguous, or inconsistent were either replaced or revised. Similar feedback discussions were held with nine professionals in psychology, organizational behavior, and human resource management who were familiar with psychometric issues, the conceptual framework, and management development.

Successive administrations of the instrument in the earlier

stages of development involved more than 3,000 managers and their subordinates. Analysis of data from these respondents included tests of internal reliability and underlying factor structure. Statements that loaded poorly or contained uninterpretable factors were either discarded or rewritten. Additional discussions with respondents resulted in further modification of the instrument.

The outcome of the above procedures is the current form of the instrument, which contains thirty statements—six statements for measuring each of the five leadership practices. There are two forms of the Leadership Practices Inventory—Self and Other—which differ only in whether the behavior described is the respondent's (Self) or that of another specific person (Other).

Sample

The sample for the current version of the Leadership Practices Inventory consists of 1,567 managers and executives involved in several public and in-company management development seminars and their subordinates. For the LPI-Self, there are 423 respondents. Their backgrounds represent a full array of functional fields from both public- and private-sector organizations. Twelve percent are female. There are approximately three subordinate respondents (LPI-Other) for each managerial subject ($N = 1,144$). A separate sample of foreign managers was also collected, including managers from Australia, England, Germany, and the Netherlands. While no attempts have been made to generate "representative" sample populations of managers, the relatively large total sample size involved increases the potential generalizability of these findings. The .01 level of probability was adopted throughout the analyses as the appropriate level of statistical significance.

Procedurally, each individual completing the LPI-Self also requests four to five other people familiar with his or her behavior to complete the LPI-Other. The LPI-Other is voluntary and confidential. The form is returned directly to the researchers (or seminar facilitators). The LPI-Self can be self-scored but is typically returned directly to the researchers for scoring and feedback purposes.

Results

Means, Standard Deviations, and Reliability. Means and standard deviations for each scale of the Leadership Practices Inventory, as well as the scores on various reliability measures, are presented in Table A. Enabling others to act was the leadership practice most frequently reported being used. This was followed by challenging the process, modeling the way, and encouraging the heart. Inspiring a shared vision was the leadership practice perceived as least frequently engaged in by managers.

Internal reliabilities on the LPI-Self ranged from .69 to .85 and on the LPI-Other from .78 to .90. Test-retest reliability from a convenience sample of fifty-seven M.B.A. students averaged better than .93. These students were employed full time and attending graduate school on a part-time basis. More than 50 percent had supervisory responsibility. Forty percent were women.

Tests for social desirability response bias were also performed with a sample of thirty middle-level managers, using the Marlowe-Crowne Social Desirability Scale, which consists of thirty-three items representing behaviors that are culturally sanctioned and approved but are improbable of occurrence. None of the correlations was statistically significant ($p < .01$).

Comparisons Between the LPI-Self and LPI-Other. Table B compares means for the LPI-Self and the LPI-Other. Frequency scores tended to be higher on the LPI-Self than on the LPI-Other, but only two were statistically significant. There was considerable difference between the frequency scores of managers and those of their subordinates on both the enabling others to act and challenging the process dimensions ($p < .01$). There were no statistically significant differences between Self and Other scores on the remaining three factors (inspiring a shared vision, modeling the way, and encouraging the heart).

Comparison Between Male and Female Respondents. Differences on the Leadership Practices Inventory for male and female respondents were investigated with a sample of seventy-three (forty-nine male and twenty-four female) senior human resource management professionals attending a national training directors' conference. Because of the relatively high percentage of females (32.9

Table A. Means, Standard Deviations, and Reliability Indices for the Leadership Practices Inventory (N = 1,567).

| | Mean | Standard Deviation | Internal Reliability | | | Test-Retest Reliability (N = 57) | Social Desirability Scale (N = 30) |
			LPI (N = 1,567)	LPI-Self (N = 423)	LPI-Other (N = 1,144)		
Challenging the process	22.63	3.85	.78	.73	.79	.93	.13
Inspiring a shared vision	20.08	4.86	.88	.84	.89	.94	.04
Enabling others to act	23.96	3.95	.83	.69	.84	.94	.24
Modeling the way	22.42	3.90	.79	.73	.80	.95	.29
Encouraging the heart	22.23	4.72	.89	.85	.90	.93	.27

Table B. *T* Tests of Differences Between Scores on the LPI-Self and LPI-Other.

	LPI-Self		LPI-Other		t
	Mean	Standard Deviation	Mean	Standard Deviation	
Challenging the process	23.12	3.20	22.41	4.04	2.64[a]
Inspiring a shared vision	20.05	4.07	19.86	5.04	.55
Enabling others to act	24.94	2.43	23.47	4.23	5.36[a]
Modeling the way	22.71	3.29	22.25	4.08	1.66
Encouraging the heart	22.72	3.82	21.93	4.92	2.41

[a] $p < .01$

Table C. Comparison Between Male and Female Managers on the LPI-Self.

	Males (N = 49)		Females (N = 24)	
	Mean	Standard Deviation	Mean	Standard Deviation
Challenging the process	24.35	2.61	24.71	3.48
Inspiring a shared vision	22.98	3.19	23.62	3.51
Enabling others to act	26.63	2.17	26.46	2.81
Modeling the way	23.94	2.66	23.67	3.28
Encouraging the heart	23.22	3.85	26.25	2.94[a]

[a] $p < .001$

percent) employed in this profession, this sample offered a unique opportunity to test for gender differences. As the results in Table C reveal, there is one significant differences between the LPI-Self scores for male and female managers. Subsequent analysis of the LPI-Other scores for female managers in the overall sample showed that they did not differ from their male counterparts, with the exception of the "encouraging the heart" factor. Female managers assessed themselves as engaging in "encouraging the heart" behaviors significantly more than did male managers.

Comparisons Between Public- and Private-Sector Managers.
Scores on the Leadership Practices Inventory for public-sector managers were compared with those of managers from the pri-

vate sector. The public-sector administrators were all senior federal government executives ($N = 137$). They were matched with two samples of senior private-sector executives ($N = 197$). The results are presented in Table D. Overall, there were no statistically significant differences. Nor were there differences between the LPI-Self and the LPI-Other scores.

Cross-Cultural Comparisons. Several cross-cultural comparisons of scores on the Leadership Practices Inventory were also conducted. A sample of ninety-five middle-level Australian managers was compared with two samples of American middle-level managers ($N = 70$) on the LPI-Self. These comparisons, reported in Table E, resulted in no statistically significant differences between the Australian managers and their American counterparts. Internal reliabilities with the Australian sample were all .72 or higher.

An earlier version of the Leadership Practices Inventory was utilized in comparing American managers ($N = 270$) from one company with their European counterparts ($N = 170$). There were 62 respondents from England, 56 respondents from the Netherlands, and 52 respondents from Germany. No statistically significant differences were found on either the LPI-Self or the LPI-Other between these European managers and their American colleagues. While some differences within the three European samples were observed, company executives found these differences consistent with cultural norms for their countries.

Factor Structure of the LPI. The factor structure of the Leadership Practices Inventory-Other is presented in Table F. Responses to the thirty leadership behavior items were factor analyzed, using principal factoring with iteration and varimax rotation. The initial analysis extracted five factors that had eigenvalues greater than or equal to 1.0 and accounted for 61.1 percent of the variance. These factors were quite consistent with a priori expectations, replicating the conceptual framework advanced from the qualitative findings from the Personal Best Survey. The individual item factor loadings were also generally as expected. The stability of the five factors was tested by factor analyzing the data from different subsamples. In each case, the factor structure was similar to the one shown in Table F.

Table D. Comparison Between Public- and Private-Sector Managers on the LPI.

	Self and Others				Self				Others			
	Public Sector (N = 137)		Private Sector (N = 197)		Public Sector (N = 22)		Private Sector (N = 35)		Public Sector (N = 115)		Private Sector (N = 162)	
	Mean	Standard Deviation	Mean	Standard Deviation	Mean	Standard Deviation	Mean	Standard Deviation	Mean	Standard Deviation	Mean	Standard Deviation
Challenging the process	22.45	4.70	22.99	3.93	24.05	3.05	23.54	3.35	22.14	4.90	22.87	4.04
Inspiring a shared vision	20.32	5.10	19.90	5.24	21.05	4.12	20.34	4.34	20.18	5.28	19.81	5.42
Enabling others to act	23.64	4.40	23.98	4.28	25.36	1.81	25.49	2.50	23.30	4.67	23.66	4.52
Modeling the way	21.74	4.36	22.44	4.29	24.27	2.05	22.83	3.27	21.25	4.52	22.36	4.49
Encouraging the heart	22.18	5.64	22.63	4.73	24.36	4.75	23.54	3.90	21.76	5.72	22.43	4.88

Table E. Comparison Between Scores of Australian and American Managers on the LPI-Self.

	Internal Reliability	Australia (N = 95)		United States (N = 70)		t
		Mean	Standard Deviation	Mean	Standard Deviation	
Challenging the process	.72	22.62	3.40	22.04	3.46	1.07
Inspiring a shared vision	.85	20.38	4.74	19.00	4.67	1.87
Enabling others to act	.74	25.22	3.05	25.24	2.17	.05
Modeling the way	.73	22.63	3.67	22.48	3.24	.28
Encouraging the heart	.83	21.95	4.26	23.31	3.60	2.23

Table F. Factor Structure for the Leadership Practices Inventory-Other (N = 1,144).

Item Number	Factor 1 Enabling others to act	Factor 2 Challenging the process	Factor 3 Encouraging the heart	Factor 4 Inspiring a shared vision	Factor 5 Modeling the way
8	.716	.020	.142	.084	.098
23	.711	.238	.228	.148	.258
18	.687	.125	.190	.155	.226
13	.519	.086	.177	.121	.026
28	.513	.213	.284	.201	.272
3	.418	.086	.189	.223	.303
16	.169	.691	.188	.224	.202
11	.069	.657	.094	.168	.189
26	.209	.604	.244	.237	.057
1	.208	.581	.124	.204	.131
21	.175	.408	.192	.144	.142
6	.367	.368	.079	.115	.146
5	.104	.117	.718	.267	.117
25	.150	.176	.711	.283	.146
20	.458	.174	.686	.098	.164
15	.409	.144	.685	.051	.116
10	.364	.166	.636	.050	.223
30	.205	.254	.562	.163	.270
7	.181	.309	.215	.684	.126
2	.144	.323	.138	.653	.171
27	.259	.466	.274	.573	.111
17	.190	.344	.258	.564	.196
22	.248	.434	.138	.469	.134
12	.128	.345	.098	.442	.122
29	.209	.183	.141	.118	.652
14	.166	.250	.201	.189	.523
9	.332	.091	.198	.033	.510
19	.067	.377	.188	.259	.439
4	.196	.277	.139	.352	.393
24	.349	.241	.114	.075	.379

Managerial Effectiveness and the Leadership Practices Inventory.
In addition to the Leadership Practices Inventory, a leadership
effectiveness scale was developed. This measure also went
through several iterations in its development. It contains six
Likert-type items on five-point scales. The questions ask about
the extent to which this manager (who requested they complete
the LPI) meets the job-related needs of his or her subordinates,
has built a committed work group, and has influence with upper
management. Additional items assess the extent to which the
respondents are satisfied with the leadership provided by the manager, satisfied that the manager's leadership practices are appropriate, and feel empowered by the manager. Coefficient alpha for
the leadership effectiveness scale is .98. The test-retest reliability
over ten days for a sample of fifty-seven M.B.A. students was better than .96. The effectiveness scale was not significantly correlated with the Marlowe-Crowne Social Desirability Scale. This
sample involved thirty middle-level managers.

Utilizing only the responses from the LPI-Other ($N = 514$),
we examined the relationship between leaders' effectiveness and
their behavior as measured on the Leadership Practices Inventory.
By including only the responses from "other people" about their
managers, we were using relatively independent assessments and
thereby minimizing any potential self-report bias. Regression
analysis was performed, with leader effectiveness as the dependent
variable and the five practices from the LPI the independent
variables. The regression equation was highly significant
($F = 318.88$), $p < .0001$). The leadership practices explained over
55 percent (adjusted $R^2 = .756$) of the variance around subordinates' assessments of their leaders' effectiveness.

Another method for examining the validity of the Leadership Practices Inventory is to determine how well LPI scores can
differentiate between high- and low-performing managers. This
issue was examined using discriminant analysis as a classification
technique. We wanted to determine how well the LPI scores
could group managers into various performance-based categories.

The lowest third and highest third of the managers on the
LPI-Other leader effectiveness scale formed the low- and high-
performance categories. Approximately 85 percent of the sample
of LPI-Other respondents ($N = 325$) was used to create the canon-

ical discriminant function, with the remaining respondents
($N = 54$) used to create a holdout sample for classification purposes. One discriminant function was derived. As shown in Table
G, the discriminant function correctly classified 92.62 percent of
the known cases. In the holdout sample, 77.78 percent of the
cases were correctly classified. Both of these results are statistically
significant ($p < .001$).

When the middle third of the sample (that is, managers
with moderate effectiveness scores) was included, the discriminant
functions derived were able to correctly classify 71.13 percent of
the cases in the known sample and 67.90 percent in the holdout
sample (see Table H). Both of these percentages are significantly
beyond probabilities due to chance ($p < .001$). That scores on the

Table G. Classification Results from Discriminant Analysis
on Effectiveness by LPI (Two Groups).

	Low	High	Percentage Correct
Known sample			
Actual members	169	156	
Predicted members	154	147	92.62
Holdout sample			
Actual members	23	31	
Predicted members	16	26	77.78

Table H. Classification Results from Discriminant Analysis
on Effectiveness by LPI (Three Groups).

	Low	Moderate	High	Percentage Correct
Known sample				
Actual members	169	108	156	
Predicted members	123	64	121	71.13
Holdout sample				
Actual members	18	28	35	
Predicted members	13	15	27	67.90

Leadership Practices Inventory are related to managerial (leader) effectiveness is reinforced by the classification results from the discriminant analyses.

Conclusions

The Leadership Practices Inventory was developed to empirically measure the conceptual framework developed in the case studies of managers' personal best experiences as leaders— times when they had accomplished something extraordinary in an organization. Various analyses suggest that the LPI has sound psychometric properties.

The factor structure of the Leadership Practices Inventory is quite consistent with the a priori conceptual model. The internal reliabilities of the LPI (both Self and Other forms) are substantial. The reliability of the LPI over time appears acceptable. Finally, the LPI does not seem to be significantly affected by possible social desirability response biases.

There are differences between respondents' self-scores and scores provided by others about the respondents (LPI-Self versus LPI-Other). In itself, this is not a remarkable finding, because this same phenomenon is characteristic of many psychological inventories. Caution, however, should be exercised when interpreting the LPI-Self scores independently of LPI-Other feedback.

For both feedback (self-development) and research purposes, the LPI-Other appears to provide relatively reliable and valid assessments of respondent behavior. Nearly one-half of subordinates' evaluations of their managers' effectiveness can be explained by their perceptions of their managers' behavior along the conceptual framework of the Leadership Practices Inventory. Moreover, significantly better than chance predictions about subordinates' assessments of their managers' effectiveness can be made on the basis of information provided by the LPI. Research is currently under way to investigate how the Leadership Practices Inventory is related to other independent measures of managerial effectiveness.

Notes

Chapter One

1. Unless otherwise noted, all quotations from leaders are taken from personal interviews or from personal best cases written for this study by the leaders and analyzed by the authors. The titles and affiliations of the leaders in this study may be different today than they were at the time of publication. We expect many to move into other leadership responsibilities.

2. Metcalfe, R., "Innovation in Industry." Presentation to the first annual conference on innovation in industry, Palo Alto, Calif., Oct. 6, 1981.

3. Bennis, W., and Nanus, B. *Leaders: The Strategies for Taking Charge.* New York: Harper & Row, 1985.

4. Kanter, R. M. "The Middle Manager as Innovator." *Harvard Business Review,* 1982, *60* (4), 95–105, p. 102.

5. Federman, I. "A Personal View of Leadership." Presentation to the Executive Seminar in Corporate Excellence, Santa Clara University, Oct. 16, 1983.

6. *First Tuesday,* Interview with Frank J. Ruck, Jr. Undated.

7. Peters, T. J. "Developing Distinctive Skills." Presentation to the Executive Seminar in Corporate Excellence, Santa Clara University, Feb. 13, 1985.

Chapter Two

1. Schmidt, W. H., and Posner, B. Z. *Managerial Values and Expectations: The Silent Power in Personal and Organizational Life.* New York: American Management Association, 1982. Also see: Posner, B. Z., Kouzes, J. M., and Schmidt, W. H.

"Shared Values Make a Difference: An Empirical Test of Corporate Culture." *Human Resource Management,* 1985, *24* (3), 293–309; and Posner, B. Z., and Schmidt, W. H. "Values and the American Manager: An Update." *California Management Review,* 1984, *26,* (3), 202–216.

2. Posner, B. Z., and Schmidt, W. H. "Values and Expectations of Federal Service Executives." *Public Administration Review,* 1986, *46,* (5), 447–454.

3. Clarke, B. Letter, April 1, 1987.

4. Clymer, A. "Low Marks for Executive Honesty." *New York Times,* June 9, 1985, p. 1F.

5. Federman, I. "A Personal View of Leadership." Presentation to the Executive Seminar in Corporate Excellence, Santa Clara University, Oct. 16, 1983.

6. Kouzes, J. M., Posner, B. Z., and Krause, M. "Summary of the Executive Challenges Survey." Unpublished manuscript, Santa Clara University, 1986.

7. Terkel, S. *Working.* New York: Pantheon Books, 1974, p. xxiv.

8. O'Reilly, C. "Charisma as Communication: The Impact of Top Management Credibility and Philosophy on Employee Involvement." Paper presented at the annual meeting of the Academy of Management, Boston, 1984, p. 15.

9. O'Reilly, "Charisma as Communication," Table 3.

10. The Times Mirror Company. *The People and The Press.* Los Angeles: The Times Mirror Company, 1986.

11. The Times Mirror Company, *The People and The Press,* p. 25.

12. "Reagan's Crusade." *Newsweek,* Dec. 15, 1986, pp. 26–35.

13. Packard, V. *The Pyramid Climbers.* New York: McGraw Hill, 1962, p. 170.

Chapter Three

1. Partridge, E. *A Short Etymological Dictionary of Modern English.* New York: Macmillan, 1977, p. 342.

2. Partridge, p. 378.

3. Carrigan, P. M. "Up from the Ashes." *OD Practitioner,* 1986, *18* (1), pp. 2–3.

4. Carrigan, "Up from the Ashes," p. 2.

5. Carrigan, P. M. Introduction as keynote speaker to the OD Network National Conference, San Francisco, Oct. 16, 1985.

6. Carrigan, P. M. Telephone conversation, Oct. 16, 1986.

7. Kanter, R. M. *The Change Masters: Innovation for Productivity in the American Corporation.* New York: Simon & Schuster, 1983, p. 125.

8. Burns, J. M. *Leadership.* New York: Harper & Row, 1978, p. 461.

9. Operation Raleigh U.S.A. recruitment poster, Raleigh, N.C., n.d.

10. Deci, E. L., and Ryan, R. M. "The Empirical Exploration of Intrinsic Motivational Processes." In L. Berkowitz (ed.), *Adventures in Experimental Social Psychology.* Vol. 13. New York: Academic Press, 1980, pp. 39–80.

11. Csikszentmihalyi, M. *Beyond Boredom and Anxiety: The Experience of Play in Work and Games.* San Francisco: Jossey-Bass, 1975.

12. Csikszentmihalyi, *Beyond Boredom and Anxiety,* p. 30.

13. Csikszentmihalyi, *Beyond Boredom and Anxiety,* p. 33.

14. Bennis, W. "View from the Top." In W. Bennis, *Leadership by Warren Bennis.* Cincinnati, Ohio: University of Cincinnati, n.d., p. 26.

15. Bennis, "View from the Top," p. 26.

16. Bennis, "View from the Top," p. 28.

17. Ackoff, R. *Management in Small Doses.* New York: Wiley, 1986, p. 110.

Chapter Four

1. Telnack, J. "How to Improve Product Design Processes." Presentation to the Executive Seminar in Corporate Excellence, Santa Clara University, Feb. 11, 1987.

2. Utterback, J. M. "Innovation in Industry and the Diffusion of Technology." In M. L. Tushman, and W. L. Moore (eds.), *Readings in the Management of Innovation.* Boston: Pitman, 1982, pp. 29–41.

3. Marquis, D. G. "The Anatomy of Successful Innova-

tions." In M. L. Tushman, and W. L. More (eds.), *Readings in the Management of Innovation.* Boston: Pitman, 1982, pp. 42–50.

4. Maidique, M. "Why Products Succeed and Why Products Fail." Presentation to the Executive Seminar in Corporate Excellence, Santa Clara University, May 29, 1985.

5. Katz, R. "The Influence of Group Longevity: High Performance Research Teams." *Wharton Magazine,* 1982, *6* (3), 28–34.

6. Katz, "The Influence of Group Longevity," p. 31.

7. Katz, "The Influence of Group Longevity," p. 32.

8. Federman, I. "A Personal View of Leadership." Presentation to the Executive Seminar in Corporate Excellence, Santa Clara University, Oct. 16, 1983.

9. Wriston, W. B. *Risk and Other Four-Letter Words.* New York: Harper & Row, 1986, pp. 219–220.

10. Abbey, A., and Dickson, J. W. "R & D Work Climate and Innovation in Semiconductors." *Academy of Management Journal,* 1983, *26* (2), 362–368.

11. Maidique, "Why Products Succeed."

12. For discussions of hardiness and health, see: Kobasa, S. C., Maddi, S. R., and Courington, S., "Personality and Constitution as Mediators in the Stress-Illness Relationship." *Journal of Health and Social Behavior,* 1981, *22,* 368–378; Kobasa, S. C., Maddi, S. R., and Kahn, S. "Hardiness and Health: A Prospective Study." *Journal of Personality and Social Psychology,* 1982, *42* (1), 168–177; Kobasa, S. C., and Puccetti, M. C. "Personality and Social Resources in Stress Resistance." *Journal of Personality and Social Psychology,* 1983, *45* (4), 839–850.

13. Maddi, S. R., and Kobasa, S. C. *The Hardy Executive: Health Under Stress.* Chicago: Dorsey Professional Books/Dow Jones–Irwin, 1984, pp. 31–32.

14. Maddi and Kobasa, *The Hardy Executive,* p. 59.

15. For another discussion of leadership and uncertainty, see: Thompson, J. D., and Tuden, A. "Strategies, Structures, and Processes of Organizational Decision." In J. D. Thompson and others (eds.), *Comparative Studies in Administration.* Pittsburgh, Pa.: University of Pittsburgh Press, 1959.

16. "Why Kodak Is Starting to Click Again." *Business Week,* Feb. 23, 1987, p. 134.

Chapter Five

1. Blum, A. *Annapurna: A Woman's Place*. San Francisco: Sierra Club Books, 1980, p. 9.

2. Blum, *Annapurna*, p. 12.

3. McDonald, J. A. "Member Profile: Mark Leslie." *Innovation Newsletter*, 1982, *2* (2), 5.

4. Bennis, W. B., and Nanus, B. *Leaders: The Strategies for Taking Charge*. New York: Harper & Row, 1985, p. 89. For other discussions of the role of vision in leadership, see: Clifford, D. K., Jr., and Cavanagh, R. E. *The Winning Performance: How American's High-Growth Midsize Companies Succeed*. New York: Bantam Books, 1985, p. 133; Kanter, R. M. *The Change Masters: Innovations for Productivity in the American Corporation*. New York: Simon & Schuster, 1983, p. 305; Levinson, H., and Rosenthal, S. *CEO: Corporate Leadership in Action*. New York: Basic Books, 1984, p. 289; Maccoby, M. *The Leader*. New York: Simon & Schuster, 1981, p. 52; Peters, T., and Austin, N. *A Passion for Excellence: The Leadership Difference*. New York: Random House, 1985, p. 284.

5. Eisenberg, L. "Taking the Long, Sharp View." *Esquire*, 1983, *100* (6), 305.

6. Shearson Lehman/American Express. "Vision." Advertisement appearing in *Business Week*, June 4, 1984, pp. 42–43.

7. For other discussions of the role of vision and purpose in leadership, see: Burns, J. M. *Leadership*. New York: Harper & Row, 1978, p. 19; Selznick, P. *Leadership and Administration: A Sociological Interpretation*. New York: Harper & Row, 1957; Barnard, C. I. *The Functions of the Executive*. Cambridge, Mass.: Harvard University Press, 1968; Vaill, P. "The Purposing of High-Performing Systems." *Organizational Dynamics*, Autumn 1982, pp. 23–39; Diebold, J. *Making the Future Work: Unleashing Our Powers of Innovation for the Decades Ahead*. New York: Simon & Schuster, 1984; Block, P. *The Empowered Manager: Positive Political Skills at Work*. San Francisco: Jossey-Bass, 1987.

8. Jacques, E. "Executive Vision: A Matter of Time." *Small Business Report*, June 1985, p. 8. For a more complete discussion of these ideas, see Jacques, E. *A General Theory of Bureaucracy*. New York: Halsted Press, 1976.

9. Madden J., with Anderson, D. *Hey, Wait a Minute: I Wrote a Book.* New York: Ballentine, 1985, pp. 225–226. Copyright © 1985, Villard Books, a Division of Random House, Inc.

10. Reprinted by permission of the *Harvard Business Review.* Excerpts from "Strategic Planning: Forward in Reverse" by Robert H. Hayes (November/December 1985, p. 113). Copyright © 1985 by the President and Fellows of Harvard College; all rights reserved.

11. Hayes, "Strategic Planning," p. 113.

12. Reprinted by permission of the *Harvard Business Review.* Excerpts from "Planning on the Left Side and Managing on the Right" by Henry Mintzberg (July/August 1976, p. 57). Copyright © 1976 by the President and Fellows of Harvard College; all rights reserved.

13. Mintzberg, "Planning on the Left Side," p. 53.

14. Rowan, R. *The Intuitive Manager.* New York: Little, Brown, 1986, p. 11.

15. Agor, W. H. "The Logic of Intuition: How Top Executives Make Important Decisions." *Organizational Dynamics,* 1986, *14* (3), 5–18, p. 7.

16. Rowan, R. *The Intuitive Manager,* p. 9.

17. Kouzes, J. M., Posner, B. Z., and Krause, M. "Summary of the Executive Challenges Survey." Unpublished manuscript, Santa Clara University, 1986.

18. El Sawy, O. A. "Temporal Perspective and Managerial Attention: A Study of Chief Executive Strategic Behavior." Unpublished doctoral dissertation, Stanford University, 1983.

19. El Sawy, "Temporal Perspective," p. VII-35.

20. El Sawy, "Temporal Perspective," p. VII-43.

21. For a useful discussion of the role of assumptions in vision creation, see Sowell, T. *A Conflict of Visions.* New York: Morrow, 1987.

22. Hayes, "Strategic Planning," p. 114.

23. Hayes, "Strategic Planning," p. 114.

24. Shepard, H. A., and Hawley, J. A. *Life Planning: Personal and Organizational.* Washington, D.C.: National Training and Development Service Press, 1974.

Chapter Six

1. Swiggett, R. L. "The Development of Kollmorgen." Presentation to graduates of the Innovation and Mastery Program of Innovation Associates, Oct. 2, 1980.

2. Swiggett, "The Development of Kollmorgen."

3. Swiggett, "The Development of Kollmorgen."

4. King, M. L., Jr. "I Have a Dream." In C. S. King (ed.), *The Words of Martin Luther King, Jr.* New York: Newmarket Press, 1983, pp. 95-98. Reprinted by permission of Joan Daves, copyright © 1963 by Martin Luther King, Jr.

5. Gardner, J. S. *The Heart of the Matter: Leader-Constituent Interaction.* Leadership Papers 3, Washington, D.C.: The Independent Sector, 1968, p. 11.

6. Cleveland, H. *The Knowledge Executive: Leadership in an Information Society.* New York: Truman Talley Books/Dutton, 1985, p. 40. Copyright © 1985, reprinted by permission of E. P. Dutton, Inc.

7. Cleveland, *The Knowledge Executive*, pp. 41-42.

8. Cleveland, *The Knowledge Executive*, p. 42.

9. Berlew, D. E. "Leadership and Organizational Excitement." *California Management Review*, 1974, *17* (2), 21-30, p. 23.

10. Renwick, P. A., and Lawler, E. E. "What You Really Want from Your Job." *Psychology Today*, 1978, *12* (5), p. 56.

11. Terkel, S. *Working.* New York: Pantheon Books, 1974, p. xxiv.

12. Terkel, *Working*, p. 589.

13. Schmidt, W. H., and Posner, B. Z. *Managerial Values in Perspective.* New York: American Management Association, 1983.

14. Burns, J. M. *Leadership.* New York: Harper & Row, 1978, p. 20.

15. King, "I Have a Dream," pp. 95-98.

16. Coggins, C. "Plain Talk Marks Reagan Skill." *Austin American Statesman*, Oct. 21, 1984, p. A14. Also see: Hart, R. P. *Verbal Style and the Presidency.* Orlando, Fla.: Academic Press, 1984.

17. Jones, E. C. "Interpreting Interpersonal Behavior: The Effects of Expectancies." *Science*, 1986, *234*, 41-46.

18. Goleman, D. "Optimism Leads to Health, Wealth, Research Shows." *San Jose Mercury News,* Feb. 5, 1987, pp. 1F-2F.

19. Bass, B. M. *Leadership and Performance Beyond Expectations.* New York: Free Press, 1985, p. 35.

20. Friedman, H. S., Prince, L. M., Riggio, R. E., and DiMatteo, M. R. "Understanding and Assessing Nonverbal Expressiveness: The Affective Communication Test." *Journal of Personality and Social Psychology,* 1980, *39* (2), 333-351.

21. Pines, M. "Children's Winning Ways." *Psychology Today,* 1984, *18* (12), 58-65.

Chapter Seven

1. Carrigan, P. M. "Up from the Ashes." *OD Practitioner,* 1986, *18* (1), 2-3.

2. Bradford, D. L., and Cohen, A. R. *Managing for Excellence.* New York: Wiley, 1984, p. 10.

3. Johnson, D. W., and Johnson, S. "The Effects of Attitude Similarity, Expectation on Interpersonal Attraction." *Journal of Experimental Social Psychology,* 1972, *8,* 197-206.

4. Tjosvold, D. "Effects of Leader Warmth and Directiveness on Subordinate Performance on a Subsequent Task." *Journal of Applied Psychology,* 1984, *69,* 422-427.

5. Lucien, R., and Amend, P. "The Turnaround." *Inc.,* Aug. 1986, pp. 45-46.

6. Kohn, A. *No Contest: The Case Against Competition.* Boston: Houghton Mifflin, 1986.

7. Tjosvold, D. *Working Together to Get Things Done.* Lexington, Mass.: Heath, 1986, p. 25.

8. Blau, P. "Cooperation and Competition in a Bureaucracy." *American Journal of Sociology,* 1954, *59,* 530-535.

9. Johnson, D. W., and others. "Effects of Cooperative, Competitive, and Individualistic Goal Structures on Achievement: A Meta-Analysis." *Psychological Bulletin,* 1981, *89,* 47-62.

10. Johnson, D. W., and Johnson, R. T. "The Socialization and Achievement Crises: Are Cooperative Learning Experiences the Solution?" In L. Bickman (ed.), *Applied Social Psychology Annual 4.* Beverly Hills, Calif.: Sage, 1983, p. 146.

11. Helmreich, R. L., Beane, W. G., Lucker, W., and Spence, J. T. "Achievement Motivation and Scientific Attainment." *Personality and Social Psychology Bulletin*, 1978, *4*, 222-226; Helmreich, R. L., Saurin, L. L., and Carsrud, A. L. "The Honeymoon Effect in Job Performance: Temporal Increases in the Productive Power of Achievement Motivation." *Journal of Applied Psychology*, 1986, *71*, 185-188; Helmreich, R. L., and others. "Making It in Academic Psychology: Demographic and Personality Correlates of Attainment." *Journal of Personality and Social Psychology*, 1980, *39*, 896-908; Helmreich, R. L. "Pilot Selection and Training." Paper presented at the annual meeting of the American Psychological Association, Washington, D.C., Aug. 1982; Spence, J. T., and Helmreich, R. L. "Achievement-Related Motives and Behavior." In T. Spence (ed.), *Achievement and Achievement Motives: Psychological and Sociological Approaches*. San Francisco: Freeman, 1983.

12. Axelrod, R. *The Evolution of Cooperation*. New York: Basic Books, 1984.

13. Homans, G. *The Human Group*. New York: Harcourt Brace Jovanovich, 1950.

14. "Companywide 'Parachute' Lifts Off." *San Jose Mercury News*, Oct. 11, 1986, p. 3F.

15. Boss, W. R. "Trust and Managerial Problem Solving Revisited." *Group & Organization Studies*, 1978, *3* (3), 331-342.

16. Cialdini, R. B. *Influence: How and Why People Agree to Things*. New York: Marrow, 1984.

17. Hay, I. *The First Hundred Thousand*. London: William Blackford, 1916, pp. 224-225.

18. Kahneman, D., and Tversky, A. "Prospect Theory: An Analysis of Decision Under Risk." *Econometrica*, 1979, *47*, 263-291; Tversky, A., and Kahneman, D. "The Framing of Decisions and the Psychology of Choice." *Science*, 1981, *211*, 453-458; Bazerman, M. H., and Neale, M. A. "Heuristics in Negotiation: Limitations to Dispute Resolution Effectiveness." In M. H. Bazerman and R. J. Lewicki (eds.), *Negotiating in Organizations*. Beverly Hills, Calif.: Sage, 1983, pp. 51-67; Neale, M. A., and Bazerman, M. H. "Systematic Deviations from Rationality in Negotiator Behavior: The Framing of Conflict and Negotiator Overconfidence." *Academy of Management Journal*, 1985, *28* (1), 34-49.

19. Bazerman, M. H. "Why Negotiations Go Wrong." *Psychology Today,* 1986, *20* (6), 54–58, p. 58. For more discussion of these ideas, see: Kanter, R. M. *Change Masters: Innovation for Productivity in the American Corporation.* New York: Simon & Schuster, 1983.

20. Kanter, R. M. Presentation on *The Change Masters,* Santa Clara University, March 26, 1984.

21. Van de Ven, A., Delbecq, A. L., and Koenig, R. J. "Determinants of Coordination Modes Within Organizations," *American Sociological Review,* 1976, *41* (2), 322–338.

22. Sheehan, W. J. "Productivity Through People at Dana." Presentation to the Executive Seminar in Corporate Excellence, Santa Clara University, June 2, 1982.

23. Rogers, C. *On Becoming a Person.* Boston: Houghton Mifflin, 1961.

24. Golembiewski, R. T., and McConkie, M. L. "The Centrality of Interpersonal Trust in Group Processes." In C. L. Cooper (ed.), *Theories of Group Processes,* New York: Wiley, 1975.

25. Deutsch, M. "Cooperation and Trust: Some Theoretical Notes." In R. Jones (ed.), *Nebraska Symposium on Motivation.* Lincoln: University of Nebraska Press, 1962, pp. 275–319; Zand, D. E. "Trust and Managerial Problem Solving." *Administrative Science Quarterly,* 1972, *17* (2), 229–239.

26. "MCI Founder Bill McGowan." *Inc.,* Aug. 1986, pp. 29–38.

27. Zand, "Trust and Managerial Problem Solving"; Boss, "Trust and Managerial Problem Solving Revisited."

28. Boss, "Trust and Managerial Problem Solving Revisited," p. 341.

29. O'Reilly, C. A., and Roberts, K. H. "Information Filtration in Organizations: Three Experiments." *Organizational Behavior and Human Performance,* 1974, *11,* 253–265.

30. Boss, "Trust and Managerial Problem Solving Revisited," p. 338.

31. Driscoll, J. W. "Trust and Participation in Organizational Decision Making as Predictors of Satisfaction." *Academy of Management Journal,* 1978, *21* (1), 44–56.

32. Rotter, J. B. "Trust and Gullibility." *Psychology Today,* 1980, *14* (5), 35–38.

33. Rotter, "Trust and Gullibility," p. 102.

34. Kelly, H. H., and Stahelski, A. J. "Social Interaction Basis of Cooperators' and Competitors' Beliefs About Others." *Journal of Personality and Social Psychology*, 1970, *16*, 66–91; Rubin, J. Z., and Brown, R. *The Social Psychology of Bargaining and Negotiation.* New York: Academic Press, 1975.

35. Kanter, *The Change Masters: Innovation for Productivity in the American Corporation.*

36. Ackoff, R. L. *Management in Small Doses.* New York: Wiley, 1986, pp. 150–152.

37. Rotter, "Trust and Gullibility"; Boss, "Trust and Managerial Problem Solving Revisited."

38. Likert, R., and Willits, J. M. *Morale and Agency Management.* Hartford, Conn.: Life Insurance Agency Management Association, 1940.

39. Rogers, *On Becoming a Person.*

40. Schmitt, C. S. "A Bean Counter with a Heart." *San Jose Mercury News*, Nov. 24, 1986, p. C1.

41. Myers, M. T., and Myers, G. E. *Managing by Communication.* New York: McGraw-Hill, 1982.

42. Fisher, R., and Ury, W. *Getting to Yes.* Boston: Houghton Mifflin, 1981.

43. Lawler, E. E., III. *High-Involvement Management: Participative Strategies for Improving Organizational Performance.* San Francisco: Jossey-Bass, 1986.

44. See Lawler, *High-Involvement Management.*

45. Myers and Myers, *Managing by Communication.*

Chapter Eight

1. Kanter, R. M. Presentation on *The Change Masters*, Santa Clara University, March 13, 1984.

2. Kipnis, D., Schmidt, S., Price, K., and Stitt, C. "Why Do I Like Thee: Is It Your Performance or My Orders?" *Journal of Applied Psychology*, 1981, *66* (3), 324–328.

3. See, for example: Tannenbaum, A. *Control in Organizations.* New York: McGraw-Hill, 1968; Tannenbaum, A., and others. *Hierarchy in Organizations: An International Comparison.* San Francisco: Jossey-Bass, 1974; Tannenbaum, A., and Cooke, R. A. "Organizational Control: A Review of Studies Employing

the Control Graph Method." In D. J. Hickson and C. J. Lammers (eds.), *Organizations Alike and Unlike*. London: Routledge & Kegan Paul, 1979.

4. Butterfield, D. A., and Posner, B. Z. "Task-Relevant Control in Organizations." *Personnel Psychology*, 1979, *32*, 725–740.

5. Telnack, J. J. "How To Improve Product Design Processes." Presentation to the Executive Seminar in Corporate Excellence, Santa Clara University, Feb. 11. 1987.

6. Bradford, D. L., and Cohen, A. R. *Managing for Excellence*. New York: Wiley, 1984.

7. Langer, E. J., and Rodin, J. "The Effects of Choice and Enhanced Personal Responsibility for the Aged: A Field Experiment in an Institutional Setting." *Journal of Personality and Social Psychology*, 1976, *34* (2), 191–198; Rodin, J., and Langer, E. J. "Long-Term Efforts of a Control-Relevant Intervention with the Institutionalized Aged." *Journal of Personality and Social Psychology*, 1977, *35* (12), 897–902.

8. McCall, M. W., Jr., and Lombardo, M. M. *Off The Track: Why and How Successful Executives Get Derailed*. Technical Report no. 21. Greensboro, N.C.: Center for Creative Leadership, 1983.

9. Hagberg, R. A., Jr., Conti, I., and Mirabile, R. J. *Profile of the Terminated Executive*. Menlo Park, Calif.: Ward, Hagberg, 1985.

10. See, for example: McClelland, D. C. *Power: The Inner Experience*. New York: Irvington, 1975; Winter, D. G. *The Power Motive*. New York: Free Press, 1973.

11. McClelland, *Power*.

12. McClelland, *Power*, p. 263.

13. See, for example: Pfeffer, J. *Power in Organizations*. Marshfield, Mass.: Pitman, 1981; Pfeffer, J., and Salancik, G. *The External Control of Organizations: A Resource Dependence Perspective*. New York: Harper & Row, 1978; Hickson, D. J., and others. "A Strategic Contingencies Theory of Intraorganizational Power." *Administrative Science Quarterly*, 1971, *16* (2), 216–229.

14. Kanter, R. M. *The Change Masters: Innovation for Productivity in the American Corporation*. New York: Simon & Schuster, 1983; Kanter, R. M. *Men and Women of the Corporation*. New York: Basic Books, 1977.

15. Mainiero, L. A. "Coping with Powerlessness: The Relationship of Gender and Job Dependency to Empowerment-Strategy Usage." *Administrative Science Quarterly,* 1986, *31* (4), 633–653.

16. Chethik, N. "After a Year, There's Still Enthusiasm at NUMMI Plant." *San Jose Mercury News,* Jan. 19, 1986, pp. 1 ff.

17. Kanter, *The Change Masters;* also see: Pfeffer, *Power in Organizations.*

18. Reprinted by permission of the *Harvard Business Review.* Excerpts from "Wide-Open Management" by Alan M. Kantrow (May/June 1986, p. 99). Copyright © 1986 by the President and Fellows of Harvard College; all rights reserved.

19. Kantrow, "Wide-Open Management," p. 102.

20. De Pree, M. "Theory Fastball." *New Management,* 1983, *1* (4), 29–36.

21. Peters, T. J. "Let the Crew Sail the Ship." *Success,* 1985, *32,* 12.

22. Suters, E. T. "Show and Tell." *Inc.,* 1987, *9* (4), 111–112.

23. Posner, B. Z., and Butterfield, D. A. "Personal Correlates of Organization Control." *The Journal of Psychology,* 1979, *102,* 299–306.

Chapter Nine

1. Schmidt, W. H., and Posner, B. Z. *Managerial Values and Expectations: The Silent Power in Personal and Organizational Life.* New York: American Management Association, 1982.

2. Fox, M. S., and Bear, J. *Cafe Beaujolais.* Berkeley: Ten Speed Press, 1984, p. 27.

3. Posner, B. Z., Kouzes, J. M., and Schmidt, W. H. "Shared Values Make a Difference: An Empirical Test of Corporate Culture. *Human Resource Management,* 1985, *24* (3), 293–310. Copyright © 1985, reprinted by permission of John Wiley & Sons, Inc.

4. Posner, B. Z., and Low, P. "Values of Australian Managers." Working paper, Santa Clara University, Apr. 1987.

5. See, for example: Kets de Vries, M.F.R. "Organizational Stress: A Call for Management Action." *Sloan Management Review,* 1979, *21* (1), 3–14; Golembiewski, R. T. "Small Groups and Large

Organizations." In J. G. March (ed.), *Handbook of Organizations.* Chicago: Rand-McNally, 1965; Newman, J. E., and Beehr, T. A. "Personal and Organizational Strategies for Handling Job Stress: A Review of Research and Opinion." *Personnel Psychology,* 1979, *32,* 1–43; Behling, O., and Darrow, A. L. *Managing Work-Related Stress.* Chicago: Science Research Associates, 1984.

6. Deal, T. E., and Kennedy, A. A. *Corporate Cultures.* Reading, Mass.: Addison-Wesley, 1982.

7. Caldwell, D. F. "The Face of Corporate Culture." *Santa Clara Today.* Nov. 1984, p. 12.

8. O'Reilly, C., and Caldwell, D. F. "The Power of Strong Corporate Cultures in Silicon Valley Firms." Presentation to the Executive Seminar in Corporate Excellence, Santa Clara University, Feb. 13, 1985.

9. Ruch, R. S., and Goodman, R. *Images at the Top.* New York: Free Press, 1983, pp. 34–40, p. 38.

10. Watson, T. J., Jr., *A Business and Its Beliefs.* New York: McGraw-Hill, 1963, p. 5.

11. Gold, K. A. *A Comparative Analysis of Successful Organizations.* Washington, D.C.: Workforce Effectiveness and Development Group, U.S. Office of Personnel Management, 1981.

12. Gardner, J. W. *Excellence: Can We Be Equal and Excellent Too?* New York: Harper & Row, 1961.

13. Argyris, C. "Double Loop Learning in Organizations." *Harvard Business Review,* 1977, *55* (5), 115–125.

14. Sanders, B. "There's No Secret to Serving the Customer." Presentation to the Executive Seminar in Corporate Excellence, Santa Clara University, Oct. 28, 1986.

15. Schein, E. H. *Organizational Culture and Leadership: A Dynamic View.* San Francisco: Jossey-Bass, 1985, p. 243.

16. Peters, T. J. "Symbols, Patterns, and Settings: An Optimistic Case for Getting Things Done." *Organizational Dynamics,* 1978, *7* (2), 2–23; Peters, T. J. "Management Systems: The Language of Organizational Characters and Competence." *Organizational Dynamics,* 1980, *9* (1), 2–26.

17. Carlzon, J. *Moments of Truth.* New York: Ballinger, 1987.

18. This discussion draws upon Peters, "Management Systems," and Schein, *Organizational Culture.*

19. Kanarick, A. F., and Dotlich, D. L. "Honeywell's Agenda for Organizational Change." *New Management*, 1984, 2 (1), 14-19.

20. Wojahn, E. "Management by Walking Away." *Inc.*, Oct. 1983, pp. 68-76.

21. Horn, J. C. "Work: Crosstalk." *Psychology Today*, 1984, *18* (80), 18.

22. Magnet, M. "Corning Glass Shapes Up." *Fortune*, Dec. 13, 1982, pp. 90-96+.

23. Kanarick and Dotlich, "Honeywell's Agenda."

24. Wilkens, A. L. "The Creation of Company Culture: The Role of Stories and Human Resource Systems." *Human Resource Management*, 1984, *23* (1), 41-60.

25. Martin, J., and Powers, M. "Organizational Stories: More Vivid and Persuasive than Quantitative Data." In B. M. Staw (ed.), *Psychological Foundations of Organizational Behavior*. Glenview, Ill.: Scott, Foresman, 1982, pp. 161-168.

26. Wilkens, A. L. "Organizational Stories as Symbols Which Control the Organization." In L. R. Pondy and others (eds.), *Organizational Symbolism*. Greenwich, Conn.: JAI Press, 1983.

27. Ornstein, S. "Organizational Symbols: A Study of Their Meanings and Influences on Perceived Psychological Climate." *Organizational Behavior and Human Decision Processes*, 1986, *38* (2), 207-229.

28. Wojahn, E. "Management by Walking Away."

29. Benner, S. "Culture Shock." *Inc.*, Aug. 1985, pp. 73-82, p. 80.

30. Peters, T. J. "Changing Habits Is the First Step to Changing Priorities." *San Jose Mercury News*, Feb. 5, 1987, p. 8C.

31. Posner, B. Z., Hall, J. L., and Harder, J. W. "People Are Our Most Important Resource, But: Encouraging Employee Development." *Business Horizons*, 1986, *29* (5), 52-54.

Chapter Ten

1. Much of the discussion of the "small win" process draws upon the theoretical basis set out in Wieck, K. E. "Small Wins: Redefining the Scale of Social Problems." *American Psychologist*, 1984, *39* (1), 40-49.

2. Similar assertions have been made by others. See, for example, Machlup, F. *The Production and Distribution of Knowledge in the United States.* Princeton, N.J.: Princeton University Press, 1962.

3. Hollander, S. *The Success of Increased Efficiency: A Study of Du Pont Rayon Plants.* Cambridge, Mass.: MIT Press, 1965.

4. Weick, "Small Wins," p. 43.

5. *The Leading Edge* (film). Santa Cruz, Calif.: Langsford Communications, 1986.

6. Barmesh, I. *For the Good of the Company.* New York: Grosset & Dunlop, 1976.

7. As quoted in Peters, T. J. "Stamp Out Risk Taking and Creativity." *Hospital Forum,* 1981, *24* (3), 6–7, 10 ff.

8. Randolph, W. A., and Posner, B. Z. *Effective Project Planning and Management.* Englewood Cliffs, N.J.: Prentice-Hall, forthcoming.

9. Mintzberg, H. *The Nature of Managerial Work.* New York: Harper & Row, 1973.

10. Randolph and Posner, *Effective Project Planning.*

11. This discussion is based upon research reported in Salancik, G. R., "Commitment and the Control of Organizational Behavior and Belief." In B. M. Staw and G. R. Salancik (eds.), *New Directions in Organizational Behavior.* Chicago: St. Clair Press, 1977; Salancik, G. R. "Commitment Is Too Easy!" *Organizational Dynamics,* 1977, *6* (1), 62–82.

12. As quoted in Peters, T. J., and Waterman, R. H. *In Search of Excellence.* New York: Harper & Row, 1982, p. 203.

13. Kidder, T. *The Soul of a New Machine.* Boston: Little, Brown, 1981.

14. Pascale, R. "Fitting New Employees into the Company Culture." *Fortune,* 1984, *109* (11), 28–40, p. 30.

15. Pascale, "Fitting New Employees into the Company Culture," p. 28.

16. Salancik, "Commitment and the Control of Organizational Behavior and Belief."

17. Finegan, J. "Four-Star Management." *Inc.,* Jan. 1987, pp. 42–51.

Chapter Eleven

1. Eden, D. "Self-Fulfilling Prophecy as a Management Tool: Harnessing Pygmalion." *Academy of Management Review,* 1984, *9* (1), 64-73.

2. Cohen, A. R., Fink, S. L., Gadon, H., and Willits, R. D. *Effective Behavior in Organizations.* (3rd ed.) Homewood, Ill.: Irwin, 1984, p. 166.

3. Brown, W. B., and Moberg, D. J. *Organization Theory and Management.* New York: Wiley, 1980, pp. 423-436.

4. Deal, T. F., and Kennedy, A. K. *Corporate Cultures.* Reading, Mass.: Addison-Wesley, 1982, p. 41.

5. For example, see Pinder, C. C. *Work Motivation: Theory, Issues and Applications.* Glenview, Ill.: Scott, Foresman, 1984, pp. 286-298.

6. Pinder, *Work Motivation,* p. 226.

7. Ivancevich, J. M., Donnelly, J. H., Jr., and Gibson, J. L. *Managing for Performance.* (3rd ed.) Plano, Tex.: Business Publications, 1986, p. 320.

8. Blanchard, K. H., and Lorber, R. *Putting the One Minute Manager to Work.* New York: Morrow, 1985.

9. Hall, J. L., Posner, B. Z., and Harder, J. W. "Performance Appraisal Systems: Matching Theory with Practice." *Human Resource Management,* forthcoming.

10. Cohen, Fink, Gadon, and Willits, *Effective Behavior,* p. 167.

11. Graham, G. "Going the Extra Mile: Motivating Your Workers Doesn't Always Involve Money." *San Jose Mercury News,* Jan. 7, 1987, p. 4C.

12. Kanter, R. M. Presentation on *The Change Masters,* Santa Clara University, March 13, 1986.

13. As quoted in VerMeulen, M. "When Employees Give Something Extra." *Parade,* Nov. 6, 1983, p. 11.

14. Dow, R. J. "Keeping Employees Focused on Customer Service." Presentation to the Executive Seminar in Corporate Excellence, Santa Clara University, Oct. 28, 1986.

15. Peters, T. J. "Boost Morale with 'Fabulous Bragging' Sessions." *San Jose Mercury News,* Jan. 31, 1985, p. 7E.

16. Deci, E. L. *Intrinsic Motivation.* New York: Plenum Press, 1975.

17. McClelland, D. C. *The Achieving Society.* New York: Van Nostrand, Reinhold, 1961.

18. Hamner, W. C., and Organ, D. S. *Organizational Behavior: An Applied Psychological Approach.* (Rev. ed.) Plano, Tex.: Business Publications, 1982.

19. This example comes from Peters, T. J., and Austin, N. K. *A Passion For Excellence.* New York: Random House, 1985.

20. Squires, S. "Clinging to Hope." *San Jose Mercury News,* Feb. 25, 1984, p. 12C. See also: Breznitz, S. "The Effect of Hope on Coping with Stress." In M. H. Appley and R. Trumbell (eds.), *Dynamics of Stress: Physiological, Psychological, and Social Perspectives.* New York: Plenum, 1986, pp. 295–306.

21. Gendron, G. "The Art of Entrepreneurship." *Inc.,* Aug. 1983, p. 7.

Chapter Twelve

1. Jones, M. O., and others. "Performing Well: The Impact of Rituals, Celebrations, and Networks of Support." Presented at the Western Academy of Management conference, Hollywood, Calif., April 10, 1987.

2. Kiechel, W., III. "Celebrating a Corporate Triumph." *Fortune,* Aug. 20, 1984, p. 262.

3. Deal, T. F., and Kennedy, A. K. *Corporate Cultures.* Reading, Mass.: Addison-Wesley, 1982, p. 63.

4. Huff, C. L., Jr. Letter, Jan. 8, 1986.

5. DeForest, C. "The Art of Conscious Celebration: A New Concept for Today's Leaders." From John D. Adams (ed.), © 1986, *Transforming Leadership: From Vision to Results.* Miles River Press, Alexandria, Va.

6. As quoted in Peters, T. J., and Waterman, R. H., Jr. *In Search of Excellence.* New York: Harper & Row, 1982, p. 229.

7. DeForest, "The Art," p. 223.

8. DeForest, "The Art," p. 224.

9. Greene, B. "Why Working For Some Bosses is a Thankless Job." *San Jose Mercury News,* Jan. 27, 1986, p. 14B.

10. See, for example: Kirmeyer, S. L., and Thung-Rung, L. "Social Support: Its Relationship to Observed Communication with Peers and Superiors." *Academy of Management Journal,* 1987, *30* (1), 138-151; Goldhaber, G. M., Yates, M. P., Porter, D. T., and Lesniak, R. "Organizational Communication: 1978." *Human Communication Research,* 1978, *5,* 76-96; Hellriegel, D., and Slocum, J. W. "Organizational Climate: Measures, Research, and Contingencies." *Academy of Management Journal,* 1974, *17,* 255-280; Schnake, M. E. "An Empirical Assessment of the Effects of Affective Response in the Measurement of Organizational Climate." *Personnel Psychology,* 1983, *36,* 791-807.

11. Tommerup, P. "Inspiring Self-Management: On Symbols, Synergism, and Excellence." Presented at the Western Academy of Management conference, Hollywood, Calif., April 10, 1987.

12. California Department of Mental Health. *Friends Can Be Good Medicine.* San Francisco: Pacificon Productions, 1981.

13. Berkman, L. F., and Syme, S. L. "Social Networks, Host Resistance, and Mortality: A Nine-Year Follow-Up Study of Alameda County Residents." *American Journal of Epidemiology,* 1979, *109* (2), 186-204.

14. Wallis, C., and others. "Stress: Can We Cope?" *Time,* June 6, 1983, p. 50.

15. See, for example: Kirmeyer and Thung-Rung, "Social Support"; Cohen, S., and Wills, T. A. "Stress, Social Support, and the Buffering Hypothesis." *Psychological Bulletin,* 1985, *98,* 310-357.

16. As quoted in Peters and Austin, *A Passion for Excellence,* p. 290.

17. California Department of Mental Health, *Friends.*

18. California Department of Mental Health, *Friends.*

Chapter Thirteen

1. Reprinted by permission of the *Harvard Business Review.* Excerpts from "Tailor Executive Development to Strategy" by James F. Bolt (November/December 1985, p. 173). Copyright © 1985 by the President and Fellows of Harvard College; all rights reserved.

2. Schlesinger, A. M., Jr. *The Cycles of American History.* Boston: Houghton Mifflin, 1986, pp. 419-420.

3. Pfeffer, J. "The Ambiguity of Leadership." *Academy of Management Review,* 1977, *2,* 104-112. See also Lieberson, S., and O'Connor, J. F. "Leadership and Organizational Performance: A Study of Large Corporations." *American Sociological Review,* 1972, *37,* 117-130.

4. Bass, B. M. *Leadership and Performance Beyond Expectations.* New York: Free Press, 1985, p. 219.

5. Smith, J. E., Carson, K. P., and Alexander, R. A. "Leadership: It Can Make a Difference." *Academy of Management Journal,* 1984, *27* (4), 765-776, p. 774.

6. McCauley, C. D. *Developmental Experiences in Managerial Work: A Literature Review.* Technical Report 26. Greensboro, N.C.: Center for Creative Leadership, 1986.

7. Zemke, R. "The Honeywell Studies How Managers Learn to Manage." *Training,* Aug. 1985, pp. 46-51.

8. McCauley, *Developmental Experiences,* p. 3.

9. Morrison, A. W., and White, R. P. "Key Events/Learning in a Manager's Life." Paper presented to the Academy of Management meeting, San Diego, Calif., Aug. 15, 1983; see also: McCall, M. W., and Lombardo, M. M. "Nobody's Perfect: An Examination of Executive Strengths and Weaknesses." Paper presented to the Academy of Management meeting, San Diego, Calif., Aug. 14, 1986.

10. Zemke, "The Honeywell Studies," p. 50.

11. Zemke, "The Honeywell Studies," p. 46.

12. For a discussion of the role of challenge in executive development, see Magierson, C., and Kakabadse, A. *How American Chief Executives Succeed.* New York: American Management Association, 1984; Bray, D. W., and Howard, A. "The AT&T Longitudinal Studies of Managers." In K. W. Shaie (ed.), *Longitudinal Studies of Adult Psychological Development.* New York: Guilford Press, 1983.

13. McCauley, *Developmental Experiences,* p. 7.

14. McCauley, *Developmental Experiences,* pp. 9-14.

15. See especially: Kanter, R. M. *Men and Women of the Corporation.* New York: Basic Books, 1977; Kram, K. E. *Mentoring at Work: Developmental Relationships in Organizational Life.*

Glenview, Ill.: Scott, Foresman, 1985; Levinson, D. J. *The Season's of a Man's Life.* New York: Knopf, 1978.

16. Gibbons, T. C. "Revisiting the Question of Born vs. Made: Toward a Theory of Development of Transformational Leaders." Unpublished doctoral dissertation, the Fielding Institute, 1986.

17. Clawson, J. G. "Mentoring in Managerial Careers." In C. B. Derr (ed.), *Work, Family and the Career.* New York: Praeger, 1980, pp. 144-165.

18. Goleman, D. "When the Boss Is Unbearable." *New York Times,* Dec. 28, 1986, pp. 3-1, 3-29.

19. Goleman, "When the Boss Is Unbearable."

20. Kotter, J. P. *The General Managers.* New York: Free Press, 1982.

21. Eurich, N. P. *Corporate Classrooms: The Learning Business.* Princeton, N.J.: Carnegie Foundation for the Advancement of Teaching, 1985.

22. Feuer, D. "Where The Dollars Go." *Training,* Oct. 1985, p. 45.

23. For a comprehensive source on leadership programs, see Freeman, F. H., Gregory, R. A., and Clark, M. B. (eds.). *Leadership Education: A Source Book for Those Planning Programs and Teaching Courses in Leadership in Higher Education.* Greensboro, N. C.: Center for Creative Leadership, 1986.

24. Drucker, P. F. *The Practice of Management.* New York: Harper & Row, 1986, p. 158.

25. Drucker, P. F. *The Practice of Management,* p. 159.

26. For a discussion of this study, see Goleman, D. "Major Personality Study Finds That Traits Are Mostly Inherited." *New York Times,* Dec. 2, 1986, pp. C1-C2.

27. Goleman, "Major Personality Study."

28. Gibbons, "Revisiting the Question." For more on transformational leadership, see Burns, J. M. *Leadership.* New York: Harper & Row, 1978.

29. Gibbons, "Revisiting the Question," p. 197.

30. Bray, D. G., Campbell, R. J., and Grant, D. L. *Formative Years in Business: A Long-Term AT&T Study of Managerial Lives.* New York: Wiley, 1974. See also Bray, D. W., and Howard, A. "The AT&T Longitudinal Studies," pp. 266-312.

31. Bray and Howard, "The AT&T Longitudinal Studies," p. 301.

32. Lee, J. "Exploring the Traits of Twins." *Time*, Jan. 12, 1987, p. 63.

33. Maccoby, M. *The Leader*. New York: Simon & Schuster, 1981, p. 60.

34. Bray and Howard, "The AT&T Longitudinal Studies," pp. 281–282.

35. For example, see Livingston, J. S. "Pygmalion in Management." *Harvard Business Review*, July–Aug. 1969, pp. 81–89; Rosenthal, R., and Jacobson, L. *Pygmalion in the Classroom*. New York: Holt, Rinehart & Winston, 1968.

36. Livingston, "Pygmalion in Management."

37. Levinson, H., and Rosenthal, S. *CEO: Corporate Leadership in Action*. New York: Basic Books, 1984, p. 12.

38. Burns, J. M. "True Leadership." *Psychology Today*, Oct. 1976, pp. 46–58, 110.

39. Schlesinger, A. M., Jr. *The Cycles of American History*. Boston: Houghton Mifflin, 1986, p. 420.

40. Gardner, J. W. *The Moral Aspect of Leadership: Leadership Papers/5*. Washington, D.C.: Independent Sector, 1987, pp. 10–18.

41. Oates, Stephen B. *Let the Trumpet Sound: The Life of Martin Luther King, Jr.* New York: Mentor/New American Library, 1985.

Index

V

Valley Times, 91–92

Value-added competence, 19–20

Values: behavior and, 12; celebrations reinforce, 260–262, 264–265, 271–272; clarifying, 102–103, 190–197, 210–212, 300–302; congruence with actions, 196–197, 197–200, 213; consensus about, 195–196; credibility and, 22; dramatizing, 200, 214–215; fitting change with, 237; honesty and, 18; importance of, 187, 190–191, 300–302; individual vs. organizational, 192–194; intensity of, 196–197; moments of truth, 200–205; qualities of, in effective companies, 195–197; setting an example of, 25, 210–216; subtle means of communicating, 205–210; symbolic reminders of, 207–210; visions as reflections of, 97–98; visions vs., 191–192; work as expression of, 115–118

Verbal Style and the Presidency (Hart), 121

Verilink, 265

Versatec, Inc., 10–11, 12, 259; challenge example from, 42–43; personal celebrations at, 266; visibility of commitment at, 229

VIP (vision-improvement-persistence) model, 7

Visibility: of choices, 228–229, 236, 237–238; commitment through, 228–229, 231–232; empowerment through, 173, 174–175, 177, 184–185; increasing, 177, 178; for leadership development, 285; for leading by example, 200; of progress, 235–236; of public statements, 203

Vision: animating, 118–125, 128; broadness of, 127; clarifying 102–103; communicating to others, 108–113; discovering a common purpose in, 113–118; encouraging cooperation with, 140–141; focus provided by, 98; importance of communicating, 100, 108; of long-term payoff, 140–141; meaning of, 85–93; purpose vs., 83–84, 85; road map vs. compass, 99; sources of, 93–99; testing assumptions underlying, 104; uniqueness of, 90–91; values vs., 191–192. *See also* Envisioning the future; Inspiring a shared vision

Vision-improvement-persistence (VIP) model, 7

Vista Test, 95

Visualization, 104–105

Voehl, T., 282

Volunteering, for leadership development, 285

Volunteers: empowering, 161; inspiring, 26; intrinsic motivation of, 44; power of choice among, 227

W

W. L. Gore & Associates, 184

Walking around, management by, 200, 208, 259

Walking away, management by, 203

Wall Street Journal, 23

War, reciprocity in, 142

Waterman, R. H., Jr., 74

Watson, N., 21

Watson, T. J., Jr., 197, 204

Watson, T. J., Sr., 275

"We," use of, 10, 133, 153–154

Weick, K., 220

Welch, J., 245

Wells Fargo Bank, 241; recognition at, 248; small win process at, 221; use of symbol by, 120

West, T., 227

Whittaker, J., 277, 298

Whittaker/O'Malley, Inc., 298

Wible, D., 282–283

Win-win solutions, 156–158

Working hours, 227–228, 242

Working (Terkel), 21, 116

World Futures Society (Washington, D. C.), 104

World War I, reciprocity in, 142

Wriston, W. B., 60

X

Xerox: egalitarian symbolism at, 209; Versatec and, 42–43